The *"Newfyjohn" Solution*:
St. John's, Newfoundland as a Case Study of Second World War Allied Naval Base Development During the Battle of the Atlantic

By
Paul W. Collins

Copyright 2014 Paul W. Collins

All Rights Reserved

This book is licensed for your personal reading enjoyment only. If you would like to share this book with others, please purchase an additional copy for each recipient.

Publisher: WriteAdvice Press (Alberta, Canada)

Editor: WriteAdvice Press

Cover Design: WriteAdvice Press

Format & Layout: Anessa Books, www.annessabooks.com

ISBN: 978-0-9878918-6-0

Paperback Edition 2.0

Library and Archives Canada Cataloguing in Publication

Collins, Paul W., 1957-, author
    The "Newfyjohn" solution : St. John's Newfoundland as a case study of Second World War allied naval base development during the Battle of the Atlantic / Paul W. Collins.

Includes bibliographical references and index.
Issued in print and electronic formats.
ISBN 978-0-9878918-6-0 (pbk.).--ISBN 978-0-9878918-5-3 (kindle)

    1. Canada. Royal Canadian Navy. HMCS Avalon. 2. Navy-yards and naval stations--Newfoundland and Labrador--St. John's. 3. World War, 1939-1945--Newfoundland and Labrador--St. John's--Naval operations. 4. World War, 1939-1945--Newfoundland and Labrador--St. John's--Logistics. 5. Logistics, Naval. 6. St. John's (N.L.)--History, Naval--20th century. I. Title.

D779.C2C65 2014	940.54'53	C2014-905507-2
		C2014-905508-0

DEDICATION

This book is dedicated to Mom, Dad, Caitlin, Ryan and, my new granddaughter, Kiera

CONTENTS

Preface	7
Introduction	10
Chapter 1: Cry "Havoc!"	19
Chapter 2: Humble Beginnings September 1939 to May 1941	26
Chapter 3: Into The Breach June 1941 to May 1942	44
Chapter 4: Holding the Line June 1942 to May 1943	95
Chapter 5: All Over but the Shouting June 1943 to May 1945	140
Conclusion	170
About the Author	175
Acknowledgements	176
Abbreviations	177
Maps and Photographs	183
Bibliography	188
Index	211

Preface

I would like to address a few issues and clarify a few points about this book. The first is that this is a narrative history. I realize that narrative history is seen by some as being a somewhat lesser form of academic investigation. As James Pritchard of Queen's University says in *Anatomy of a Naval Disaster*[1], narrative history has long been disparagingly referred to as "Histoire Evenmentielle," simply a history of events. This is unfortunate as I think asking "what happened?" is a perfectly valid question. From the mid-1980s when I first learned that St. John's was the Royal Canadian Navy's (RCN) main Second World War trans-Atlantic escort base, I wanted to know how Canada managed to develop a major naval base in such a small, isolated, and already congested port. In other words, I wanted to know "what happened?" Unfortunately, other than Gilbert Tucker's section in *The Naval Service of Canada*[2] and eventually Bernard Ransom's "Canada's 'Newfyjohn' Tenancy"[3] article some forty years later (1996), there was really very little written about it.[4] This surprised me, as I knew that events at sea often depend significantly on the facilities ashore. Consequently, I look at my study as a sort of addendum to the operational histories of the RCN in the North Atlantic during the Second World War. If someone reading *No Higher Purpose*[5] or any of the other excellent examinations of RCN operations was curious as to why a certain escort group during a certain convoy battle only had three out of six working asdic sets, or had been put together at the last moment, or was missing its senior officer, I wanted to provide a source that could possibly offer some answers. Consequently, I attempted to write as detailed a study as I could as to how HMCS *Avalon* developed and operated. As Pritchard says, I wanted to bring order to chaos. I endeavoured to gather as much information as I could on HMCS *Avalon*, organize it into some sort of order, and make it available to anyone interested in how St. John's evolved into one of the most important escort bases developed during the Battle of the Atlantic.

Pritchard also argues that how the story is told is important. Whether it is told romantically–making it glorious; or passively–making it dismal; or obliquely–which could reduce it to a cheap farce, the story is still the thing. And ideology can get in the way of its telling. I did not want to approach my topic from a Newfoundland or Canadian nationalist point of view. I did not want to put any sort of Marxist spin on it. I attempted to present the story as objectively, in as much detail, and with as much documentation as I possibly could. I did not have any sort of ideological agenda. I tried to limit my explanations and commentary (some may say tangents) to what I thought directly affected the evolution and operation of HMCS *Avalon*, whether it was ulterior motives, personality conflicts, command decisions, developments with the war at sea, or simply the weather. Having said that, I do argue that HMCS *Avalon* was not the "seat of the pants" operation that much of the literature portrays. This brings me to the form I chose to write this study.

Perhaps I should have put all my Battle of the Atlantic discussion into a separate chapter or eliminated it altogether instead of jumping back and forth between the Atlantic war and HMCS *Avalon*. I did so because all during my graduate studies I was impressed as to how important context is to any discussion. (Thanks Dr. Hiller!) While I could include general contextual and historical material in one chapter, I felt that as the evolution of HMCS *Avalon* was so inextricably linked to the events at sea, this context had to be immediate. Referring to events a chapter or two previous as mitigating factors in another chapter, in my opinion, somehow dilutes the impact of those events in the reader's eye. Consequently, I felt it was more important to include the Battle of the Atlantic alongside my discussions of HMCS *Avalon*.

Some may have concerns that I relied too heavily on the Flag Officer Newfoundland Force's (FONF) Monthly Reports (RG24). Be assured, the monthly reports are not simply the observations of the Flag Officer alone but also include reports submitted by the various department heads below him: the Maintenance Captain, the Captain of the Port, Captain (D), the Barracks Commander, Training Officer, Medical Officer, and even the Chaplain. I could have looked at each department's individual files, and in many cases I did, but FONF's monthly reports are generally complete, concise, and supplied the type of information that Naval Service Headquarters (NSHQ) in Ottawa required and thus, I felt, also gave me what I needed to know. This was confirmed by the significant number of FONF and Admiralty (ADM 1 & 116) files I also examined. Of the Commission of Government files (GN 38), I paid particular attention to the Department of Justice and Defence files because this was the department most involved with the war effort, although the Department of Public Utilities in the person of Commissioner Wilfred Woods was concerned with port facilities, land acquisition and compensation. I examined Dominion Office (DO 35) files both at PANL and the PRO/TNA and found the Governor's quarterly reports particularly enlightening. I did not concentrate on the other Newfoundland Government departments, although I examined all, because I was not writing on the Home Front. I would like to make this clear–even though HMCS *Avalon* was located in Newfoundland and therefore is part of the province's history, this is primarily a military topic. My book examines HMCS *Avalon* as a case study in Allied Second World War naval base development. HMCS *Avalon* could have been situated anywhere in the North Atlantic and would have had to deal with many of the challenges experienced at St. John's. Consequently, I was mainly concerned with those files that had a direct impact on the evolution and operation of HMCS *Avalon* as a naval establishment.

In most ways, I am a traditional military historian. I think one has to start with the "big picture" and work your way down from there. To that end, Canadian historians have examined North Atlantic operations, the U–boat attacks in Canadian coastal waters, the equipment crisis that hit the RCN during 1942, and the leadership crisis of 1943, as well as the commanders, losses, logistics, and ships' designs. As HMCS *Avalon* was the RCN's main trans-Atlantic escort base during the Second World War and it has not been widely explored, I thought it was something that also needed further investigation. Having said that, I wrote my study the way I wanted to, the way I thought I had to, and I accept full responsibility for its form, function and its flaws.

---

[1] James Pritchard, *Anatomy of a Naval Disaster: The 1746 French Expedition to North America* (Montreal and Kingston: McGill-Queen's University Press, 1995).

[2] Gilbert Tucker, *The Naval Service of Canada*. 2 vols (Ottawa: King's Printer, 1952).

[3] Bernard Ransom, "Canada's 'Newfyjohn' Tenancy: The Royal Canadian Navy in St. John's 1941-1945." *Acadiensis*, XXIII, No. 2 (Spring 1994), 58-81.

[4] Tony German has a small section in his 1990 history *The Sea is at Our Gates*. See German, Tony, *The Sea is at Our Gates: The History of the Canadian Navy*. (Toronto: McClelland and Stewart, 1990), 93-4.

[5] W.A.B. Douglas *et al*, *No Higher Purpose: The Official Operational History of the Royal Canadian Navy in the Second World War, 1939-1945*, Volume II, Part 1 (St. Catharines: Vanwell Publishing, 2002).

Introduction

The "Newfyjohn" Solution: St John's, Newfoundland as a Case Study of Second World War Allied Naval Base Development During the Battle of the Atlantic

Contrary to popular belief, St. John's, Newfoundland–not Halifax, Nova Scotia–was Canada's major convoy escort base during the Second World War. Indeed, the myth that Halifax-based warships escorted the vital convoys across the Atlantic is constantly repeated.[6] That it was St. John's and not Halifax is significant for a number of reasons. Chief among them is that Newfoundland was a separate dominion at the time, and the base–commissioned HMCS *Avalon*[7]–was built and operated by the Royal Canadian Navy (RCN) but actually owned by the British Admiralty. Further, the RCN managed to create such a major naval facility in the heart of a capital city with a civilian population of 40,000 at a time when American and Canadian Armed Forces already occupied most of the available vacant land.

This study seeks to answer two questions. The first is how St. John's, better known as "Newfyjohn" during the war, developed from merely a poorly defended port in September 1939 into Canada's main trans-Atlantic escort base, with particular attention to the crucial May 1941/May 1943 period. The RCN accomplished this despite inter-governmental tensions, conflicting personalities, a convoluted command structure, labour difficulties, enemy action, and even the weather. Often, the forces that dictated the development and operation of the base at St. John's were completely out of the control of the Flag Officer, Newfoundland Force (FONF) or even Naval Service Headquarters (NSHQ) in Ottawa. Secondly, if the RCN "solved the problem of the Atlantic convoys" as posited by Admiral Sir Percy Noble RN, Commander-in-Chief (C-in-C), Northwest Approaches,[8] then what contribution did HMCS *Avalon* make to this success? This examination argues that HMCS *Avalon* accomplished all it was designed to do. It asserted Canada's special interest in Newfoundland while at the same time highlighting the country's contribution to the Allied war effort.

The "Newfyjohn" Solution

Even more important, HMCS *Avalon* facilitated the safe and timely arrival of over 25,000 RCN-escorted merchant ships in the United Kingdom during the course of the war–it also "solved the problem of the Atlantic convoys."

Marc Milner suggests that "the establishment of the Newfoundland Escort Force (NEF) in May 1941 was a milestone in Canadian naval history."[9] Michael Hadley points out that the creation of the NEF elevated the RCN from a minor role in coastal defence to a major participant in ocean operations.[10] The RCN's two official historians, Gilbert Tucker and Joseph Schull, argue respectively that the importance of St. John's as a naval base "can hardly be exaggerated" and was actually "the key to the western defence system."[11] Yet relatively little has been written on how an escort base of such strategic importance arose from what originally was merely a defended harbour. This is really not surprising. While much has appeared on the ships and men involved in the Battle of the Atlantic, the various bases from which they operated have received scant attention. Even in St. John's, both the historiography and popular consciousness remember the presence of the American army more so than the RCN, despite the fact that thousands of sailors and hundreds of warships were stationed here during the war.[12] This may be due to the longevity of the American residency in Newfoundland and the haste with which the Canadian facilities were dismantled at the end of hostilities. Or perhaps it is a lingering hangover from Newfoundland's still contentious decision to join Canada in 1949.[13] Regardless, an in-depth study of the evolution of St. John's from a defended harbour–similar to hundreds of others in the North Atlantic–to a major Allied escort base makes an important contribution to both Royal Canadian Navy and Newfoundland historiography as well as our understanding of Allied naval base development during the Battle of the Atlantic.

The creation of the NEF at St. John's in May 1941 facilitated the continuous escort of Britain's vital convoys across the Atlantic Ocean. Previously, convoys had been escorted by Halifax- or Sydney-based warships only as far as the Western Ocean Meeting Point (WESTOMP) northeast of the Grand Banks. Past this point, until they met their Royal Navy (RN) protectors at the Eastern Ocean Meeting Point (EASTOMP) just south of Iceland, convoys were basically on their own. As a result of the establishment of HMCS *Avalon*, convoys were escorted to the Mid-Ocean Meeting Point (MOMP) southwest of Iceland, where they were picked up by ships of the British Western Approaches Command (WAC) based in Liverpool. From the Canadian perspective, the establishment of an RCN escort base at St. John's enabled Canada to assert its presence on the international scene, forcing the United States and Britain to recognize its important contribution to the war effort. Equally significant, it allowed Canada to press its national interest in Newfoundland. As the American presence in Newfoundland grew, thanks to the 1940 "destroyers for bases" deal giving the United States the right to establish bases on British-controlled territory,[14] Canada became anxious that it might find an American protectorate on its front doorstep by war's end. Consequently, the establishment of the NEF was as important to Canada politically as it was to the prosecution of the war in the Atlantic.

Why HMCS *Avalon* was established is adequately addressed in the literature, but how this was done is not.[15] Indeed, how any North Atlantic base–Allied or Axis–was put in place and operated has not been widely explored.[16] Most often historians simply state it as a *fait accompli*– wharves were built, oil tanks installed, ships repaired, etc.– without any explanation of how this occurred. Questions as to how the land for the wharves was procured, how long it took for the oil tanks to be fabricated and what was used in the meantime, or how ships were repaired and by whom, have seldom been posed and even less frequently answered. All the myriad details of how something was accomplished are conspicuous by their absence in the literature. This is important because how the forces fared at sea was often bound up inextricably with the creation and operation of the facilities ashore. This was especially so for the RCN as a result of its tremendous expansion during the war years. Its performance in defence of the convoy network was a direct reflection of the efficiency, maintenance and training capabilities of the shore establishments. This was certainly the case with HMCS *Avalon*; thus, it is odd that Canadian historians tend generally to describe the facilities at St. John's in disparaging terms. They suggest that the port "had little to offer the Escort Force" and that the base had the appearance of a "travelling tent show" with the naval staff working out of rooms at the Newfoundland Hotel and warships tied up at "rickety South Side wharves."[17] It almost seems as if these historians, consciously or not, are presenting the base as a mitigating factor in the RCN's performance in the first few years of the Battle of the Atlantic. While the RCN did have to rely heavily on the available facilities at St. John's in the first year, by the summer of 1942, the Flag Officer, Newfoundland Force had moved into the new combined RCN/RCAF administration building, the RCN hospital was fully operational, as were the RCN Dockyard and barracks, and the wharfing along the Southside was up to naval standards. Certainly, HMCS *Avalon* was born out of crisis, and FONF was continually forced to play catch-up by the ever-changing war at sea and decisions made in Argentia, Ottawa, Washington and London, often without any consultation. Regardless, despite tremendous challenges,

HMCS *Avalon* was a reasonably efficient, well-run operation, not the "seat of the pants" arrangement suggested by the literature.

Establishing and developing HMCS *Avalon* was certainly problematic, and there were many complications to its evolution and operation. For one, three separate governments were involved: Great Britain, Canada and Newfoundland. The Newfoundland government was very suspicious of the Canadians, and not without reason.[18] Moreover, both preferred to bypass each other and to deal directly with the British. Furthermore, the base was built in a relatively small harbour with limited facilities that were already fully utilized and congested with mercantile interests. The procurement of this prime waterfront land tended to be convoluted and involved the co-operation of all three governments and the landowners themselves, who for the most part, just wanted to be left alone, war or no war. In many cases, facilities were rented for $1/year plus improvements and shared with the owners. How did this work? In addition, almost all materials and most of the skilled labour required to build the base's facilities–barracks, administration buildings, dockyard, hospital, wireless stations, etc.–were imported from Canada and/or the United States through U-boat-infested waters. How was this accomplished? How were the necessary personnel housed, fed and entertained? It was really quite an accomplishment on all levels that the base was built. That it also functioned in a reasonably efficient manner and allowed the RCN–notwithstanding the criticisms leveled at it–to hold the line during the darkest days of the Battle of the Atlantic, is a truly remarkable story.

Even after the subject of the ownership of the base was agreed, the difficulties in actually building it seemed insurmountable. Unlike the Americans, who developed their facilities in uninhabited or sparsely populated areas, the RCN attempted to construct a major naval facility in the middle of a densely populated urban centre. Most of the skilled labour, building materials and equipment had to be imported, at the same time, operations had to begin immediately. Consequently, the RCN initially relied heavily on the population and facilities of St. John's. That both were already severely taxed by the Canadian and American Armies' presence did not seem to concern Naval Service Headquarters (NSHQ) in Ottawa. Regardless, relations and co-operation between the various forces, governments and the local population were generally remarkably smooth. There were no VE Day riots in St. John's at war's end.

Wars tend to follow a seasonal cycle. Offensives generally start in the spring, and hostilities take a hiatus during the winter, recommencing with the onset of fine weather the following spring.

Despite being a global conflict, the Second World War and the Battle of the Atlantic followed a similar model. The "Phony War" ended in May 1940 with the invasion and defeat of France and the Low Countries, giving U-boat chief Admiral Karl Dönitz bases on the French Atlantic coast. As a result, full end-to-end convoy escort commenced in June 1941 to counter the subsequent westward expansion of the U-boat war. With the American entry into the war in December 1941, Dönitz pulled his forces out of the mid-Atlantic and assigned them to the poorly defended eastern seaboard of the United States and the Caribbean. The United States Navy (USN) finally halted the resulting hemorrhage of shipping (with unacknowledged help from the RCN)[19] by June 1942, and the U-boats once more moved back into the mid-Atlantic. It was here that the "clash of titans," so to speak, took place, resulting in the strategic defeat of the U-boats in May 1943. With the U-boat threat now contained, the Allies were able to increase the build-up of forces and supplies in Britain, and in June 1944, American, British and Canadian forces assaulted Fortress Europe. The resulting defeat of German forces in Normandy compelled Dönitz to abandon his French Atlantic bases and retreat to Norway. Ultimately, the Battle of the Atlantic ended with the war in Europe in May 1945.

As operations and the development of HMCS *Avalon* reflected events at sea, it seemed only logical for the chronology of this book to follow the same May/June axis. Chapter 1 sets the immediate context of this study, examining Newfoundland's early history from the Vikings at L'Anse-aux-Meadows to the beginning of the Second World War, plus the main players in the Battle of the Atlantic on the Allied side. Chapter 2 examines St. John's at the start of hostilities in September 1939 and the Newfoundland government's attempts to acquire some means of defence from both the British and Canadian governments. It also discusses the arrival of the Americans in Newfoundland as part of the Anglo-American "destroyers for bases" deal and the appearance of the RCN in May 1941. The main component of Chapter 3 is the actual establishment of HMCS *Avalon*. Escort operations started even before Commodore Murray, the Flag Officer, Newfoundland Force (FONF), arrived in June 1941. How this was done even before the first nail for the base was hammered was an amazing accomplishment in itself. This chapter also examines the American entry into the war in December 1941 and the start of U-boat operations in Canadian and American waters in the winter of 1942. Chapter 4 deals with what many historians consider the critical year of the Battle of the Atlantic. With the Americans in control of their eastern seaboard by spring 1942 and the establishment of escorted convoys in the Caribbean, the U-boats moved back into the North Atlantic by the fall of 1942 in greater numbers than ever before. They exacted tremendous losses on the Allies, especially against RCN-escorted convoys. While acknowledging that the RCN had sustained the majority of U-boat attacks but at the same time blaming poor leadership and training for the losses, the Admiralty pulled the RCN out of the North Atlantic for retraining and modernization. Consequently, Canadian forces did not participate in the disastrous March convoys nor the strategic defeat of the U-boats in May 1943. Regardless, the U-boats were still a threat and convoys still had to be escorted, and the RCN accepted more and more responsibility as British and American forces went on the offensive. Chapter 5 examines the last two years of the Atlantic war. Ship repair became critical during this period as both naval and merchant shipping overwhelmed available facilities. The Canadian government had been derelict in concentrating all its vessel repair facilities in central Canada while ignoring those on the east coast until the ship repair problem had reached crisis proportions. Unfortunately, by then, most of the local skilled labour had moved to the larger centres or joined the military, and shipyards and associated industries needed time to restart and retool.[20] Nevertheless, repair capacity at St. John's was expanded and improved by the acquisition of a floating drydock and the development of an overflow facility at Bay Bulls, and HMCS *Avalon* did its best to meet the demand. An added benefit was that for the first time, training could now take a priority and by now St. John's had first class training facilities. How times had changed! Convoys were still escorted, but other than the very real threat of lone wolf attacks in coastal waters, the days of the epic convoy battles were over and there was time to adequately train both men and ships.

Ultimately, the Battle of the Atlantic ended with Germany's defeat. That it was won by the Allied side was due in no small measure to the RCN and its base at St. John's, Newfoundland. When the RCN arrived in May 1941, the port did have only "the leanest of facilities" to offer the newly formed NEF.[21] However, by the time Hitler's U-boats surfaced and raised their black flags of surrender in May 1945, over 500 warships and thousands of naval personnel had passed through St. John's.[22] Overall, these forces were well served by HMCS *Avalon*, but not without difficulty. The evolving war in the Atlantic and decisions made in Argentia, Ottawa, Washington and London all impacted the development and operation of HMCS *Avalon*. Nevertheless, the base at St. John's accomplished all that it set out to do. It asserted Canada's special interest in Newfoundland while at the same time highlighting the country's contribution to the war effort. Further, the RCN accomplished this despite tensions between the various governments, a convoluted command structure, labour difficulties, enemy action and even the weather. The RCN's success in keeping the trans-Atlantic lines of communication open during the Second World War cannot be determined by the number of U-boats sunk but rather by the safe and timely arrival of the thousands of merchant ships convoyed across the North Atlantic by St. John's-based escorts. Consequently, if the RCN solved the problem of the Atlantic convoys, then *Newfyjohn* was the key to that solution.

---

[6] William D. Naftel, *Halifax at War: Searchlights, Squadrons and Submarines, 1939-1945* (Halifax: Formac Publishing, 2008), 71.

[7] It is actually the barracks complex that is commissioned, not the base itself. However, for the purpose of this study the entire naval base will be referenced as HMCS *Avalon*. This will also be the case for all other Canadian naval facilities discussed. Consequently, HMCS *Stadacona* refers to the whole Halifax naval base rather than just the barracks complex.

[8] Marc Milner, *Canada's Navy: The First Century* (Toronto: University of Toronto Press, 1999), 92.

[9] *Ibid.*, 89-90.

[10] Michael Hadley, *U-Boats against Canada*, 29.

[11] Gilbert Tucker, *The Naval Service of Canada*, (2 vols., Ottawa: King's Printer, 1952), II, 203; and Joseph Schull, *Far Distant Ships: An Official Account of Canadian Naval Operations in World War II* (Ottawa: Edmond Cloutier, 1950; 2nd ed., Toronto: Stoddart Publishing, 1987), 68.

[12] In his history of St. John's, Paul O'Neill devoted one and a half pages to the American army presence in the city while assigning less than two paragraphs to all three Canadian services. See Paul O'Neill, *The Oldest City: The Story of St. John's, Newfoundland* (Erin, ON: Press Porcepic, 1975), 110-112. Similarly, Kevin Major allocated only three paragraphs to the Canadian occupation compared to almost five pages about the Americans. Indeed, Major contends that the Americans made a more lasting impression on the residents of St. John's than either the Canadians or the British. See Kevin Major, *As Near to Heaven by Sea: A History of Newfoundland and Labrador* (Toronto: Penguin Books, 2001), 371-377. Former St. John's Fire Commissioner John Cardolis has written two books on the American tenure in Newfoundland and Labrador. See John N. Cardolis, *A Friendly Invasion: The American Military in Newfoundland, 1940-1990* (St. John's: Breakwater Books, 1990); and Cardolis, *A Friendly Invasion II: A Personal Touch* (St. John's, NL: Creative Publishers, 1993).

[13] The most recent material on Newfoundland's decision to join Canada in 1949 is found in Sean T. Cadigan, *Newfoundland and Labrador: A History* (Toronto: University of Toronto Press, 2009), 235-240. Jeff Webb devoted an entire chapter on the broadcast debates in his recent book on the Broadcasting Corporation of Newfoundland. See Jeff A. Webb, *The Voice of Newfoundland: A Social History of the Broadcasting Corporation of Newfoundland, 1939-1949* (Toronto: University of Toronto Press, 2008), 142-169. The standard work on

the Commission of Government years and the debate surrounding Newfoundland's entry into confederation with Canada is Peter Neary, *Newfoundland in the North Atlantic World, 1929-1949* (Montreal: McGill-Queen's University Press, 1988; 2nd ed., Montreal: McGill-Queen's University Press, 1996), especially 278-345.

[14] Steven High, *Base Colonies in the Western Hemisphere, 1940-1967* (New York: Palgrave Macmillan, 2009), 17-42; Neary, *Newfoundland in the North Atlantic World*, 135-153; David MacKenzie, "A North American Outpost: The American Military in Newfoundland, 1941-1945," *War & Society*, XXII, No. 2 (October 2004), 51-74: Peter Neary, "Newfoundland and the Anglo-American Leased Bases Agreement of 27 March 1941," *Canadian Historical Review*, LXVII, No. 4 (1986), 491-519; Stetson Conn, Rose C. Engelman and Byron Fairchild. *Guarding the United States and Its Outposts* (Washington, DC: Office of the Chief of Military History, 1964; reprint, Washington, DC: US Government Printing Office, 2000), 354-408; and Philip Goodhart, *Fifty Ships that Saved the World: The Foundation of the Anglo-American Alliance* (New York: Doubleday and Co., 1965).

[15] W.A.B. Douglas, *et al.*, *No Higher Purpose: The Official History of the Royal Canadian Navy in the Second World War, 1939-1943* (St. Catharines: Vanwell Publishing, 2002), II, Part 1, 183-189; Marc Milner, *North Atlantic Run: The Royal Canadian Navy and the Battle for the Convoys* (Toronto: University of Toronto Press, 1985), 32-34; Tucker, *Naval Service of Canada*, II, 186-208; and Schull, *Far Distant Ships*, 65-69.

[16] What has been published on the various Allied and Axis bases has been preoccupied with U-Boat bunkers on the German side and operations on the Allied side. Steven High recently edited a social history of wartime St. John's and also examined the social impact, especially in Newfoundland, of the American bases leased from the British in the Western Hemisphere during WWII. Brian Tennyson and Roger Sarty have perhaps most closely examined Allied naval base development in their work on Sydney, Cape Breton, although that base was mostly a convoy assembly point and local escort base during the Second World War. See High (ed.), *Occupied St. John's: A Social History of a City at War, 1939-1945* (Montréal: McGill-Queen's University Press, 2010); and High, *Base Colonies*. See also Jak P. Mallmann Showell, *Hitler's U-Boat Bases* (Stroud: Sutton Press, 2007); Gordon Williamson, *U-Boat Bases and Bunkers, 1941-45* (Oxford: Osprey Publishing, 2003); Randolf Bradham, *Hitler's U-Boat Fortresses* (Westport, CT: Praeger Press, 2003); Stetson, Engelman and Fairchild, *Guarding the United States and Its Outposts*; Brian Tennyson and Roger Sarty, *Guardian of the Gulf: Sydney, Cape Breton, and the Atlantic Wars* (Toronto: University of Toronto Press, 2000); and Roger Sarty, *The Maritime Defence of Canada* (Toronto: Canadian Institute of Strategic Studies, 1996).

[17] Tony German, *The Sea is at Our Gates: The History of the Canadian Navy* (Toronto: McClelland and Stewart, 1990), 93. James B. Lamb, *The Corvette Navy: True Stories from Canada's Atlantic War* (Toronto: Macmillan

of Canada, 1977; 2nd ed., Toronto: Fitzhenry and Whiteside, 2000), 91; and Lamb, *On the Triangle Run* (Toronto: Macmillan of Canada, 1986), 13. See also Bernard Ransom, "Canada's 'Newfyjohn' Tenancy: The Royal Canadian Navy in St. John's, 1941-1945," *Acadiensis*, XXIII, No. 2 (Spring 1994), pp. 58-81. Milner, *North Atlantic Run*, 43 and 215.

[18] From 1934 to 1949, Newfoundland was governed by a Commission of six London-appointed bureaucrats, three British and three Newfoundlanders, headed by the Governor. There had been tensions between Newfoundland and Canada over trade and fishing rights dating back to the nineteenth century. The Canadians exacerbated these by making contingency plans for Newfoundland with the Americans in 1940 without consulting the Newfoundland government. See Cadigan, *Newfoundland and Labrador*, 209-234. See also Webb, *Voice of Newfoundland*; and Neary, *Newfoundland in the North Atlantic World*.

[19] Marc Milner, "Royal Canadian Navy Participation in the Battle of the Atlantic Crisis of 1943," in James A. Boutilier (ed.), *The RCN in Retrospect, 1910-1968* (Vancouver: University of British Columbia Press, 1982), 166-167.

[20] Ernest R. Forbes, "Consolidating Disparity: The Maritimes and the Industrialization of Canada during the Second World War," *Acadiensis*, XV, No. 2 (Spring 1986), 3-27. See also Michael Whitby, "Instruments of Security: The Royal Canadian Navy's Procurement of the Tribal-Class Destroyers, 1938-1943," *The Northern Mariner/Le Marin du nord*, II, No. 3 (July 1992), 1-15.

[21] German, *The Sea is at Our Gates*, 93.

[22] In April 1945, over 2000 men were accommodated at the naval barracks alone. LAC, FONF, RG 24, Vol. 11,505, file 1445-102/3, sub 1, vol. 1, Administrative War Diary, April 1945.

Chapter 1

Cry "Havoc!"

When the Second World War erupted in September 1939, Newfoundland was little more than a minor British outpost off Canada's east coast.[23] It was famous for its Grand Banks, which was a source of friction between a number of countries, and as the most easterly point on the North American continent, it was the location of many important wireless and trans-Atlantic cable stations. But with its fragile economy and under-employed and largely under-educated population, it was ruled by a London-appointed Commission of Government and kept afloat by grants and loans from the British government. Newfoundland, despite being intensely loyal, was in some ways the unwanted child of the British Empire. This changed, however, as the Battle of the Atlantic moved further west, and Britain's vital lifelines to the New World were seriously threatened. A full escort system was needed to protect the flow of supplies, and one end had to start in the Western Atlantic. Suddenly, Newfoundland became important.

No discussion of "Newfyjohn"–as military personnel affectionately called Newfoundland, and St. John's in particular, during the war–can make sense without a brief review of the island's 500-year history as a British outpost. Officially "discovered" in 1497 by John Cabot, Newfoundland already had a prosperous indigenous population, and indeed was actually settled 500 years earlier by Vikings who built a thriving, if ultimately doomed, community at L'Anse-aux-Meadows on the Great Northern Peninsula. In the intervening period, the island was largely forgotten until the late Fifteenth Century when Cabot returned to England with tales of codfish so plentiful that they could be hauled aboard in baskets. Within a short period, most of the major European nations fished on the Grand Banks, and in 1583 Sir Francis Drake sailed into St. John's harbour and claimed the island for England. Two years later, Sir Bernard Drake (no relation) firmly established English control by destroying the Spanish fishing fleet. From that time forward only English and French vessels were allowed in Newfoundland waters.

France, initially confined to the west coast, slowly realized the strategic importance of Newfoundland, and in 1662 established a garrison at Plaisance (Placentia) in Placentia Bay. It was designated as the seat of government in Newfoundland and the base for all French activities in the region. The French attacked and burned St. John's to the ground in 1696, and again in 1708. Indeed, until the Treaty of Utrecht (1713), France controlled Newfoundland. Under the treaty, however, France lost Newfoundland but retained rights to an area between Cape Bonavista and Riche Point which became known as the French Shore. This did not end English/French tensions, though, and St. John's once again fell briefly to the French in 1762. Under the Treaty of Paris in 1763, the French relinquished Newfoundland but retained fishing rights on the French Shore and ownership of the islands of St. Pierre and Miquelon. With the peace, structured settlement and proper government was soon forthcoming, especially when inexpensive exports from the American colonies immediately before the American Revolution lowered the cost of provisions. The period between 1763 and the end of the Napoleonic wars was the greatest period of in-migration in the island's history.

The first half of the nineteenth century was reasonably stable and prosperous. By mid-century, responsible government was in place, and Phillip Little became Newfoundland's first Prime Minister. The next half was not quite as stable as the colony suffered through several financial disasters and a major fire almost completely destroyed St. John's in 1892. Things improved with the dawn of the new century, and in 1904 France relinquished its claim to the French Shore, and the Permanent Court of Arbitration in The Hague upheld Newfoundland's right to regulate American fishing on the Grand Banks. However, there were war clouds on the horizon.

When war was declared in August 1914, Newfoundland quickly answered the call to arms. Nevertheless, such patriotism came at a tremendous cost: by the end of the war almost every family had a friend or relative killed or wounded in action, and the island's war debt, combined with the liabilities assumed when the government took over the Newfoundland Railway, eventually led to the dominion's near financial collapse and the imposition of Commission of Government in 1934. The London-appointed Commission, comprising three Newfoundlanders and three Britons, acting in cooperation with the Governor, instituted economic reforms, reorganized the civil service and improved health, education and other social services. The economy responded, but the real recovery came from the Second World War. Newfoundland's strategic location played a major role in world events, and once again the country was "occupied" by foreign armed forces.[24]

When First Sea Lord Winston Churchill ordered His Majesty's ships to commence hostilities against Germany on 3 September 1939 neither he nor anyone in the Royal Navy (RN) could foresee the kind of sea war they would eventually fight. The RN still ruled the waves, but naval strategy continued to be centered on the battleship and the set-piece naval engagement. The U-boat experience of World War I was still remembered, and convoys were immediately initiated, but the Admiralty considered the U-boat threat to be minimal; ASDIC–the newly developed underwater detection device now known as Sonar–supposedly guaranteed that. As a result, the RN regarded the German surface fleet as the main threat.[25]

To face the German fleet, Britain had several forces. First, there was the Home Fleet comprising five battleships, two battle cruisers, two carriers, twelve cruisers, seventeen destroyers, seven large minesweepers and two submarine flotillas. The Channel Force fielded two battleships, two carriers, three cruisers and nine destroyers. The carriers, like their aircraft, were almost all obsolete, and a U-boat sank HMS *Courageous* early in the war while on anti-submarine patrol. Britain had numerical superiority in ASDIC-equipped escorts compared to Germany's U-boats by a ratio of almost four to one, but the ratio of merchantmen, the U-boats' targets, to escorts was a daunting twenty to one. Churchill's misguided decision early in the war to create hunting groups to search out U-boats "like cavalry divisions" further depleted the number of escorts available for convoying.[26] Because it was as difficult for a hunting group to find a U-boat in the vast expanse of the Atlantic as it was for a U-boat to find a victim, the best place for both parties to intercept their targets was around the convoy itself. Indeed, this became the strategy pursued by both foes as the war progressed.

Britain depended upon imports for survival, especially in wartime, and its position was much the same at the beginning of the Second World War as it had been at the start of the Great War. The country still relied heavily on its overseas empire and imported approximately fifty million tons of goods per year, including all its oil and half its food and industrial raw materials. The merchant navy contained 160,000 men, including 4,500 masters, 13,000 officers and 20,000 engineers, and numbered approximately 3,000 ocean-going and 1,000 coastal vessels totaling 21,000,000 tons of shipping. At any one time, 2,500 British merchant vessels were at sea. Despite its size, however, the British merchant navy could carry only three-quarters of the country's imports, and foreign hulls supplied the remainder. For the

Admiralty, protection of Britain's vital lifelines, as represented by its merchant fleet, proved a prodigious task, especially given the escort-to-merchant vessel ratio. As a result, the Admiralty sought other means to protect the ships from attack.[27]

As the risk of U-boat attacks was thought to be minimal at this time, the main threat was considered to be surface raiders. The Admiralty revived its Trade Division in 1936 and a year later appointed a Shipping Defence Advisory Committee with liaison officers to instruct the merchant marine in defensive measures. By the beginning of the war, 10,000 officers had undergone training–2,000 in gunnery–and 1,500 seamen had been instructed on how to maintain and operate large calibre guns. As the likelihood of war became more apparent, the Admiralty set up the Defensively Equipped Merchant Ship (DEMS) program to find and install old naval, anti-aircraft and machine guns on merchant ships, as well as to recruit the personnel to man them. This was a daunting task considering that there were 5,500 such ships to be armed, but by the end of 1940, some 3,400 ships were converted to DEMS. Ultimately, this program absorbed 190,000 men from the merchant and Royal navies, the Royal Marines and even the army–more men than served in the pre-war merchant navy.[28]

The Admiralty did not forget the first naval lesson of the First World War–that the most effective way to protect merchant ships was to convoy them. Unfortunately, available resources often did not match requirements; as a result, early convoys were often inadequately defended and subject to severe losses. Regardless, sinkings of independently routed ships outstripped those traveling in convoy by a margin of more than five to one. This trend continued into 1940, but it started to decline in the middle of the year as more and more ships were put into convoys.[29] However, escorts for these convoys became a problem and this was one area where Canada could fill the breach.

As international tensions had risen in the late 1930s, Prime Minister Mackenzie King faced the possibility that Canada would once again find itself embroiled in a European war as part of the British Commonwealth. Remembering that the country had been almost brought to the point of civil war by the conscription issue during the Great War, he did not want to find himself in the same position as his predecessor, Sir Robert Borden. King's answer was to support the less personnel-intensive branches of the armed forces: the air force and the navy. He also intended that any war would benefit Canada industrially. Anything that could be built in Canada for the war effort would be constructed domestically. Consequently, when the RCN submitted its naval

The "Newfyjohn" Solution

construction program in September 1939, Cabinet immediately approved it. The first program called for twenty-eight of the newly designed Flower-class corvettes to be built by twelve shipyards from the Maritimes to the west coast, all delivered by the end of the 1940 navigation season. Another order for thirty-six quickly followed, bringing the total to sixty-four. British Prime Minister Winston Churchill referred to these little warships as "cheap and nasties." The nasty was debatable but they were at least inexpensive: depending on the location of the building yard and adjustments to specifications, contract prices never exceeded $606,000 per vessel.[30]

At the same time, US President Franklin Delano Roosevelt desperately wanted to send Churchill "all aid short of war" after the fall of France. However, the deep isolationist sentiment in the United States hamstrung him. In order to aid Britain he had to make it appear to be in America's national interest to do so.[31] In August, Roosevelt met with Mackenzie King in Ogdensburg, New York, and agreed to form the Permanent Joint Board on Defence (PJBD) aimed at the defence of the Western Hemisphere should Britain be forced to capitulate. Shortly thereafter, Britain and the US concluded a deal whereby the US would turn over fifty mothballed WW I destroyers in return for bases on British territory in the Western Hemisphere. Six of the destroyers, narrow of beam and flush-decked for the relatively calm Pacific Ocean, were immediately transferred to the RCN. Manning these ships–and ten corvettes originally planned for the Admiralty–exhausted the RCN's supply of disposable manpower. As 1940 drew to a close and the ships of the first building program were coming off the ways in rapid succession, the RCN was looking at having to find trained crews for fifty-four corvettes, twenty-five minesweepers and an assortment of motor launches, a total of approximately 7,000 officers and men. This number did not include personnel to man new shore establishments.[32]

By this point, U-boats were attacking convoys on the surface, using the *Rudeltaktik*, and exacted a heavy toll on shipping. In late September 1940, Convoy HX-72 lost eleven ships 350 miles west of Ireland. SC 7 was decimated off Rockall in mid-October, followed a few days later by HX-79. In these three convoys alone, forty-three ships were sunk, accounting for almost a quarter of a million tons of British shipping. Not one of the attacking U-boats was lost.[33]

The British responded to this new development by extending escort coverage further west into the Atlantic. Previously, escorts left their outgoing charges and picked up their inbound ones at roughly 22 degrees West longitude, but by April 1941 escort coverage extended to

35 degrees West, aided by the British occupation of Iceland. This produced a drop in losses of convoyed ships but led to a corresponding increase in sinkings of independently routed ships (IRS). By May 1941, this ratio was 2.5 IRS to 1 ship in convoy.[34] The answer was to include more ships in convoy and extend escort coverage further into the Atlantic from the western end. Newfoundland was the obvious location to set up a new naval base.

The RCN developed eight escort bases on the east coast of Canada during the Second World War; half serviced merchant ships and non-operational warships, and rest provided for the repair and re-supply of operational warships. Although initially conceived as just a temporary forward base, HMCS *Avalon* would ultimately incorporate the features of both. But this was all in the future, and when war was declared in September 1939, few Canadians and even fewer naval officers could anticipate how the destinies of the RCN and Newfoundland were inextricably linked. To most Canadians, Newfoundland was a backward, economically depressed rock jutting out into the North Atlantic off the coast of Canada. Yet in less than two years it would become an integral part of Canada's most important military commitment of the Second World War.

---

[23] Newfoundland's situation was somewhat ambiguous during the first half of the 20th Century. Along with most of the British Commonwealth, Newfoundland was granted Dominion status in 1907. However, it retained and continued to refer to itself both formally and informally as The Colony of Newfoundland. Furthermore, it did not send a delegation to the Paris Peace Conference in 1919, despite its contribution towards the Great War, or ratify the Statues of Westminster in 1932, as did most of the other dominions, and gave up responsible government altogether in 1934 in favour of a London-appointed Commission of Government headed by the Governor. Consequently, it was both a colony and "a dominion in suspension". William C. Gilmore, "Law, Constitutional Convention, and the Union of Newfoundland with Canada," *Acadiensis*, Vol. XVIII, No. 2 (Spring 1989), 111-126.

[24] The most recent general history of Newfoundland and Labrador is Sean T. Cadigan, *Newfoundland and Labrador: A History* (Toronto: University of Toronto Press, 2009). For an in-depth study of settlement and government in Newfoundland during the seventeenth and eighteenth centuries, see Peter E. Pope, *Fish Into Wine: The Newfoundland Plantation in the Seventeenth Century* (Chapel Hill: University of North Carolina Press, 2004); and Jerry Bannister, *The Rule of the Admirals: Law, Custom and Naval Government in Newfoundland, 1699-1832* (Toronto: University of Toronto Press, 2003). The classic work on the Commission of Government/Second World War years is Peter Neary, *Newfoundland in the North Atlantic World, 1929-1949* (Montreal: McGill-Queen's University Press, 1988; 2nd ed., Montreal: McGill-Queen's

University Press, 1996). An excellent examination of recruitment for the (Royal) Newfoundland Regiment during WW I is Mike O'Brien, "Out of a Clear Sky: The Mobilization of the Newfoundland Regiment, 1914-1915," *Newfoundland and Labrador Studies*, XXII, No. 2 (Fall 2007), 401-427. On the Royal Naval Reserve in Newfoundland, see Mark C. Hunter, *To Employ and Uplift Them: The Newfoundland Naval Reserve, 1899-1926* (St. John's: Institute of Social and Economic Research, 2009); and Bernard Ransom, "A Nursery of Fighting Seamen? The Newfoundland Royal Naval Reserve, 1901-1920," in Michael L. Hadley, Rob Huebert and Fred W. Crickard (eds.), *A Nation's Navy: In Quest of Canadian Naval Identity* (Montreal: McGill-Queen's University Press, 1996), 239-255.

[25] Dan van der Vat, *The Atlantic Campaign: The Great Struggle at Sea, 1939-1945* (New York: Harper and Row, 1988), 164-167.

[26] *Ibid.*; and David J. Lyon, "The British Order of Battle," in Stephen Howarth and Derek Law (eds.), *The Battle of the Atlantic, 1939-1945: The 50th Anniversary International Naval Conference* (Annapolis: Naval Institute Press, 1994), 266-275.

[27] *Ibid.*, 184. See also Thomas A. Adams, "The Control of British Merchant Shipping," in Howarth and Law (eds.), *Battle of the Atlantic*, 158-178; Tony Lane, "The Human Economy of the British Merchant Navy," in Howarth and Law (eds.), *Battle of the Atlantic*, 45-59; and Philip Pugh, "Military Needs and Civil Necessity," in Howarth and Law (eds.), *Battle of the Atlantic*, 30-44.

[28] *Ibid.*, 184-186. See also Alan J. Scarth, "Liverpool as HQ and Base," in Howarth and Law (eds.), *Battle of the Atlantic*, 240-251.

[29] V.E. Tarrant, *The U-Boat Offensive, 1914 -1945* (Annapolis: Naval Institute Press, 1989), 89.

[30] *Ibid.*

[31] Peter Neary, "Newfoundland and the Anglo-American Leased Bases Agreement of 27 March 1941," *Canadian Historical Review*, LXVII, No. 2 (December 1986), 495.

[32] Milner, *North Atlantic Run*, 27.

[33] *Ibid.* 87.

[34] Tarrant, *U-Boat Offensive*, 101.

Chapter 2

Humble Beginnings: September 1939 to May 1941

When it entered the Second World War as part of the British Empire in September 1939, Newfoundland was totally defenceless. The colony had always relied on the protection of the Royal Navy (RN) and again looked to Britain for security. The Admiralty, however, felt that the threat to Newfoundland was slight and, as during the Great War, promised to come to the rescue when danger actually materialized.[35] As a retired Royal Navy Vice-Admiral, Newfoundland's Governor Sir Humphrey Walwyn probably recognized the hollowness of these assurances and, deeply concerned about the vulnerability of shipping in St. John's Harbour, requested keeping the four-inch gun off the damaged *SS King Edward* which was being repaired at the Newfoundland Dockyard.[36] In the event, the Newfoundland Commission of Government could take its own measures, and these were immediately initiated. The British Overseas Defence Committee had formulated a *Newfoundland Defence Scheme* in 1936 which dictated steps to be taken at each stage up to and including the outbreak of war: The Peace Stage speaks for itself; The Precautionary Stage was defined as when relations with another power were so strained as to take precautions against hostilities; and The War Stage, when war had actually broken out. The scheme set out when and how various warning telegrams would be sent and what actions should be taken upon receipt. Amongst the immediate measures to be initiated were the seizure of all ships belonging to the enemy, the detention of all British and neutral ships loaded with contraband believed to be destined for the enemy, and, finally, the prevention of any British ships clearing port headed for an enemy port.[37] As St. John's and many of Newfoundland's ports were international in nature, these instructions had significant repercussions. Much of the iron ore mined at Wabana, Bell Island, and the lead and zinc mined at Buchans was shipped to Germany, and German vessels were constant visitors at Botwood, Lewisporte and Corner Brook.[38] Captain CMR Schwerdt, RN, Walwyn's Private Secretary was appointed Naval Officer in Charge (NOIC) and immediately established a Naval Control Service office and set about implementing the *Newfoundland Defence Scheme*.[39] Indeed, one of his first actions as NOIC was to order the seizure of the *Christoph von Doornum* at Botwood and the internment of her crew.[40]

While Governor Humphrey Walwyn had not been an exceptional, or even popular, figure as head of the Commission of Government before September 1939, the former navy man came into his own during the war years. Walwyn initiated committees to examine such serious matters as censorship, recruitment, currency, rationing, and of course, defence.[41] Among his major concerns were the two airports. The Newfoundland Airport at Gander and the trans-Atlantic seaplane base at Botwood were developed during the 1930s for civilian purposes by the Newfoundland and British governments. The fear was that the Germans might want to neutralize both facilities as a strictly defensive measure or, even more worrisome, to acquire them for their own use in hostilities against Canada and the United States. Should the Nazis get a foothold in Newfoundland, the whole east coast of Canada and the United States could be threatened[42] Indeed, Ottawa worried that if the Germans "were given six hours on a piece of land where they intended to establish an air base they could never be dislodged."[43] Walwyn discussed the formation of a Newfoundland Defence Force to protect such vital installations with the Dominions Office (DO) in May 1939 and requested funds and equipment.[44] The DO approved the request, and dispatched training officers and a limited amount of equipment from Britain.[45] The Newfoundland Government, however, put the plan on hold in August until the force could be fully outfitted.[46] In the meantime, Walwyn suggested that the Canadians be invited to take over the protection of both facilities for the duration.[47] The British Air Ministry rejected this, as London was afraid that once they got in, the Canadians would be as hard to dislodge as the Germans, and these two airports would be very important to civil aviation after the war.[48]

Actually, Canada made the commitment to defend Newfoundland even before it entered the war against Germany.[49] Where once Ottawa considered Newfoundland to be a "liability,"[50] it now saw its neighbour as an "essential Canadian interest" and an important part of the "Canadian orbit."[51] Indeed, Prime Minister Mackenzie King argued in September 1939 that not only was the defense of Newfoundland and Labrador "essential to the security of Canada" but also by guaranteeing its integrity, Canada would actually be assisting Britain and France's war effort by relieving the former of that responsibility.[52] Yet despite these altruistic sentiments, the reality was that Newfoundland presented a number of potential targets important to Canada: Newfoundland's bountiful forestry and fisheries resources, the numerous trans-Atlantic cable and wireless stations along its coast, the paper mills at Corner Brook and Grand Falls, and the fluorspar mine at St. Lawrence and the iron ore mine on Bell Island, supplying Cape Breton's steel mills which produced one-third of Canada's steel output, as well as, the airport at Gander; the seaplane base at Botwood; and of course, the city of St. John's, the economic and political centre of Newfoundland. Furthermore, thanks to its geographical position, Ottawa viewed Newfoundland as the "key to the gulf of Canada" and "in many ways [its] first line of defence."[53] Indeed, Governor Walwyn lamented that it was "quite apparent that Newfoundland [was] being considered only in so far as the defence of Canada is concerned."[54]

During the "Phony War" in Europe,[55] the Canadian government did not act upon its commitment to Newfoundland's defence. In fact, after visiting Ottawa in March 1940 to discuss Canada's defence plans for Newfoundland, Commissioner L.E. Emerson complained that no preparations had been made.[56] In meetings with the Chief of the General Staff Major-General T.V. Anderson, the head of the Royal Canadian Navy (RCN) Rear-Admiral Percy Nelles, and Royal Canadian Air Force (RCAF) Chief Air Vice Marshal G.M. Croil, Emerson discovered that no instructions had been issued relating to Newfoundland other than for the defence of Bell Island and those parts of the coast that were important to the defence of Canada. No provisions at all had been made to base anything in Newfoundland to protect the populous but very vulnerable coast stretching from Cape Freels at the head of Bonavista Bay to Cape Race at the southern tip of the Avalon Peninsula.[57] During his March meetings, Emerson suggested basing reconnaissance seaplanes at Bay Bulls or Trepassey on the Southern Shore, or even somewhere in St. Mary's or Placentia Bays. The Canadians regretted that "they did not have any planes to spare," but they did offer to train men to man the guns on Bell Island.[58]

This state of affairs changed as the German *Blitzkrieg* swept through France and the Low Countries in the spring of 1940. In June, Ottawa dispatched the 1st Battalion of the Black Watch of Canada to Botwood and stationed five Douglas Digby bombers from RCAF No. 10 Squadron at Gander.[59] Nevertheless, it did not take long before the first invasion scare occurred. In early July, authorities received intelligence that U-boats were going to set up an advance base at Cape Bauld at the tip of the Great Northern Peninsula. Canadian troops were landed, aided by HMCS *Ottawa*, but no evidence of a German incursion was found and the troops withdrew.[60] In the meantime, at a meeting held at the Colonial Building in St. John's, Major-General Anderson and various government and local military officials discussed defensive measures in the event of

The "Newfyjohn" Solution

an enemy incursion. Lewisporte was seen as a likely insertion point for any enemy force intent on capturing the Newfoundland Airport. Commissioner of Public Utilities, Sir Wilfrid Woods informed the meeting that arrangements were being made, including an all-night telegraph watch, to immediately alert the airport should the enemy land at Lewisporte. Anderson also recommended that Canadian troops draw up demolition plans for the Newfoundland Railway and guard certain focal points along the line in the event that an invading force tried to seize one or more locomotives. The General further worried that the runway at Harbour Grace was long enough to accommodate enemy aircraft. Unwilling to make the site permanently unusable, he suggested temporary measures be utilized and Commissioner Woods recommended that large boulders be place along the ground to temporarily block it.[61]

In any event, by November 1940, the newly appointed Commander, Combined Newfoundland and Canadian Military Forces, Brigadier P Earnshaw, arrived in St. John's and Canadian contractors were building Camp Lester on the outskirts of the city. By the end of the year, 775 men from the Canadian 53rd Infantry Battalion arrived to defend St. John's.[62] In the meantime, the sites for two 4.7- and 10-inch guns had been selected at Signal Hill and Cape Spear, respectively, and a further two 6-inch guns were proposed on top of the 75-mm examination battery already in place at Fort Amherst.[63] Even so, Schwerdt worried that an enemy cruiser with 6-inch guns could park just outside the Narrows and after quickly silencing the Fort Amherst battery, systematically pound the harbour and town for at least an hour before planes from Gander, 135 miles distant, arrived, assuming the weather co-operated.[64] His fears were somewhat alleviated with the news that four 155-mm mobile guns, four 3-inch Anti-Aircraft (AA) guns and a number of smaller AA guns as well as an ample supply of ammunition were due at St. John's along with 1000 American troops on *Edmund B Alexander* in January 1941 as part of the Anglo-American "destroyers for bases" deal.[65]

The RCN was also making plans for Newfoundland, especially for St. John's. In October 1940, Naval Service Headquarters (NSHQ) decided to institute a Naval Examination Service at the port, commencing 1 December, to control shipping entering St. John's Harbour and provide further defence for the facilities. It proposed that HMCS *Amber* would proceed to St. John's for duty as an examination vessel and that a Port War Signal Station be installed at Cabot Tower. NSHQ requested that the Naval Officer in Charge (NOIC), Captain C.M.R. Schwerdt, RN,[66] make arrangements for their accommodation. NSHQ assumed these plans would meet the approval of the

Newfoundland government,[67] but in what may have been a portent of things to come, Ottawa neglected to make arrangements to pay for them.[68] Regardless, the Newfoundland Government approved the request, and by the end of the year the Examination Service was up and running. As well, the anti-torpedo defences for St. John's harbour were on site and ready for installation in the spring.[69]

By the time the first ships of the Newfoundland Escort Force (NEF)–HMC Ships *Agassiz, Alberni, Chambly, Cobalt, Collingwood, Orillia* and *Wetaskiwin*–under the command of Commander J.D. "Chummy" Prentice, RCN, on *Chambly*–sailed through the Narrows at the end of May 1941, St. John's was well on its way to being a well-defended harbour. It was already the base for the Newfoundland Defence Force (NDF) comprising five corvettes, two minesweepers and four Fairmile patrol boats.[70] Captain Schwerdt and his small staff arranged to install the anti-torpedo baffle at the entrance to the harbour, and enlarged the Examination Service by enlisting two former Newfoundland Customs cutters, *Marvita* and *Shulamite*, complete with their crews. A 4000-ton Admiralty fuel tank was under construction, and a Port War Signal Station planned at Cape Spear along with a High Frequency Direction Finding (HF/DF, or Huff Duff) station and a radio beacon.[71] Under NSHQ instructions, one RCN leading signalman and five ratings manned the Cabot Tower Port War Signal Station, and Fort Amherst was sited as an Examination Battery including four RCN signalmen.[72] The Canadian Army completed this battery in the fall of 1941; in the interim, American troops manned four mobile 155-millimetre guns and two 8-inch railway guns in and around St. John's for defence.[73] By the spring of 1941, St. John's was an armed camp, and the Battle of the Atlantic had entered an important stage.

Despite tremendous successes by the U-boats in the Battle of the Atlantic during the first part of the war, the tide actually started to turn during the winter of 1941. This is not to say that both sides failed to have some spectacular successes as well as tragic failures during this period. Rather, by the time the first ships of the NEF sailed into St. John's harbour, the Atlantic war had reached a new phase that started to favour the Allies. The year began well for the Germans when in early January 1941, the *Oberkommando der Wehrmacht* (Supreme High Command of the Armed Forces or OKW) put I/KG 40 with Focke-Wulf Fw200 Condor long-range bombers under Dönitz's command. For the first time, the U-Boat chief had aircraft to help direct his wolfpacks to the vital convoys feeding Britain's war effort. With a range of almost 600 miles, these aircraft roamed far out into the Atlantic to search out targets. Once found, the aircrews reported the convoy's position to U-boat Command

The "Newfyjohn" Solution

or guided the U-boats to their targets directly. Also in January, the heavy cruisers *Gneisenua* and *Scharnhorst* left Brest for an anti-shipping campaign in the North Atlantic. Shortly thereafter, their sister ship, *Admiral Hipper*, also sortied, and all three broke into the Atlantic through the Denmark Strait without being detected by the Allies in early February. *Hipper* sank eight ships before her return in mid-February[74] and by the end of their mission in March, *Gneisenua* and *Scharnhorst* had sunk twenty-two ships for a total of 115,622 tons.[75]

Despite such successes, the potential of the Condors' anti-shipping patrols was never realized. In the main, this was due to their difficulty in giving the U-boats correct navigational data on the location of a convoy. Consequently, even if a plane detected a convoy, the wolfpack could not find it unless the Condor homed it in with radio signals. Given the time it took for the pack to reach the datum point, as well as Allied anti-aircraft measures, the Condors often had to depart before the U-boats located their target. Nevertheless, during the first three months of 1941, U-boats sank 620,000 tons of Allied shipping. However, with the gales of March came disaster. In quick succession, Germany's three most famous U-boat aces–Prien, Kretschmer and Schepke–were all sunk. Only Kretschmer survived his sinking, and he was eventually interned at Camp Bowmanville in Ontario. So disastrous was the loss of "The Bull of Scapa Flow" that Prien's death was kept secret for months. To many historians, these losses capped off what was known as "The Happy Time" for the U-boats. Up to this point, the Battle of the Atlantic seemed to be going all Germany's way–successes were many, while casualties were relatively low. Despite being serious blows to morale–Prien, Kretschmer and Schepke were national heroes–their losses were only the thirty-sixth, thirty-seventh and thirty-eighth of thirty-nine U-boats sunk in the eighteen months since the beginning of the war. But from April to the end of the year, monthly successes diminished, and by the end of 1941 a further thirty U-boats had been lost.[76]

Historians point to two important measures which were largely responsible for the change in Allied fortunes. One is how Coastal Command operated its aircraft. In April, Coastal Command came under the control of the Admiralty and tactics changed. To this point, aircraft gave only close escort protection to convoys, meaning that they patrolled either over or in front of the formation. This did not take advantage of the aircrafts' range and speed or the fact that the wolfpacks were homed into the convoy by a shadower to the rear of, or running parallel to, the convoy just beyond the horizon. Coastal Command discovered that most U-boat sightings around convoys were made by aircraft coming or going to intercept their convoys rather than when they got there. Consequently, from the spring of 1941, Coastal Command sent aircraft further afield to detect and at least put down shadowing U-boats, or if the pack had already gathered, to drive off the attackers before they could do much damage. The other measure altering the balance of power in the Atlantic was the increase in the number of escorts per convoy. Escorts now formed into groups with the Senior Officer Escort (SOE) giving instructions through short-range radio-telephone. This was facilitated in large measure by the introduction of fifty ex-USN destroyers Britain received in exchange for giving the US bases on British territory in the Western Hemisphere.[77]

In the summer of 1940, the British were dangerously short of destroyers for convoy escort duty. The Royal Navy (RN) lost a large number during the ill-fated Norwegian campaign and the evacuation at Dunkirk, with still more being sunk or damaged while held in port to counter the expected German invasion of Britain. Prime Minister Winston Churchill appealed to President Franklin Roosevelt in May for "forty or fifty of [his] older destroyers" to fill the breach until new construction compensated for the losses.[78] Roosevelt was more than willing to do this, but the United States was officially neutral and such a transfer would contravene international law as well as inflame isolationist sentiment in the US. The answer seemed to be an exchange of sorts. As a gesture of friendship, Churchill proposed that Britain would allow the US to lease land on British territory in the Western Hemisphere for bases, and a reciprocal gesture would be made of the destroyers as well as other military hardware. Unfortunately, this remedy was too subtle for American policymakers, who preferred a more direct and documented swap. On the other hand, a straight exchange of assets would not have gone down well in the territories involved or in Britain. Indeed, British Minister of Supply Lord Beaverbrook (1st Baron Beaverbrook William Maxwell "Max" Aitken from New Brunswick) opined that if the British were going to make a bargain, he did not want to make a bad one, and in his opinion, granting British territory to the Americans for ninety-nine years in exchange for fifty WWI-vintage destroyers was a bad deal.[79] The solution came in a compromise that gave the British their gesture and the Americans their business deal. Leases would be given "freely and without consideration" to the Americans in Newfoundland and Bermuda, while similar facilities would be traded in Jamaica, Trinidad, British Guiana, St. Lucia and Antigua for the fifty destroyers. This solved the problem, and the "destroyers for bases" deal, as it became known, was announced on 3 September 1940.[80]

In January 1941, the first of the Americans arrived at St. John's, to set up naval and air bases on the island under arrangements made by the Greenslade Board in the fall. The Board, named after its head, Rear-Admiral John W. Greenslade, and including Brigadier-General Jacob L Devers, Lieutenant-Colonel Harry J. Malony and Major Townsend Griffiss toured the various territories in the Western Hemisphere included in the Anglo-American Leased Bases Agreement throughout September 1940 in order to choose appropriate sites for the proposed US bases.[81] Two months later, the USN formed Support Force Atlantic Fleet under Admiral A.L. Bristol, operating out of Argentia, in Placentia Bay, ostensibly to escort American convoys to Greenland and Iceland. While doing so, on 10 April USS *Niblack* attacked a submerged contact with depth charges. While no results were forthcoming, this was the first recorded instance of American action against the U-boats in the Battle of the Atlantic. The boundary of the Western Hemisphere was advanced to 30 degrees West a week later. At the same time, the US naval base at Bermuda opened for operation, and US *TG 7.3* under the command of Rear-Admiral Cook arrived to commence the Central Atlantic Neutrality Patrol.[82] On the other side of the Atlantic, despite continued heavy bombing, Western Approaches Command (WAC) moved to Liverpool from Plymouth which allowed closer co-operation between staff and the men at sea. However, these were not the only reasons behind the Allies' change in fortunes.

The Allies started to win the technology war in early 1941. One major component, radar, became more readily available to escorts, although Canadian forces habitually lagged behind the RN in this area.[83] Radar-equipped escorts were able to penetrate the cloak of invisibility that night surface attacks gave the U-boats in wolfpack operations. In addition, miniaturization of Huff Duff systems allowed the SOE to detect U-boat radio signals long before an attack commenced. This permitted the Convoy Commodore to alter course while one or more escorts converged on the triangulated signal's point of origin, usually a shadowing submarine, and sink it or at least drive it down.

These advances facilitated a number of intelligence captures on the high seas during the first few months of 1941. On 4 March, HMS *Somalia* captured secret German naval codes from NN04 *Krebs* which allowed the Government Code and Cipher School[84] at Bletchley Park, just outside London, to decode selected German Enigma messages over the next few months. However, it was the capture of *U-110* and the recovery of an intact naval Enigma machine and codebooks that really gave British code breakers an insight into the German naval codes. On 9 May, U-110 was blown to the surface while attacking HX-123 and abandoned. A party from HMS *Bulldog* boarded the U-boat and recovered a treasure trove of secret papers, codes and an Enigma machine. The U-boat was taken in tow but sank en route to Iceland. The recovered intelligence, combined with that salvaged from the German weathership *München* near Jan Mayan Island two days previous, allowed Bletchley Park to read Enigma messages for most of June. Still, this did not come in time to counter Operation *Rheinübung*, the Atlantic breakout of the German battleship *Bismarck* and heavy cruiser *Prinz Eugen* under Admiral Lütjens.[85]

On 22 May, British reconnaissance aircraft confirmed the departure of the two capital ships from Norway. Thus alerted, the British Home Fleet under Admiral John Cronyn "Jack" Tovey sortied from Scapa Flow and intercepted the German ships in the Denmark Strait two days later. During the ensuing engagement, *Bismarck* sank HMS *Hood* with the loss of over 1400 men but was itself damaged, causing a reduction in speed. Over the next several days, the RN subjected *Bismarck* to carrier-borne torpedo plane attacks which finally resulted in two hits on the steering gear rendering the battleship un-manoeuvrable. Unable to escape and ordering its consort *Prinz Eugen* home, Bismarck was surrounded the next day and battered to a blazing hulk by shells from the battleships *King George V* and *Rodney*. *Bismarck* ultimately scuttled itself leaving many of its crew in the water. RN ships rescued 110 men, but a U-boat scare forced the British to leave the rest to their fate. Only five were found several hours later by a U-boat and a weathership.[86]

While the British rejoiced at this spectacular victory, it was still tinged with salt due to the destruction of HMS *Hood* and continuing losses of merchant shipping in the Atlantic. During May, the Allies lost sixty-three ships.[87] Although almost half of these were attacked in the Freetown area of Africa, the remainder were sunk in the North Atlantic, many in convoy. OB-318 outward-bound from Britain was attacked at the beginning of the month with the loss of five ships and OB-126 was set upon by a pack of six U-boats and suffered a total of nine ships sunk. This last attack prompted the Admiralty to instigate end-to-end convoy escort and decide that the western end would be based at St. John's.[88]

Initially, the RN escorted convoys to 22 degrees West, but as the U-boats advanced westward, Britain pushed this to 35 degrees West and occupied Iceland, to both deny it to the Germans and use it as a forward escort base. The RCN, based out of Halifax, Nova Scotia, could only provide escort as far as the Grand Banks, which left approximately 1200 miles where convoys travelled with little or no protection. This area became known as "The Pit" and this was the stretch of ocean where the

The "Newfyjohn" Solution

U-boats now operated with apparent impunity. It soon became clear that establishing a forward base at St. John's, as had been done at Hvalfjordhur, Iceland, would extend coverage more than 600 miles further east into the Atlantic.

Towards the end of May, the British Admiralty sent a message to Captain Schwerdt, the NOIC at St. John's, explaining that due to the advance of the U-boats they were "now forced to use a base on the Western side of the Atlantic for escorting destroyers and corvettes." They indicated that they were interested in using St. John's for this and asked his opinion on whether it was feasible as an escort base, and if not, what was his next choice.[89] Schwerdt had long demonstrated his ability both as the Governor's personal secretary and as the NOIC at St. John's. Indeed, Canadian historian Roger Sarty has correctly suggested that the fine job that Schwerdt and his small staff did in preparing the ex-USN destroyers for their trans-Atlantic crossing to Britain probably helped introduce St. John's as a possible escort base.[90] Schwerdt replied that St. John's was the best choice in Newfoundland and optimistically suggested that it was only hampered by fog "two or three days per month." It also featured a soon-to-be-completed 4,000-ton Admiralty fuel tank. His next choice was Botwood, which had less fog but was undefended and had no fuel storage facilities.[91] On the other hand, at the time, convoys were routed through the Strait of Belle Isle into the Labrador Sea, which made Botwood much closer than St. John's, which was on the other side of the island.[92] With St. John's being Schwerdt's clear choice, the Admiralty asked him whether St. John's could accommodate a depot ship, an oiler, a 500-foot supply ship, five destroyers, five corvettes, a sloop, and a cutter at the same time.[93]

The Admiralty also asked Naval Service Headquarters as to the number of new-construction corvettes it could provide for a force in the "Newfoundland focal area."[94] The Admiralty received NSHQ's enthusiastic reply that seven corvettes were immediately available for posting at St. John's with fifteen more in a month and a total of forty-eight in six months. Ottawa also offered to "undertake [the] task of anti-submarine convoys...which would involve utilization of all R.C.N. destroyers."[95] To sweeten the pie, CNS Admiral Percy Nelles offered to establish the base from "Canadian sources."[96] Commander E.R. Mainguy (soon to be Captain) was offered as commander of this force.[97] The Admiralty thought Mainguy was too junior, but Captain L.W. Murray, then in London as Commodore Commanding Canadian Ships (CCCS), was perfectly acceptable.[98] Ottawa readily agreed.

The RCN and the Government of Canada in particular, had a

number of reasons for wanting the base in St. John's to be a "Canadian" enterprise. For one, the protection of the vital trans-Atlantic convoys was the single most important responsibility of the Battle of the Atlantic. Without the "safe and timely arrival" of the convoys in the UK, the war in Europe would be lost. The RN had been derelict in its preparation in this area. The Admiralty thought that the menace to trade would come from surface raiders and that any submarine threat would be nullified by the development of ASDIC. Nonetheless, within the first few months of the war, it was evident that German U-boats were more than just a mere nuisance and that the RN was woefully short of escort craft.[99] The government of Prime Minister Mackenzie King saw trade protection as an area where Canada could make a major contribution to the war effort without suffering the horrendous casualties of the First World War. Furthermore, the prospect of concentrating all of Canada's available naval forces in one area and with one vital and well-defined objective, under a Canadian officer, was very attractive to both the RCN brass and their political bosses.[100] Canadian Minister of Defence J.L. Ralston suggested at a meeting of the War Cabinet that it offered the RCN the opportunity to play "an important and vital role in the Western Atlantic."[101] From the onset of the war, Canada resisted any British attempt to subordinate its sovereignty and the autonomy of its armed forces. Unlike the governments of the other Commonwealth and occupied nations, the Mackenzie King government refused the suggestion that the RCN simply operate as part of the RN. The country's small fleet was built to protect Canada's extensive coastline, and was only transferred to UK waters at the personal appeal of Winston Churchill. The creation of the NEF and the establishment of the RCN base at St. John's could be seen as a move directly related to the defence of Canada.[102]

Another reason that the Canadians wanted a major naval force operating out of St. John's was because by this time the American presence in Newfoundland was increasing as the US built bases and outposts from coast to coast. By war's end, tens of thousands of American servicemen were stationed in Newfoundland and Labrador, and hundreds of thousands of military personnel and passengers had passed through the various US facilities in the colony.[103] Furthermore, thanks to the Anglo-American Staff Agreement (ABC 1), signed without Canadian participation in early 1941, the United States was assigned strategic control over the Western Atlantic and all the naval forces therein, including Canadian, when they entered the war. The Canadian government feared that this agreement was a further attempt to oust Canada from Newfoundland.[104] Consequently, Canadian authorities worried about both a permanent American presence in Newfoundland and also that the RCN's more experienced forces would be under American direction.[105] Canada needed both to impress upon its allies the "vital nature" of its interest in Newfoundland and to project itself on the world scene.[106] As Malcolm MacLeod noted, "Canada was determined to become a weighty presence in Newfoundland, both for the sake of winning the war and for future considerations."[107]

Meanwhile, Schwerdt replied that St. John's harbour could accommodate no more than ten ships moored mid-harbour because the meteorological ships *City of Toronto* and *Arakaka* were based in St. John's, and that the Americans were anticipating a continual flow of transports, not to mention regular merchant ship traffic. He suggested that wharfage for the some of the destroyers, the corvettes, and depot ships could be requisitioned but that dredging and repairs to the wharves would be necessary. The remaining destroyers and the oiler would have to anchor in the middle of the harbour. Schwerdt concluded that space for any more than the aforementioned would be "most difficult to arrange with any security of tenure."[108]

This state of affairs did not seem to deter the Admiralty, which concluded that while "facilities may be lacking at first...this can be accepted in view of the urgent necessity to establish [the] base." It then laid out a long list of requirements which included six buildings for ordnance and 50,000 square feet for naval and victualling stores including refrigeration. The proposed force also grew to thirty destroyers and corvettes (fifteen each) and six sloops.[109] Support would consist of a depot ship, an oiler and a store ship and personnel totalling forty-six officers and 1000 men. The 4000-ton Admiralty oil tank would be used for refuelling the force. Despite knowing that the local hospital could barely service the civilian population, the Admiralty thought it would suffice for the naval personnel as well.[110]

In a very short period of time, Newfoundland went from a helpless outpost in the North Atlantic to being "the key to the western defence system."[111] Whereas in 1939 the Commission of Government worried about how to cope with its own defence, by May 1941 Newfoundland had become an armed camp, occupied by Canadian and American armed forces. However, this was, and would continue to be, an uneasy relationship as the United States and Canada both pursued their own agendas in Newfoundland, while the Newfoundland government tried to look after the colony's interests. These tensions were quite evident in the establishment of HMCS *Avalon* at St. John's. Canada saw the escort base as both an opportunity to improve its international presence and a means to protect its interests in Newfoundland from the Americans. As we will see in the next chapter, the Newfoundland government, not without justification, was suspicious of Canadian intentions and did not want to give that country any greater hold over the colony than was absolutely necessary. This caused delays and frustrations on all sides and would continue to do so for the remainder of the war.

---

[35] Great Britain, National Archives (TNA/PRO), Admiralty (ADM) 1/10608, Admiralty minute, Director of Plans, 15 March 1940. See also TNA/PRO, ADM 1/10608, Admiralty to Dreyer, 2 May 1940.

[36] London denied the request. Public Archives of Newfoundland and Labrador (PANL), GN38, File 2: J23-40, Memorandum for Commission, 23 May 1940. See also Governor to Dominions Secretary, 25 May 1940 in Paul Bridle (ed.), *Documents on Relations between Canada and Newfoundland* (2 vols., Ottawa: Department of External Affairs, 1974-1984), I, 76; and Dominions Secretary to Governor, 10 June 1940 in Bridle (ed.), *Documents*, I, 80.

[37] PANL, GN38, Dept. of Justice and Defence, S4-2-1.2, File 14, *Newfoundland Defence Scheme 1936*.

[38] Gerhard Bassler, *Vikings to U-Boats: The German Experience in Newfoundland and Labrador* (Montreal & Kingston: McGill-Queen's University Press, 2006), 194-6, 225-7.

[39] PANL, DO 35/725, B5012, Governor's Quarterly Report for the Period Ending 30 September 1939.

[40] Bassler, *Vikings to U-Boats*, 194-6, 225-7.

[41] "Newfoundland Emergency Defence Measures," *Evening Telegram* (St. John's), 2 September 1939.

[42] Air Officer Commanding, Eastern Air Command, to Secretary, Department of National Defence, 29 May 1940, in Paul Bridle (ed.), *Documents on Relations between Canada and Newfoundland* (2 vols., Ottawa: Department of External Affairs, 1974-1984), I, 77-78.

[43] This assessment was based on Allied experience in Norway. PANL, GN38, S4-2-4, File 2, A.S. Brand, Director of Naval Intelligence to C.M.R. Schwerdt, 3 July 1940.

[44] Governor of Newfoundland to Dominions Secretary, 22 May 1939 in *Ibid.*, I, 35.

[45] Dominions Secretary to Governor, 26 June 1939, and Dominions Secretary to Governor, 30 August 1939 in *Ibid.*, I, 37.

[46] Commissioner of Justice to Commission of Government for Newfoundland, 31 August 1939, in *Ibid.*, I, 39-41.

[47] Governor to Dominions Secretary, 15 September 1939 in *Ibid.*, I, 45-46.

[48] Peter Neary, *Newfoundland in the North Atlantic World, 1929-1949* (Montreal: McGill-Queen's University Press, 1988; 2nd ed., Montreal: McGill-

Queen's University Press, 1996), 116. See also Neary, "Newfoundland and the Anglo-American Leased Bases Agreement of 27 March 1941," *Canadian Historical Review*, LXVII, No. 4 (December 1986), 493.

[49] Secretary of State for External Affairs to Governor of Newfoundland, 2 September 1939, in Bridle (ed.), *Documents*, I, 41. See also Extract from a Speech by Prime Minister, 8 September 1939, in *Ibid., Documents*, I, 43.

[50] During a meeting with Prime Minister Mackenzie King at Hyde Park in April 1941, President Roosevelt suggested that Canada should take over Newfoundland. Mackenzie King replied that Newfoundland had not been included in Confederation before that because it was a liability and Canada would have to make it into an asset. J.W. Pickersgill, *The Mackenzie King Record*, Vol. I (Toronto: University of Toronto Press, 1960), 202. See also David Mackenzie, *Inside the Atlantic Triangle: Canada and the Entrance of Newfoundland into Confederation, 1939-1949* (Toronto: University of Toronto Press, 1986), 65. In 1933, Canadian Minister of Finance Edgar N. Rhodes summed up Ottawa's view of Newfoundland when he declared that, if part of Canada, it "would really in effect become another Ireland...a nuisance and always grumbling and wanting something." Peter Neary, *Newfoundland in the North Atlantic World, 1929-1949* (Montreal: McGill-Queen's University Press, 1988; 2nd ed., Montreal: McGill-Queen's University Press, 1996), 20. See also Peter Neary, "'A Mortgaged Property': The Impact of the United States on Newfoundland, 1940-1949," in *Twentieth Century Newfoundland: Explorations*, James Hiller and Peter Neary, eds. (St. John's, NL: Breakwater, 1994) 179-193.

[51] High Commissioner for Newfoundland to Secretary of State for External Affairs, 3 December 1941, in *Ibid.*, I, 115.

[52] Extract from a Speech by Prime Minister, 8 September 1939, in *Ibid.*, I, 43.

[53] J.W. Pickersgill, *The Mackenzie King Record* (4 vols., Toronto: University of Toronto Press, 1960), I, 202; and Minutes of a Meeting of War Cabinet Committee, 17 September 1940, in Bridle (ed.), *Documents*, I, 99. See also Minutes of a Meeting of War Cabinet Committee, 10 June 1941, in Bridle (ed.), *Documents*, 571; High Commissioner in Newfoundland to Secretary of State for External Affairs, 3 December 1941, in Bridle (ed.), *Documents*, I, 115; and Secretary of State for External Affairs to Dominions Secretary, 2 March 1941, in Bridle (ed.), *Documents*, 103. For a further examination of Newfoundland's strategic importance, see A.R.M Lower, "Transition to Atlantic Bastion," in R.A. MacKay (ed.), *Newfoundland: Economic, Diplomatic, Strategic Studies* (Toronto: Oxford University Press, 1946), 484-508.

[54] Provincial Archives of Newfoundland and Labrador (PANL), GN 38, S4-1-2, File 2: J12(a)-40, Governor to Secretary of State For Dominion Affairs, 5 April 1940.

[55] The period from the end of the invasion of Poland in September 1939 to the start of the *Blitzkrieg* in the West in May 1940 is also known as the *Sitzkrieg* due to the lack of any fighting in Europe.

[56] PANL , Memorandum for Commission, GN 38, S4-1-2, File 2:J12-

49, 23 March 1940.

[57] During the First World War, plans were made to establish a naval air station at Cape Race to counter the threat of German U-boats. Stuart E. Soward, *Hands to Flying Stations; A Recollective History of Canadian Naval Aviation, Vol. I, 1945—1954* (Victoria, BC: Neptune Developments, 1993), 3.

[58] *Ibid.*, PANL, GN38, S4-1-4, File 5: J12-40, Memorandum for Commission, 23 March 1940.

[59] C.P. Stacey, *Six Years of War: The Army in Canada, Britain and the Pacific* (Ottawa: Queen's Printer, 1955), 178-180. See also David MacKenzie, *Inside The Atlantic Triangle: Canada and the Entrance of Newfoundland into Confederation, 1939-1949* (Toronto: University of Toronto Press, 1986); and Robert Kavanagh, "W Force: The Canadian Army and the Defence of Newfoundland in the Second World War" (Unpublished MA thesis, Memorial University of Newfoundland, 1995).

[60] PANL, DO35/725, B-5012, Governor's Monthly Report for the period ending 30 September 1940. A German U-boat actually did land an unmanned weather station in Northern Labrador in 1943 that was not discovered until decades after the end of the war. Michael Hadley, *U-Boats Against Canada* (Kingston: McGill-Queen's University Press, 1985), 163-5.

[61] PANL. DO35/725, B-5012, Minutes of Meeting Held at the Department of Justice, July 29, 1940, in Governor's Monthly Report for the period ending 30 September 1940.

[62] Permanent Joint Board on Defence, Journal of Discussions and Decisions, Report of Service Members, 17 December 1940, in Bridle (ed.), *Documents*, I, 136-137. See also Governor of Newfoundland to Secretary of State for External Affairs, 7 January, 1941 in Bridle (ed.), *Documents*, I, 139-140.

[63] Permanent Joint Board on Defence, Journal of Discussions and Decisions, Report of Service Members, 17 December 1940, in Bridle (ed.), *Documents*, I, 136-137. See also Governor of Newfoundland to Secretary of State for External Affairs 7 January 1941, in Bridle (ed.), *Documents*, I, 139-140; Library and Archives Canada (LAC), Record Group (RG) 24, Naval Officer in Charge (NOIC), Vol. 11,956, C.M.R. Schwerdt to Governor, 31 December 1940; and Stacey, *Six Years of War*, 541.

[64] LAC, RG 24, NOIC, Vol. 11,956, Schwerdt to Governor, 31 December 1940.

[65] Secretary of State for Dominion Affairs to Dominions Secretary, 16 February 1941, in Bridle (ed.), *Documents*, I, 164. The famous "destroyers for bases deal" negotiated in 1940 gave the Americans base rights in British territory in the Western Hemisphere in return of 50 surplus destroyers. For the most recent investigation into the Anglo-American Leased Bases Agreement see Steven High, *Base Colonies in the Western Hemisphere, 1940-1967* (New York: Palgrave Macmillan, 2009).

[66] Capt. Schwedt had been serving as the Governor's secretary and took over as NOIC at the start of hostilities.

[67] National Defence Headquarters to Naval Officer in Charge, St. John's, 31 October 1940, in Bridle (ed.), *Documents*, I, 135.
[68] Governor to Secretary of State for External Affairs, 6 November 1940 in *Ibid.*, I, 136.
[69] Permanent Joint Board on Defence, Journal of Discussions and Decisions, Report of Service Members, 17 December 1940 in *Ibid.*, I, 136-137.
[70] Department of National Defence (DND). Directorate of History and Heritage (DHH), NSS-1000-5-20, Vol. 1, Flag Officer Newfoundland (FONF), monthly report, CCNF to NSHQ, 30 June 1941.
[71] *Ibid.*
[72] *Ibid.*, NSS-1000-5-13.5, Monthly report on proceedings, Lt-Cdr. R.U. Langston, RCNR (for NOIC), to NSHQ, 31 March 1941.
[73] Roger Sarty (ed.), *The Maritime Defence of Canada* (Toronto: Canadian Institute of Strategic Studies, 1996), 155.
[74] Robert Jackson, *The German Navy in World War II* (London: Brown Books, 1999), 86.
[75] Jürgen Rohwer and Gerhard Hummelchen, *Chronology of the War At Sea, 1939-1945: The Naval History of World War Two* (London: Ian Allan, 1972; 3rd rev. ed., London: Chatham Publishing, 1992), 55.
[76] V.E. Tarrant, *The U-Boat Offensive, 1914-1945* (Annapolis: Naval Institute Press, 1989), 97-103.
[77] Eric J. Grove (ed.), *The Defeat of the Enemy Attack on Shipping, 1939-1945* (Aldershot: Ashgate Publishing, 1997), 66-69.
[78] H. Duncan Hall, *North American Supply* (London: HMSO, 1955), 139.
[79] Philip Goodhart, *Fifty Ships that Saved The World: The Foundation of the Anglo-American Alliance* (New York: Doubleday and Co., 1965), 172.
[80] Stetson Conn, Rose C. Engelman and Bryon Fairchild, *Guarding the United States and Its Outposts* (Washington, DC: Office of the Chief of Military History, 1964; reprint, Washington, DC: US Government Printing Office, 2000), 359.
[81] *Ibid.*, 359.
[82] Rohwer and Hummelchen, Chronology, 58.
[83] David Zimmerman, *The Great Naval Battle of Ottawa: How Admirals, Scientists, and Politicians Impeded the Development of High Technology in Canada's Wartime Navy* (Toronto: University of Toronto Press, 1989), 84, notes that by December 1942, of the fifty-seven warships in the North Atlantic without radar, forty-five (seventy-five percent) were Canadian.
[84] Facetiously nicknamed the Golf, Cheese and Chess Society
[85] Rohwer and Hummelchen, *Chronology*, 53-62. See also F.H. Hinsley, *et al., British Intelligence in the Second World War: Its Influence on Strategy and Operations* (4 vols., London: HMSO, 1979-1990), I, 336-339.
[86] *Ibid.*, 62-64. See also Hinsley, *et al., British Intelligence*, I, 339-345.
[87] Tarrant, U-Boat Offensive, 101.
[88] W.A.B. Douglas, *et al., No Higher Purpose: The Operational*

History of the Royal Canadian Navy in the Second World War, 1939-1943, Volume II, Part 1 (St. Catharines, ON: Vanwell Publishing Ltd., 2002), 183.

[89] TNA/PRO, ADM 116/4526, Admiralty to NOIC, St. John's, 20 May 1941.

[90] Roger Sarty, personal communication, May 2006. In a message to the First Sea Lord, the C-in-C, American and West Indies Station recognized the Admiralty's fortune at having Schwerdt at St. John's. *Ibid.*, ADM 1/4526, C-in-C, American and West Indies to Admiralty (For First Sea Lord), 15 June 1941.

[91] *Ibid.*, ADM 116/4526, NOIC St. John's to Admiralty, 20 May 1941.

[92] Marc Milner, *North Atlantic Run: The Royal Canadian Navy and the Battle for the Convoys* (Toronto: University of Toronto Press, 1985), 62.

[93] TNA/PRO, ADM 116/4526, CNS to Admiralty, 26 May 1941.

[94] LAC, RG 24, FONF, Vol. 3892, NSS 1033-6-1, part 1, Newfoundland Convoy Escort Forces, General Data and Correspondence, NSHQ to Admiralty, 21 May 1941.

[95] *Ibid.*

[96] TNA/PRO ADM 116/4526, CNS to Admiralty, 26 May 1941.

[97] PANL, GN 38, S4-2-4, file 2, NSHQ to Admiralty, 21 May 1941. E. Rollo Mainguy was a member of the Class of 1915 at the Royal Naval College of Canada. At the start of the Second World War, Mainguy took command of HMCS *Assinaboine* and in 1940 was appointed to HMCS *Ottawa*. It was in *Ottawa* that Maninguy claimed the RCN's first U-boat kill, although it was not awarded until forty-two years after the war. He joined the NEF in June 1941, was promoted to Captain and appointed as Capt. (D) at HMCS *Avalon* in July 1941. He served in that post until 1942, also serving briefly as FONF before moving to Ottawa as the Chief of Naval Personnel. He commanded the cruiser HMCS *Uganda* in the Pacific theatre until 1946 and became Canada's sixth CNS in 1951. Wilfred G.D.Lund, "Vice-Admiral E. Rollo Mainguy: Sailors' Sailor," in Michael Whitby, Richard H. Gimblett and Peter Haydon (eds.), *The Admirals: Canada's Senior Naval Leadership in the Twentieth Century* (Toronto: Dundurn Press, 2006), 186-212.

[98] TNA/PRO, ADM 116/4526, CNS to Admiralty, 26 May 1941.

[99] During the first four months of the war (September-December 1939), U-boats sank over half a million tons of British shipping, including the aircraft carrier HMS *Courageous* and the battleship HMS *Royal Oak*, the latter at the fleet anchorage at Scapa Flow, Scotland. See Tarrant, U-Boat Offensive, 84.

[100] Gilbert Tucker, *The Naval Service of Canada* (2 vols., Ottawa: King's Printers, 1952), II, 189.

[101] Minutes of Meeting of Cabinet War Committee, June 20, 1941 in Bridle (ed.), Documents, 572.

[102]

[103] LAC, RG 24, Vol. 3892, NSS 1033-6-1, part 1, Nfld. Convoy Escort Force, General Data and Correspondence, Lt-Col. K.S. Maclachlan, Assistant Deputy Minister of Naval Service, and Admiral Percy Nelles, CNS, "Notes for Minister of National Defence," 1 July 1941. See also C.P. Stacey, *Arms, Men*

and Governments: The War Policies of Canada, 1939-1945 (Ottawa: Queen's Printer, 1970), 311.

[104] Milner, North Atlantic Run, 33.

[105] W.A.B. Douglas, *The Creation of a National Air Force* (Toronto: University of Toronto Press, 1986), 386.

[106] Minutes of a Meeting of Cabinet War Committee, 29 October 1941, in Bridle (ed.), *Documents*, 110.

[107] Malcolm MacLeod, *Peace of the Continent: The Impact of the Second World War Canadian and American Bases in Newfoundland* (St. John's: Harry Cuff Publishing, 1986), 18.

[108] PANL, GN 38, S4-2-4, file 2, NOIC, St. John's, to Admiralty, 23 May 1941.

[109] *Ibid.*

[110] TNA/PRO Cabinet Papers (CAB) 122/85, "Use of St. John's Newfoundland as Base," 24 May 1941.

[111] Joseph Schull, *Far Distant Ships: An Official Account of Canadian Naval Operations in World War II* (Ottawa: Edmond Cloutier, 1950; 2nd ed., Toronto: Stoddart Publishing, 1987), 430.

Chapter 3

Into The Breach: June 1941 to May 1942

It was not long before the plans for the proposed base at St. John's started to snowball. Initially, the Admiralty had proposed to run a sort of shuttle service between Newfoundland and Iceland. The Newfoundland Escort Force (NEF) would escort a convoy to the Western Ocean Meeting Point (WESTOMP) west of Iceland; from there an Iceland-based force would escort it to the Eastern Ocean Meeting Point (EASTOMP) where it would be passed to the Royal Navy. This plan was shelved when the Admiralty decided that it was a more effective use of scarce resources to extend both the WESTOMP and EASTOMP into a Mid-Ocean Meeting Point (MOMP) and to use Iceland only for refuelling. To facilitate this, the strength of the NEF was increased to thirty destroyers, twenty-four corvettes and nine sloops; of this number, the Admiralty optimistically estimated that only sixteen would be in St. John's at any one time. The Newfoundland Commission of Government doubted whether St. John's could handle the increased force without extensive improvements to the proposed facilities, while the British Ministry of War Transport (MWT) questioned its impact on the repair and maintenance of merchant vessels. Canada did not balk at the increase in forces, but when the estimates came in at around CAN $10 million, the government backtracked from its original offer to underwrite the base.[112] This decision caused some embarrassment to all parties.[113] The Admiralty realized it would have to make a "substantial contribution to its capital cost" and suggested that a fifty/fifty split (five million dollars apiece) would be acceptable.[114] For its part, the Newfoundland government felt it was preferable from "the point of view of the future of Newfoundland," as well as for popular support, for the base to be totally owned and operated by the Admiralty.[115] Tensions had long existed between the governments of Canada and Newfoundland, and the local population was suspicious of any further Canadian involvement in Newfoundland. While the presence of army and air force personnel could be viewed as being involved directly in the defence of Newfoundland, a naval base could not. Establishing the NEF was getting more complicated by the day and was going to become more so.

The existing facilities at St. John's were totally inadequate for the maintenance and supply of a major naval force, and until they were upgraded the NEF would have to depend on supply and repair facilities afloat. Moreover, any improvements ashore would take time to construct, and a substantial portion would have to be completed before the onset of winter, which gave the Admiralty no more than six months. As some of the necessary materials had to come from the United States through the Lend-Lease Program, Military Branch (M Branch) wondered if it would be easier to just ask the Americans to construct the base as they were then doing in Londonderry, Northern Ireland, and at Gareloch, Scotland. The Admiralty knew, however, that the Newfoundland government would "strongly object to the U.S. having a hold over the base."[116]

Nonetheless, the Americans were already constructing facilities at the northeast corner of the harbour. If the Americans developed the proposed escort base, the US would have control over a sizable portion of St. John's Harbour. Actually, the Admiralty knew that the Newfoundland government was very sensitive to either the US or Canada having a larger presence in Newfoundland than they already had. It was well aware that both countries had shown "scant regard for the views of the Newfoundland Government" when they created the US-Canada Permanent Joint Board on Defence (PJBD) the year before.[117] Prime Minister Mackenzie King and President Roosevelt agreed to form the PJBD when they met in Ogdensburg, New York, in August 1940. One of the Board's first duties was to produce a worst-case plan, code-named "Black," to be instituted in the event that Britain fell and North America lay open to Nazi attack. This plan included the occupation of Newfoundland.[118] Learning of this second hand from the American mission investigating locations for the proposed bases, the Commission of Government complained to London that the Canadians were making plans without consultation and warned that this could cause a public backlash if it were made public.[119]

Furthermore, Newfoundland's treatment in the Anglo-American "Destroyers for Bases" agreement, signed on 17 March 1941, had left the Commission of Government with a bad taste in its mouth. Although announced the previous September, the deal was actually negotiated at the same time that President Roosevelt was pushing his Lend-Lease Bill (passed 11 March 1941) through Congress, and this had a serious impact on the negotiations for bases in Newfoundland.[120] It was obvious from the start that the Americans had definite ideas as to what they wanted in any agreement. Knowing Britain's desperate need for war materials, they pressed their advantage, sometimes not very subtly.[121] Of particular concern to Newfoundland's government representatives were the "general powers" insisted upon by the Americans. These essentially granted the US total autonomy over the areas to be leased, giving it unprecedented authority over the property and inhabitants of a sovereign country.[122] The Newfoundland government had also hoped to acquire economic considerations from the United States as compensation for its contribution to the deal, but it was sadly disappointed. The best the Americans offered was the promise to "consider sympathetically" the development of mutual trade between the two countries.[123]

Newfoundland's representatives in the negotiations, L.E. Emerson and J.G. Penson, recognized that the terms of the agreement were "one-sided throughout and often extremely harsh" and might not be well received when made public.[124] Acting on Governor Walwyn's suggestion,[125] they requested that Prime Minister Churchill address a personal letter to the people of Newfoundland acknowledging "the considerable sacrifices" that the American plan represented and portraying acceptance of the agreement as a matter of patriotic duty.[126] In public, the Newfoundland government presented the agreement as fair and equitable, and the accord was accepted without serious objection once it was made public. Regardless, Newfoundland had taken "some hard diplomatic knocks,"[127] an experience that coloured the Commission's attitude when it came to giving either the US or Canada a further hold over Newfoundland.[128]

Ironically, as it turned out, the Admiralty thought that the Newfoundland government might prefer the Americans over the Canadians because the US occupancy would in all likelihood be less permanent.[129] By this time, however, the Canadians had already "set preparations in motion and it [was] too late to make other arrangements."[130] London decided that in order to prevent further delay, the cost of establishing the base should be shared between the British and Canadian governments with the Newfoundland Commission as agent, and asked the Americans for assistance under Lend-Lease. The Admiralty asked the Dominions Office to put pressure on both the Canadian and Newfoundland governments to agree to this arrangement, stressing the importance of speed in establishing the base and asking for cooperation to achieve this.[131]

While this was going on, a committee comprised of Admiral Sheridan, RN, Captain Schwerdt and Engineer Captain Stephens, RCN, met with the Newfoundland Commission of Government to discuss Rear-Admiral SS Bonham-Carter's appreciation of the potential for St.

The "Newfyjohn" Solution

John's to meet Admiralty requirements. Bonham-Carter was the RN's Flag Officer, North Atlantic Escort Squadron, based in Halifax and had previously visited St. John's. Bonham-Carter felt that St. John's harbour could accommodate the force envisioned by the Admiralty but only with considerable dredging and wharf construction. The Admiral further suggested that Harbour Grace could also be used to handle any overflow, at least for vessels up to the size of a corvette. Still, acquiring the waterfront property necessary for the base was not going to be easy. The Commission warned the Admiralty of the "great cost which will be involved in compensating the owners of the waterfront properties for the damages which will be caused to them by the requisitioning of their premises."[132]

Later in the month, the Base Planning Committee met to "make specific recommendations" for facilities for St. John's.[133] The committee proposed that the Knights of Columbus Building be purchased, that leases on the Reid and Angel Buildings continue on a six-month basis, and that a new administration building with a combined Royal Canadian Navy (RCN)/Royal Canadian Air Force (RCAF) operations room be constructed. With the planned move of the Royal Rifles of Canada to Valcartier, Quebec, accommodation for approximately twenty-five officers and 1000 enlisted men would be provided in the Canadian Army barracks, but canteens, sports and recreational facilities would have to be built. Most of the committee's attention, however, was directed at the operational needs of the NEF. Improvements to the harbour included approximately 3450 feet of wharf frontage–thirty-feet wide–along the Southside, and another 2065 linear feet of the same width on the north side, both of which would require dredging. Magazines would be built on Crown lands outside the city. Approximately 85,400 square feet of storage space (including 2400 square feet of refrigeration) was to be built in the dockyard area along with 18,800 square feet for repair shops and another 5000 square feet for torpedo stores. A 250-bed hospital was proposed for a site next to the city's General Hospital, along with a separate sickbay near the army barracks. It further recommended that the existing army hospital "be set aside for V.D. cases."[134] While the committee recognized that it was impossible to estimate the total cost of the plan, it suggested that it "should not exceed" six million dollars.[135] This figure did not include the cost of acquiring the sites, and this was where the problem lay.

London recognized that the Newfoundland government was not happy about the Canadian encroachment and suspected that the cost estimates were probably "swollen by the figures which [the Newfoundland Government were] in a position to charge the Canadians for requisitioned property, and compensation to owners, and other local services."[136] This suspicion would continue to cloud Canadian and British relations with the Newfoundland government during the war. The British High Commissioner to Canada warned the Admiralty in July of his "apprehension [over the] use of the Newfoundland Government as purchasing agent" for just this reason.[137] Indeed, Admiralty officials soon "strongly suspect[ed that] the U.S. Government [had] been soaked" by the Newfoundland government's compensation board.[138] Not surprisingly, Ottawa wanted to bypass the Newfoundland government altogether and deal directly with the British government.[139] The Admiralty was getting tired of all the "complications [that had] arisen on the other side of the Atlantic."[140] From the very beginning, and in spite of the Canadian offer which started the confusion, it never harboured "any doubt that the capital cost should be [the Admiralty's] liability." Finally, after a month of bickering, the Admiralty reverted to its original proposal to develop the base at St. John's itself and invited the Canadian government "to assist with materials and transferable equipment." London also thought that the Americans could help under the Lend-Lease Program. To allay the Newfoundland government's concerns, title to the sites of the new facilities would rest with either it or the British government.[141]

The arrangement was finalized in a message to all parties at the end of June. Noting particularly that the Newfoundland government was in agreement, the Admiralty announced that it would be responsible for providing the naval facilities and services for basing the NEF at St. John's. These facilities and services would be arranged between the British and Newfoundland governments on an agency basis per Admiralty plans and estimates. The occupation of existing premises and title to new ones, as well as all associated sites and improvements, would be vested in either the Newfoundland government or the Admiralty. The Admiralty would be responsible for all capital costs of these new works and services. Canada, in turn, would be responsible for the "administration and maintenance of the naval base," which would also be under the command of an RCN Commodore (Murray).[142] Ever conscious of cost, the Canadian government requested clarification that the RCN's maintenance responsibilities were limited to operations and not physical maintenance. Regardless, even though its actual capital investment was now minimal, Ottawa still felt it should have first right of refusal on the base if the Admiralty should decide to transfer its share of the assets.[143]

The NEF was inaugurated on 2 June 1941 when HMC ships *Chambly, Orillia* and *Collingwood* rendezvoused with HX-129, the first HX convoy to receive full trans-Atlantic escort, northeast of

The "Newfyjohn" Solution

Newfoundland.[144] As the Commodore Commanding, Newfoundland Force (CCNF) had not yet arrived, this was done under the authority of the Naval Officer in Charge (NOIC), the able Captain Schwerdt. Commodore Murray arrived shortly thereafter and set up his office in the Newfoundland Hotel along with Schwerdt.[145] Murray had been Commodore Commanding Canadian Ships (CCCS) in the UK and had attended a series of naval staff meetings at the Admiralty as the RN pushed convoy escort further west in the winter of 1940/1941. It was Murray who persuaded the C-in-C Western Approaches Command, Admiral Sir Percy Noble, his old captain in HMS *Calcutta*, that the gap in the trans-Atlantic escort system could be solved by creating a Canadian base in Newfoundland. No doubt this played a great part in his appointment to the post of CCNF over Mainguy, although Murray himself modestly contended that he was merely "in the right place at the right time.[146] " Considering the size of Schwerdt's staff at St. John's when Murray arrived, CCNF was lucky the depot ship HMS *Forth* arrived the next day, and he was able to draft some of the crew to handle the greatly increased code and cipher traffic and to man the Staff Office (Operations) full time.[147]

During July, the NEF was organized into twelve groups, eleven for regular convoy escort and one for special convoys, such as those for troopships, and an operational schedule based on a 110-day cycle commenced on 12 July. Six RCN corvettes were allocated to the Newfoundland Defence Force, but while the first patrols of the Strait of Belle Isle were started, CCNF discontinued them after only two convoys due to fog. However, five local convoys from Wabana were escorted during the month. Progress was made with the anti-torpedo baffle at the entrance to St. John's harbour, with buoys being laid out to mark the extremities of the two northern barriers and steps taken to put attachments in the rocks to hold the inshore end.[148] The baffle was completed by the end of August despite being damaged by HMS *Chesterfield* on 24 August.[149] By the end of the month, 129 warships had passed through St. John's, consuming 14,000 tons of fuel oil. Commodore Murray reported that even with this number of ships, the supply of fuel was adequate and fuelling arrangements were working well. This service, however, was provided by facilities afloat, and Murray argued that more permanent facilities ashore were "an urgent necessity."[150] Also during July, approval was given to construct the naval hospital, but in the interim, temporary accommodations were arranged in the basement of the Memorial College on Parade Street.[151]

At the same time, a delegation consisting of Rear Admiral Sheridan, Mr. R C Thompson of the Ministry of War Transport (MWT),

Mr. Andrews, the Officer in Charge of Works in Bermuda and Mr. E. A. Seal (codenamed Britman), head of the British Admiralty Delegation (BAD) in Washington, arrived in St. John's. The purpose of the visit was to provide the Admiralty with an on-the-ground appraisal as to what was required to establish the escort base.[152] The first issue was the small size of St. John's harbour and the resulting congestion. Seal observed that the harbour was so congested that the introduction of naval vessels would result in a decrease in space for merchant ships (and *vice versa*). The biggest problem was providing alongside accommodation for the NEF.[153] The north side of the harbour was occupied by the town, and the various commercial firms were crowded together along the waterfront. Sir Wilfred Woods, Commissioner of Public Utilities with the Newfoundland Government advised the delegation that expropriation of this waterfront property would not only detrimentally impact on the economy of Newfoundland but also would be "extremely expensive." The Americans were already developing the east side just west of the entrance to the harbour to accommodate their shipping. The Southside was occupied by commercial firms, the main ones being Imperial Oil, Job Brothers and Bowring Brothers Ltd. The jetties, Seal observed, were "in an extremely ramshackle condition" and required extensive improvements to meet naval standards. The only bright spot was the Newfoundland Dockyard, owned by the Newfoundland government, which MWT representative Thompson concluded was "efficiently and keenly run."[154]

In the course of their investigations, the delegation discovered that Canadian authorities planned to take over a large parcel of land at the extreme northwest corner of the harbour. This property was utilized by two coal import companies and occupied by "extremely old and decrepit buildings" which would require demolition. It would also be necessary to build a breastwork around the property to provide berthing for two destroyers alongside and to accommodate the workshops on shore. Seal quoted Lt. A.W. Jeckell, RCNR, a Canadian civil engineer, who suggested that buildings of standard Canadian design could be constructed on the site for seventeen cents a cubic foot.[155] The only practical plan for providing space alongside for the ships of the NEF, the delegation concluded, was to improve and extend the existing wharfage on the Southside of the harbour. With that view in mind, Seal thought that if the British government were going to invest so much money on improving the owners' sites, this should be reflected in the rent they were charged. The problem was that the owners wanted to be left alone and not have their premises improved because they felt that use by the Admiralty would cause them a "considerable amount of inconvenience

The "Newfyjohn" Solution

and extra expense." From the other side, the need to juggle naval berthing to accommodate commercial maritime activity would necessitate more wharfage than was required for naval purposes. On this subject, there seems to have been some confusion as to the size and composition of the proposed NEF. Seal and his comrades appear to have been under the impression that they were seeking to accommodate only the thirty-four destroyers assigned to the NEF, only seven of which would be in the harbour at any one time. They thought that the remainder of the force–the corvettes and sloops–would be based in Halifax. They did, however, recognize that a local defence force of five corvettes, six minesweepers, four Fairmile patrol boats, a boom lighter, a tug and four harbour craft also had to be accommodated.[156]

On 10 July 1941, Seal presented his report to Sir Wilfred Woods for approval by the Commission.[157] At the same time, Woods submitted Thompson's report to the Commission members, informing them that it dealt "entirely with the dockyard and other requirements of merchant ships in St. John's harbour." Thompson's report pointed out the difficulty caused by the congestion in the harbour. He suggested that even though forty-six merchant vessels were present in the harbour at one point during the previous year, this did not mean that the harbour could accommodate such a large number consistently or safely. He felt that thirty was the maximum number under normal circumstances and suggested that this would be further reduced to twenty-five when the RCN was using some of the harbour facilities. Thompson made a number of recommendations for improving the efficiency of the port, including straightening and enlarging berthing facilities on the north (or town) side of the harbour, building new shops, and appointing a full-time hull and machinery surveyor to determine the type of repair work that needed to be undertaken and its priority. The estimated cost of this work was $750,000.[158]

None of this would work, however, without Thompson's most important recommendation–the recruitment and training of additional labour to facilitate current and future ship repair needs. Thompson suggested that the British experience of ensuring that there was always a sufficient number of ships undergoing repairs to keep the expanded workforce occupied should lessen any union resistance to the plan.[159] The British government accepted the responsibility for the cost of training up to 200 men and asked the Newfoundland government to arrange it. London also suggested that Newfoundland might want to adopt measures that had been undertaken in British shipyards, where the Emergency Powers Defence Order provided that every worker employed in shipbuilding or repair was to be paid for every week he was "capable and available for work," even if he did not actually work.[160] This provision appeased trade union concerns, and thus with the "complete agreement" of the unions involved, the Newfoundland government proposed to start the program with an initial intake of twenty-five men in mid-September, increasing to "100 or more if we find such numbers can be handled."[161] Although reservations about the success of the scheme lingered, and some delays were experienced, the first twenty-five apprentices were taken on by the middle of November[162].

Meanwhile, during August, twenty-one convoys were escorted without loss using no fewer than four escorts each. Further protection was provided when combined RCN/RCAF operations commenced, facilitated by situating an RCAF operations room next to the RCN operations room, with a direct line to the telegraph room of the Department of Posts and Telegraphs and two city lines. In addition, a continuous listening watch was instituted at several Department of Posts and Telegraph wireless stations outside St. John's which were in contact with approximately 100 low-power wireless stations throughout the coastal regions of Newfoundland. Observers were instructed to report any and all aircraft–especially at night–as well as any unidentified ships, gear or wreckage.[163] This led to a mine being reported by a Newfoundland Ranger in La Scie on the Baie Verte Peninsula in mid-August. It had been picked up off Horse Islands by a local resident and towed ashore. Apparently the finder had hoisted it on to the pier and with the help of several of the local men then rolled it a considerable distance to his store house. The ranger suggested that it was miraculous that "all the people living in the little cove...were not blown to pieces."[164]

But the high point of the month was the arrival in Newfoundland of HMS *Prince of Wales* carrying Prime Minister Churchill and USS *Augusta* with President Roosevelt on board. Up to this point, all Allied convoys and their escorts were under Admiralty control. This changed in August when Churchill arrived in Placentia Bay to meet with Roosevelt to plan war objectives which ultimately produced the Atlantic Charter.[165] As a result of this conference, the US Navy (USN) assumed strategic control over the Western Atlantic and took over the escort of all HX convoys and fast westbound convoys, leaving the slow SC convoys for the RCN.

Meanwhile, plans for the escort base were also finalized, and towards the end of the month Murray presented the Commission of Government with the actual drawings for the proposed development for approval. On them he noted the harbour improvements–the Naval Dockyard and wharves on the northeast side of the harbour next to the

Newfoundland Dockyard, plus the wharves, refuelling facilities and the underground magazine on the Southside. The naval barracks would be built just north of Prince of Wales College (between Golf Avenue and Prince of Wales Street), the naval hospital adjacent to the Fever Hospital (Cavell Street) and the combined officer's accommodation and administration building next to the Newfoundland Hotel (Plymouth Road). He informed the Commission that all construction contracts were placed with the ECM Cape Company and that dredging would be undertaken by J.P. Porter and Sons. Ever mindful of local sensitivities, Murray also informed the commission that all parties had been reminded of the necessity of obtaining the "requisite permission of the Municipal Authorities."[166] This eventually led to some problems when the City Council demanded payment for building permits and the Canadian Department of National Defence refused to send them the plans because parts were considered secret.[167]

In September, there were a couple of major changes in the Newfoundland Command. First, Murray was promoted to Rear-Admiral and became Flag Officer Newfoundland Force (FONF). The second was the re-organization of the NEF into six six-ship escort groups in anticipation of the planned withdrawal of all RN ships from the NEF as a result of the USN taking over responsibility for the HX convoys and fast westbound convoys. Initially, the Admiralty thought that the American assumption of jurisdiction would release RN forces for service in the eastern Atlantic. However, it soon became evident that the NEF did not have the forces, most particularly destroyers, to protect the SC convoys properly, and the Admiralty agreed instead to detail five more RN destroyers and seven corvettes to the NEF.[168] Even so, Murray felt his forces were still inadequate for the job at hand, especially since of the twelve RN ships committed, only three were immediately available. The rest were refitting or had suffered serious breakdowns and were under repair. In addition, two destroyers were detached from the NEF to escort the hospital ship *Pasteur* and as part of the protection for the troop convoy TC-14. Nevertheless, Murray hoped it would be possible to maintain escort groups of eight warships, including two destroyers, in each group.[169] At the same time, Murray tried to accommodate the new American command arrangement in the Western Atlantic.

To this end, "excellent liaison" was maintained during the month between Murray and his staff and that of the Commander of US Task Force 4 (TF4), Argentia, Admiral Bristol, and his staff. Both senior officers exchanged courtesy visits, and held conferences to iron out the strategic changes agreed upon between London and Washington the month before. To lubricate the transition, and to encourage good relations, Bristol and Murray appointed permanent liaison officers to each others' staffs. As well, he sent commanders of RN and RCN destroyers to Argentia for informal discussions with their American counterparts.[170]

With the re-organization of the Western Atlantic convoying system, the sailing schedules for fast and slow convoys departing from Halifax and Sydney, respectively, were also changed. They now left every six days, as would the corresponding fast and slow outward bound (ON) convoys from the UK. HX convoys took the Cape Sable route along the south coast of Newfoundland to the WESTOMP, while the SC convoys travelled the more round-about route through the Strait of Belle Isle. While Murray could not maintain a full-time patrol of the Strait, he did detach ships of the Newfoundland Defence Force to perform anti-submarine (A/S) sweeps for SC-44 and SC-45 during the month.[171]

The NEF also scored its first victory over the U-boats during September. As HMCS *Chambly* (Commander Prentice, SO) and HMCS *Moose Jaw* were the only two ships assigned to the Newfoundland Defence Force at the time, they sailed in company early in the month on a training cruise along the convoy routes so that they could offer immediate assistance if required. The two corvettes sailed from St. John's on 5 September and were consequently well placed when U-boats attacked SC-42 on the 9th. *Chambly* and *Moose Jaw* proceeded to a point approximately five miles ahead of the convoy, and in a brief but wild melee that included the U-boat captain climbing onto *Chambly* from his conning tower, they sank *U-501*. While *Chambly* returned home with its prisoners, *Moose Jaw* remained with the convoy for the remainder of its voyage.[172]

Meanwhile, base construction ashore was proceeding slowly. Bad weather at the beginning of September resulted in the loss in transit of two scows owned by J.P. Porter and Sons. This considerably delayed progress in dredging various parts of St. John's harbour because a replacement did not arrive until the third week of September. No sooner had work commenced when problems arose over where to dump the dredged materials. Without asking the Newfoundland government, the contractor assumed that the spoils from the dredging could be dumped back into the harbour. This was not the case, and it was only after numerous appeals to the Commission that permission to do so—with minor conditions such as clearing any floating debris—was given.[173]

By the end of September the site for the administration building was cleared; the foundation walls of the six central wings of the hospital were poured and some of the framing completed; the excavation and some of the foundation for the barracks were partially completed; and the concrete walls and some of the roof rafters for the barracks garage were in place. In addition, the clearance of the dockyard site was ninety-five percent complete, and construction of the wireless station and the Port War Signal Station were progressing well. In the interim, HMS *Greenwich* and HMS *Georgian* (renamed *Avalon II* and used for accommodation) arrived to take over from *Forth*, which left on 18 September.[174] Unfortunately, *Avalon II* was overcrowded until the passenger vessel, HMCS *Prince Henry*, which had been requisitioned by the Canadian government, arrived in November to take the overflow.[175]

In October the re-organization of the NEF into six groups of eight ships was completed, and Murray expressed his hope to keep each group intact. The arrival of three Free French corvettes assigned to the NEF helped facilitated this. He also hoped to give the groups more time in port. The operational schedule allowed each group to have a short turnaround in Iceland and then about eleven days at St. John's. This longer period in port not only gave the crews a respite from the rigours of the Battle of the Atlantic but also allowed the repair and upgrading of equipment, particularly RDF (radar). The North Atlantic was hard on the ships of the NEF, most especially the delicate electronic gear. The heavy pounding of the Atlantic swells damaged asdic domes and rattled delicate vacuum tubes, and the salt water corroded contacts and wiring. Furthermore, engines and boilers often needed attention after every crossing, guns required routining, and the scraping and painting of rust spots on exposed surfaces was a constant necessity. Layovers also provided the opportunity for training. To achieve this, FONF sent the British submarine *L-27* to Harbour Grace to train escort crews in anti-submarine detection and tactics. Murray also suggested that ships visiting Harbour Grace should not only train in A/S but also carry out all around "work-outs" (general drill, gunnery practice, etc.).

About this time, the contractor assigned to build the RCN facilities began to have difficulties with the local longshoremen's union. In a letter to Capt. Schwerdt, Edgar Gilbert of the Canadian Department of National Defence (DND) complained that a crew of longshoremen unloading piles from a ship had taken a week to handle only half of the cargo. In addition, they halted work in the middle of one afternoon to attend a meeting, but they returned intoxicated and quit working two hours later, having accomplished little. The following day, he claimed that longshoremen prevented the contractor from unloading railway cars to transport materials off-site, threatening a work stoppage if the contractor did so.[176] On another occasion, having demanded the job of unloading lumber for dock construction, local longshoremen left the job incomplete, requiring it to be finished by the contractor whose men unloaded the lumber at a rate three times faster than the local longshoremen.[177] Gilbert charged that the longshoremen were causing unnecessary delays and expense and that their actions practically "amount[ed] to sabotage." He enquired whether it was "possible to prohibit longshoremen, as a union, from handling defence materials?"[178] Murray had expressed the same view to Sir Wilfred Woods several months earlier when, on a couple of occasions, valuable ships missed their sailings because longshoremen refused to work during bad weather. If the men knew the importance of the cargoes, Murray told the commissioner they probably would have continued working, but rather caustically he pointed out that it was not navy policy to "take the whole water-front into our confidence."[179] A possible contributing factor to this obstinacy was the ill-will that was created among the local population by the Commission of Government's two-tier wage scale where American and Canadian workmen were paid a higher rate than a local worker doing the same job.[180]

Delays in acquiring the required sites added to these tensions, with the Newfoundland government blaming the Canadians, and *vice versa*, for the hold-ups. A flurry of correspondence during the month between the Newfoundland Commissioner of Public Utilities, Sir Wilfred Woods and Murray clearly illustrate the frustration on the part of both sides. Woods accused the Canadian authorities of leaving arrangements in a "half-baked condition,"[181] to which the FONF retorted that Woods was "inclined to feel hurt at being left with no one to hold his hand in these arrangements."[182] The root of the problem was the issue of compensation for landowners affected by the establishment of the RCN base. An Arbitration Board was originally set up in mid-1941 to assess compensation for parties with claims against the US associated with the Anglo-American Leased Bases Agreement.[183] The Newfoundland Government detailed this same board to assess compensation for people who were dislocated or otherwise inconvenienced by the establishment of HMCS *Avalon*. The head of the BAD, E.R. Seal, expressed concern about the board's awards as early as the summer of 1941, whereby he stated that he thought that the Americans had been "soaked."[184] Seal felt that the board had made "excessive awards," charging that it had shown "a scandalously biassed [sic] and casual manner." He was equally as critical of the Newfoundland government's lawyer, who Seal saw as "incompetent, if not worse."[185] The difficulty lay mainly with the interpretation of "market value." The Americans, British and Canadians viewed it as simply what a property was worth on the open market without due consideration to local conditions. The Newfoundland

The "Newfyjohn" Solution

government, on the other hand, felt it also had to include what is now termed "injurious affection" and awarded compensation for such things as lost business, loss of a vegetable garden, or relocation of a fishing stage. In one case it even awarded compensation for a haystack.[186] This difference of opinion continued to cause problems and in August 1942, R.W. Rankin, a Canadian government real estate advisor, arrived to report on the workings of the arbitration board for the Canadian government.[187]

November turned out to be a rough month for both the NEF and the Newfoundland Command in general. First of all, the weather was continuously bad. This had a detrimental effect on both the men and the ships of the NEF, not only due to actual weather and/or battle damage but also because crossings took longer, which meant that there was less time in harbour for the escorts and their crews. To offset this, Naval Service Headquarters (NSHQ) suggested that the number of groups in the NEF be increased. Murray had reservations about this because there were not enough destroyers to go around as it was. Indeed, during November only six of the thirteen destroyers assigned to the NEF were operational, and Murray did not expect this situation to improve. He complained that the ex-USN Town-class destroyers were undependable and that even the River-class destroyers were enduring punishment at sea.[188] Lord Beaverbrook's reservations about trading British territory for fifty obsolete destroyers in the Anglo-American Leased Bases Agreement seem to have been justified.

Aside from the difficulties with the weather, it soon became evident that the U-boats were venturing further westward in search of targets. On 3 November, SC-52 was attacked off the northeast coast of Newfoundland, losing four ships in two attacks. The convoy scattered and returned to Sydney, but by this time the movements of U-boats southward towards Cape Race had sparked some special patrols off St. John's. Unfortunately, while the Special Harbour Patrols did not encounter any U-boats, HMCS *Ouganda* was lost when, while on patrol at the inner baffles, the engine backfired and burst into flames. The depth charges were rendered safe and dropped overboard, and the crew taken off without injury before the vessel sank.[189]

Construction of the base continued satisfactorily during the month, and Capt. Schwerdt travelled to Ottawa to report on progress. Murray was gratified to learn that the Admiralty had agreed to the construction of the hospital as originally envisioned, namely without a section reserved for merchant seamen casualties and with a separate accommodation block for nurses. The Admiralty also agreed to a third seamen's block at the naval barracks and the completion of a new wharf on the Southside of the harbour, opposite the Bowring Brothers' and Job Brothers' properties. Further progress was made in dredging the harbour, and construction was started on the RCN wharf on the Southside. Unfortunately, some of the original wharf along the Cashin property had to be demolished to build cribwork, which reduced the space available for berthing warships by 150 feet. In addition, three tunnels of approximately thirty feet each were blasted into the Southside Hills for the magazines.[190] Work on the foundations and sidewalls at the naval dockyard had also commenced. Most important, the Mobile Training Unit (MTU) garage was finished and now housed the training bus. The wireless building and the Port War Signal Station at Cape Spear were also well advanced. The six centre wings and the four north wings of the hospital were shelled and roofed but still needed windows and doors, all of which were on order. Building #2 (workshop) of the naval barracks was at a similar stage, while Building #1 (the sickbay and guardhouse) was weather-tight and now used as sleeping quarters for the mechanics. According to Captain Schwerdt's report, work on the rest of the naval barracks complex was "proceeding satisfactorily."[191] However, HMCS *Avalon* almost suffered a serious setback in November when a major fire threatened the officers' administration and accommodations block next to the Newfoundland Hotel.

During the Second World War, there were a number of devastating fires in St. John's.[192] Probably the most notorious occurred at the new Knights of Columbus hostel on Harvey Road just before Christmas 1942, but in a town comprised of mainly old, attached, wooden-frame buildings, any fire could be catastrophic. The one at "The Arena" on the night of 28 November 1941 was no different. Formerly known as the Prince's Rink, the building was located just behind the Newfoundland Hotel and was owned by the Arena Rink Company of which prominent St. John's businessmen Chesley Crosbie and Chesley Pippy were the major shareholders. The fire started early in the evening, and the Central and Eastern Fire Stations responded. Before long, however, it was evident that more equipment was needed and, for the first time in eight years, a second alarm was rung, signifying that all available fire equipment was required. All the armed forces in the city responded. The Americans sent two pumper trucks from Fort Pepperrell, and American and Canadian army, air force and naval personnel grabbed shovels, axes, and buckets to help contain the fire. Sparks and flaming debris fell among the lumber at the RCN administration/officers' accommodation building, which was located adjacent to the arena, but fortunately servicemen posted there prevented the fire from spreading to the partially constructed building. Ultimately, the surrounding structures were saved with little smoke or fire damage, but the forty-two-year-old skating arena and the adjacent St. John's Curling Club buildings were both total losses, a severe blow to both the civilian population and the various armed forces in the city. Ten thousand dollars insurance was carried on the Curling Club building and eighty thousand on the Arena.[193]

On the same day as the fire, an "extremely interesting meeting" took place, presided over by Chairman of the Harbours Board, Sir Wilfred Woods. Capt. Schwerdt, Commander E.L. Armstrong, RCN, local Ministry of War Transport representative Eric Bowring attended, as well as the Marine Superintendent of the Newfoundland Railway and a number of shipping agents and wharf owners. The purpose of the meeting was ostensibly to discuss the problem of congestion in St. John's harbour. The problem had two main causes: ships were waiting too long to be unloaded and it was taking too long to clear warehouse and wharf space of cargo. The first was the result of the second, and the second was due to plain old human greed.[194]

Knowing of the large orders being placed by American and Canadian authorities, firms both large and small were hoarding stock in anticipation of shipping difficulties, thus occupying warehouse and dock space that was needed for other purposes. As a result, ships idled in the middle of the harbour waiting for sufficient space to become available to unload. Combined with the difficulties with local longshoremen, it is easy to understand the frustration of naval authorities. In the end, the Chairman of the Customs Board promised to tackle the immediate problem of the clearance of cargo currently on wharves and in warehouses and undertook to investigate the construction of a bonded warehouse to facilitate faster clearance of goods from these areas, presumably by providing alternate secure storage facilities.[195]

December was a fairly quiet month for the Newfoundland Command. Continuing bad weather throughout the month caused damage and delays among the NEF, but there were no attacks on NEF-escorted convoys. FONF decided at the end of the December to re-organize the NEF into seven groups from six, thus reducing the composition of each group to six warships. While this was not ideal, Murray felt that at least this scheme provided for a reasonable period between crossings for ship repair and rest and training for the crew. To help compensate for the weaker group strength, Murray proposed that ships from other "longest off" convoys could detach temporarily to assist ones that were clearly threatened. In addition, four ex-Sydney Force corvettes were due to join in January, bringing the force up to sixty corvettes, and NSHQ promised that five Modified Corvettes were earmarked for the NEF when they became available. Unfortunately, some of the older corvettes would be detached to Charleston, South Carolina, for modification. The first six-ship group sailed from St. John's on 22 December to escort SC-61.[196]

Of course, in December 1941, after the Japanese bombing of Pearl Harbor, the Americans officially joined the war. This did not have much initial impact on the operations of the NEF, although the Commander of Task Force 4 (TF 4), under whose command the NEF operated, did order the ships of the NEF to commence hostilities with Japan forthwith.[197] This caused a bit of confusion at the time because Canada had yet to issue its own declaration of war against Japan.[198] Such embarrassments illustrate the difficult command-and-control situation facing the Newfoundland Command. While Murray co-operated quite well with Admiral Bristol in Argentia, the same could not be said about the officer commanding US ground forces in Newfoundland, Major-General G.C. Brant. At a meeting with the heads of the Canadian army and air force in Newfoundland, Brigadier Earnshaw and Group Captain McEwen, Brant expressed displeasure at his treatment, complaining that even though he was the ranking officer in St. John's he was being treated "like a Second Lieutenant."[199] Governor Walwyn thought him to be very co-operative and efficient and "like[d] him very much personally,"[200] but the heads of the Canadian services found Brant to be belligerent, inconsistent and prone to "sit by himself and nurse imagined wrongs." Murray suggested that he should be kept "sweet" by keeping him constantly informed. To this end, Brant assigned a Major Meyer as a liaison officer on Murray's staff.[201]

With the Americans now full participants in the conflict and their facilities in Newfoundland an integral part of western hemispheric defence, local military authorities addressed the issue of Newfoundland's vulnerability to attack. Brant felt that an attack was not only possible "but very probable." After Pearl Harbor, he was concerned that aircraft catapulted from merchant ships would spearhead any attack.[202] With this in mind, Murray and Brant, along with all the other service heads, met with Newfoundland Commissioners Emerson, Puddester, Wild and Winter at Emerson's office to discuss defence arrangements for Newfoundland. All agreed that an attack would have to come from the sea and would likely take the form of an air assault.[203] The *Kriegsmarine* had four aircraft catapult ships which Murray felt would be the most likely vehicles for any attack on St. John's. They had the range and endurance, and two could carry multiple aircraft. The others carried at least one aircraft each, and all could be used as mother ships for a larger force. Murray forwarded this intelligence to Brant.[204] Consequently, a comprehensive blackout regime was discussed. Emerson proposed that a two-week continuous blackout be tried at the end of January. Notice would be given in newspapers, and the regulations would cover all of St. John's and surrounding area, including Conception Bay. During the blackout, local radio stations would be asked to suspend their broadcasts so that enemy forces could not use them to home in on their targets. The committee concluded that air raid shelters were impractical since an effective shelter needed to be at least thirty feet underground to protect against high-explosive bombs and St. John's, for the most part, sits on solid rock. Further, as an air assault would come from the sea and thus be limited in size, a sustained attack was not anticipated, and because radar had not yet been installed, the raid would probably be over before people could take shelter. Thus, the committee felt that the main cause of casualties would be falling debris and splinters. Experience in Britain showed that the best defence against this was for people to stay in their homes, under stairs or in closets or pantries, and to tape or board up windows.[205] However, the committee thought that any attacking forces would probably use incendiaries as opposed to high-explosive bombs, so fire actually posed the biggest danger.[206]

Any attack on St. John's would probably concentrate on shipping in the harbour and the docks. But since the city was built up around the harbour with mainly wooden buildings and homes, any attack, especially with incendiaries, would pose a serious fire hazard to the whole area. To combat this threat, the committee had at its disposal the St. John's Fire Department's Central, East and West End Fire Halls plus the local Auxiliary Fire Service, the RCAF fire unit at Torbay and the US fire unit at Fort Pepperrell. In addition, homes and businesses would be encouraged to take their own fire precautions, including the provision of stirrup pumps and bags of sand. Fire wardens could also be organized and called out in the event of attack.

The other problem facing the authorities in St. John's was what to do with those left homeless by an attack.[207] It was easy to anticipate that any serious incursion would leave several thousand people homeless. The Americans offered Camp Alexander as emergency accommodation for up to 2000 people, as well as their facilities at Torbay Airport and Argentia. Evacuees would need to be fed, and US military authorities also offered mobile kitchens to feed fire fighters and those forced to evacuate their homes. To this end, food supplies would have to be stockpiled. The committee hoped that the merchants of St. John's could arrange for the storage and distribution of foodstuffs. In the meantime, homeowners would be asked to stockpile several days' essential supplies for an emergency. The meeting adjourned with arrangements apparently well in hand.[208]

In December HMCS *Prince Henry*, which had been providing overflow accommodation space for the Newfoundland Command, departed for Halifax in anticipation of resuming seagoing operations. While approximately 295 men were billeted on board HMCS *Avalon II*, eighty men had to be accommodated ashore at the Knights of Columbus and YMCA hostels. These men were mainly engine room ratings responsible for repair work and boiler cleaning for the ships alongside. While Murray recognized that boarding men at the two hostels was not conducive to naval discipline, he felt it was "preferable to and more economical than the provision of another chartered vessel."[209] *Prince Henry*'s departure for Halifax presented the opportunity to send Lt.-Commander P.E. Heseltine, RN, the base Ordnance Officer, and Lt. L.A. Bown, RCNVR, to Halifax to investigate the laying of an indicator loop and associated minefield at the approaches to St. John's. While there, both officers met with the Director of the Technical Division of the RCN, Captain G. Hibbard, and they agreed upon a plan to install two guard loops to cover the channels from the end of the outer and middle baffles and a visually controlled minefield in the narrows opposite Chain Rock. A light net would indicate the presence of a submarine in the minefield and a patrol craft fitted with depth charges would destroy it. This plan had the advantage of positively indicating a submarine in the minefield, and the depth charges would sink the submarine without blocking the harbour while minimizing any collateral damage. The control station for the minefield would also be close to the Port War Signal Station to speed communication. The FONF hoped that the various cables, mine loops, mines and nets could be collected and ready for shipment by the end of December.[210]

Base construction slowed as Christmas drew near, prompting "a large number of Newfoundland workmen to take their leave." Regardless, by that point the naval hospital was sixty percent complete, the administration building was thirty percent finished, and the officers' quarters seventy percent done. The naval barracks were almost finished but were being held up because of delays in receiving millwork (windows, doors, etc.) and heating equipment. Naval authorities blamed this on the still unresolved problem of congestion in St. John's harbour. In December, 165 merchant vessels arrived at St. John's, and on any given day approximately seventeen warships were in the harbour. Work on the Naval Dockyard was also slow, dependent on the progress of the breastwork. However, work on the garage, canteen, inflammable stores,

The "Newfyjohn" Solution

machine shop and guard house was proceeding satisfactorily. The wireless station was completed, but the Cape Spear Port War Signal Station was only sixty percent finished, progress having been impeded by bad weather.[211] Yet while things were progressing at HMCS *Avalon*, the Battle of the Atlantic was entering a new phase that would severely challenge the Allied war effort in the Western Atlantic.

When Hitler finally declared war on the United States on 11 December 1941, it brought a sense of relief to Admiral Karl Dönitz, the *Befelschaber der Uboote* (BdU) or Commander-in-Chief of U-boats.[212] This was because the declaration finally ended the guerrilla war that had been raging for months between his U-boats and American forces in the North Atlantic.[213] What had started as the Americans' maintaining a "neutrality patrol" had slowly but surely progressed to the blatant escort of British convoys. This had not been without cost to the United States. In September, *U-652* torpedoed USS *Greer*, USS *Kearney* had been hit on 10 October, and on 31 October USS *Reuben James* was sunk by *U-522*. Now that the US was officially in the war, Dönitz reasoned that with the Americans' attention diverted to the Pacific, the whole east coast of the United States was wide open for attack.[214] He was absolutely correct. The USN was totally unprepared for the onslaught that enveloped it in early 1942. Whether the Commander-in-Chief of the US fleet, Admiral Ernest J. King, was Anglophobic, as some have suggested, or just did not appreciate the potential of Dönitz's U-boats, he refused to institute coastal convoys along the eastern seaboard. This caused what some have suggested was a defeat for the USN equal in scale to the attack on Pearl Harbor.[215]

The opening salvo of Dönitz's U-boat offensive against the US was fired by *Kapitänleutnant* Rienhard Hardegan in *U-123*. On 12 January 1942, he sank the British steamer *Cyclops* approximately 100 miles southeast of Cape Sable, Nova Scotia. Hardegan was in command of one of eight U-boats that comprised the first of three waves of the initial assault on North America, code-named *Paukenschlag* or "drumbeat." For the next six months, the U-boats caused havoc along the eastern seaboard of North America and even into the Caribbean. The USN, like the pre-war RN, had not prepared for a war against the U-boats and was also woefully short of escort vessels. This seems incredible, considering the British experience, as does Admiral King's refusal to institute convoys. He felt that an inadequately escorted convoy was worse than no convoy at all.[216] The British, on the other hand, had found just the opposite. The best–really the only–defence against U-boat attack was convoy, regardless of the inadequacies of the escort. Admiral King's view prevailed, however, and when Hardegan and his cohorts arrived in American waters they not only found plenty of targets but also shipping lanes that were still operating under peacetime conditions. Ships were not darkened, beacons and lighthouses were still lit, and wireless messages were being sent in the clear.

The Commander of the Eastern Sea Frontier had a difficult job on his hands. To battle the onslaught, Admiral Adolphus "Dolly" Andrews USN had a force of only twenty anti-submarine vessels, including seven Coast Guard cutters, three WW I-vintage *Eagle*-class sub-chasers and two pre-WW I patrol boats.[217] Andrews had no air cover to speak of, and the patrol planes he did have were too few to make a difference. Civilian watercraft (author Ernest Hemmingway was a volunteer) and airplanes were ultimately added to Andrews' resources with little effect. Of course, the main reason for this scarcity was the Pacific War. With the Japanese advance continuing almost unchecked, the USN hauled most of its assets out of the Atlantic for duty in the Pacific. The other problem lay in USN doctrine. Like the pre-war RN, destroyers and other escort vessels were reserved for the protection of capital ships. Consequently, while there were escort vessels available on the Atlantic coast for convoy escort, they were reserved for the USN's heavy units and special assignments.[218]

By the end of the first wave of the U-boat offensive in early February, fifty ships had been sunk with no German casualties.[219] The British were alarmed and at a loss as to why the Americans did not institute the well-proven convoy system. Several missions were sent to Washington to investigate the problem and found a number of difficulties. The Americans had no experience in the rigours of locating and sinking U-boats, and unlike within the British system, there was little co-ordination between the USN and the Army Air Force (USAAF). Likewise, there was no central body to formulate anti-submarine doctrine, and research in the field was still in its infancy. In short, the Americans were in trouble.[220]

During the first quarter of 1942, U-boats sank over 1.25 million tons of shipping in the North Atlantic, most of it in areas under American control. Shipping that was, at great expense in men and materiel, safely convoyed across the North Atlantic by the RN and RCN was being sunk just short of its destination. Some have suggested that this situation almost completely negated the advantage that America's joining the war gave the Allies.[221] Growing ever more alarmed, the Admiralty sent experts such as Roger Winn, Head of the Admiralty's Submarine Tracking Room, to Washington to help combat the mounting losses and offered ten corvettes and two dozen anti-submarine trawlers with their

The "Newfyjohn" Solution

crews to help stop the slaughter.[222] The USN accepted the trawlers but turned down the corvettes because the navy felt that US shipyards could supply these in short order.[223] Regardless, a partial convoy system, soon dubbed the "bucket brigade," was initiated so that ships received some protection during the day and sought refuge at night at the nearest port. This system caused serious delays in the arrival of cargoes, but it did cut losses. Over the next few months, a full-fledged interlocking system was developed from Halifax to ports in South America as the U-boats continued to move south into the Caribbean.[224] By the time this system became fully operational in June 1942, however, almost three million tons of shipping had been lost off the American east coast and in the Caribbean.[225]

While most of the losses during the first four months of 1942 were in American territorial waters, attacks in Canadian waters were also part of Dönitz's strategy.[226] The first sinking in "Canadian" waters was actually Reinhard Hardegan's sinking of the British steamer *Cyclops* southeast of Cape Sable, Nova Scotia on 12 January.[227] This was really an "act of opportunity" because Hardegan was just passing through Canadian waters on his way to his station off New York, as Operation *Paukenschlag* was not supposed to start until the next day when the rest of his group was expected to be in position. But *Cyclops* was just too good a target to let go, and Admiral Dönitz had given permission to attack large vessels if the opportunity presented itself.[228] *Cyclops* was in the wrong place at the wrong time. Regardless, three medium-sized U-boats were detached from Group *Seydilitz* in mid-Atlantic in early January and ordered to Canadian waters.[229] Eric Topp in *U-552* patrolled approximately fifty miles off Cape Race, Newfoundland; Heinrich Bleichrodt in *U-109* took station south of the Grand Banks; and Ernst Kals in *U-130* guarded the Cabot Strait between Newfoundland and Nova Scotia.[230] Kals drew first blood, sinking both *Frisco* and *Friar Rock* on 14 January. Next was Topp, who sank *Dayrose* on the 15th and *Frances Salman* on the 18th. By this time, Walter Schug in *U-86* had also arrived in position near Cape St. Francis at the tip of the Avalon Peninsula, where he sank the 4271-ton Greek steamship *Dimitrios O. Thermiotis*. Meanwhile, Bleichrodt's *U-109* had reached a position 110 miles southeast of Halifax, and on the 19th he sank *Empire Kingfisher* just south of Cape Sable. On the 23rd he sank the 4887-ton British steamer *Thilby* with one torpedo.[231] Of the four boats, *U-109* would have the least success in Canadian waters, being constantly plagued with defective torpedoes, as were all of those in the *Paukenschlag* first wave.[232] It got so bad that Eric Topp's *U-522* was supposedly forced to hold up one freighter with nothing more than a machine gun. After letting the crew abandon ship, Topp sank the vessel with 126 rounds from his 8.8-mm deck gun.[233]

Hot on the heels of the first wave of *Paukenschlag* were the boats of the second. Although most were destined for the still mostly virgin waters off the US eastern seaboard, all traversed Canadian waters and some claimed victims. Those boats ordered to the east coast of Canada were concentrated in three areas: the east coast of Newfoundland, the western side of the Cabot Strait, and the Halifax Approaches. Operating from 21 January to 19 February, nine U-boats sank a total of thirteen ships and damaged two others. In one notable episode, *U-754*, commanded by Gerhard Bigalk, sank the 3876-ton Greek steamship *Mount Kithern* with two torpedoes a mere two miles from St. John's harbour.[234]

By the time the third wave hit Canadian waters in early February, targets were not as plentiful, and air surveillance frequently forced the boats to dive. While *U-96* under Heinrich Lehmann-Willenbrock had considerable success, sinking five ships in eighteen days, the rest did not fare as well. The third wave produced the first U-boat losses in North American waters. On 1 March, Naval Reserve Ensign William Tapuni, flying a Lockheed Hudson out of Argentia, surprised *U-656* (Kröning) on the surface approximately twenty-five miles south of Cape Race. Taken totally unprepared, the U-boat was sunk with all hands. Fifteen days later, another patrol from Argentia sank *U-503* (Gericke) south of the Virgin Rocks approximately 300 miles east of St. John's.[235]

Despite these losses, Dönitz's offensive on the east coast of Canada had been successful. Between January and March 1942, U-boats sank a total of forty-four ships in Canadian waters.[236] As this figure represented twenty percent of the total sunk worldwide, the Canadian government could not keep such news from the public.[237] In the face of growing sensationalism in the press, on 5 March, Lt.-Cdr. William Strange, RCNVR, of Plans and Operations,[238] admitted to a local Canadian Club audience and the press that U-boats were operating in Canadian waters. However, he added that this was to be expected and not to give such incursions "unreasonable prominence." Furthermore, he stated that the government would in future refrain from making announcements concerning "maritime operations" so as not to reveal any information to the enemy.[239] As a result, the public were not informed when *Kapitänleutnant* Karl Thurmann's *U-553* started the next series of attacks in the early hours of 12 May 1942. At approximately 0615 GMT (about 3:15 AM Canadian Atlantic time), Thurmann sank the 5364-ton

The "Newfyjohn" Solution

British steamer *Nicoya* ten miles north of Pointe á la Frégate on the Gaspé Peninsula. He followed this up a few hours later by sinking the 4712-ton Dutch ship *Leto* en route from the UK to Montreal. Thurmann also claimed a hit on a 3000-ton vessel, although official records do not indicate a sinking at this time.[240] Canadian authorities immediately initiated convoys and prompted the Eastern Air Command to increase air patrols both inside and outside the Gulf of St. Lawrence. As well, on 21 May, Cape Gaspé Light, including its outer beacons, was extinguished.[241] By this time, however, *U-553* was on her way out of the Gulf headed for the Bay of Fundy and the east coast of the United States.

This sharp increase in U-boat activity had serious consequences for the NEF and its base at St. John's. Admiral Murray noted the sudden concentration of U-boats in January and the increased attacks in the Western Atlantic. Local escorts of ocean convoys were strengthened, and as far as possible, coastal shipping was also put in convoy. From mid-January to the end of the month, forty-four merchant ships were escorted to various destinations. Murray well knew the lessons that the Americans had yet to learn–"in very few cases have escorted merchant ships been attacked, however small or inadequate the escort." Even if the escort only consisted of a minesweeper, its presence seemed to have the "requisite deterrent effect." Indeed, warships in transit to Halifax were co-opted to provide escort to coastal convoys along their routes. In addition, precautions were taken to protect shipping loading or at anchor at Wabana, Conception Bay and at Bay Bulls. Regardless, a number of sinkings occurred in Newfoundland waters which the FONF attributed mainly to the dispersal of a number of ON convoys due to "exceptionally bad weather." This weather, especially the hurricane that hit the North Atlantic mid-month, caused considerable damage to ships of the NEF, resulting in only four destroyers being available for duty during most of the month.[242]

The increased U-boat concentrations in the Western Atlantic also hastened changes in the North Atlantic escort system. At meetings held in Washington, the RN, RCN and USN decided to push the WESTOMP further east to 45 degrees West and to change the eastern terminus for the NEF from Iceland to Londonderry. The US groups would remain in Iceland. This allowed a strengthened escort for both the western and eastern legs of the journey as the renamed Mid-Ocean Escort Force (MOEF) accompanied the Halifax-based Western Local Escort Force (WLEF) to the new WESTOMP and reinforced the British Eastern Local Escort Force (ELEF) from the EASTOMP to the newly completed escort base at Londonderry in Northern Ireland.[243] As Londonderry played such an important role in later events impacting HMCS *Avalon*, a brief discussion of this base is necessary.

Similar to HMCS *Avalon*, the escort base in Londonderry was a product of necessity more than planning. Denied the use of ports in Eamon de Valera's neutral Eire, Londonderry was the most westerly port suitable for development as a naval base. Similar to St. John's, it had the leanest of facilities at the time, but within a very short period it became the most important repair, maintenance and training base in the United Kingdom.

During World War I, Britain had used several Irish "Treaty Ports" for its anti-submarine war, the most notable being Queenstown in Cork Harbour on Ireland's south coast.[244] But thanks to a gross miscalculation by the British General Staff and Prime Minister Neville Chamberlain, these ports were returned to Ireland in 1938.[245] Churchill seethed at what he considered this "feckless act," and in his memoirs suggested that many lives were needlessly lost as a consequence of this "improvident example of appeasement."[246] As a result, convoys were routed to the north of Ireland to come within the protection of the RN and Coastal Command aircraft. This sufficed for the short term, but barring the forcible retaking of the Treaty Ports, the Admiralty needed a base in Ireland, and its one real choice was Londonderry.[247]

For the first couple of years, the naval base at Londonderry was just "an obscure little organisation" called HMS *Ferret*, devoted to the conversion of fishing trawlers to minesweepers and coastal escorts.[248] It was not until late 1940, as the convoy battles became more ferocious, that the Admiralty decided to upgrade the facilities to accommodate and repair larger warships.[249] As Dönitz's U-boats ventured farther into the Atlantic and Iceland was occupied as a forward base, Northern Ireland, like Newfoundland, became strategically important. As Churchill said later, "[t]here by the grace of God, Ulster stood like a faithful sentinel."[250] Escort forces began running between Iceland and Londonderry, and by early 1942 Londonderry forces were taking over convoys that had been escorted as far as the MOMP by ships of the NEF. In the meantime, the US had entered the fray and was building its own facilities at Lisahally.

In January 1941, almost a year before it actually entered the war on the Allied side, the United States drew up plans to develop "Derry" as a trans-Atlantic convoy terminal. On 30 June 1941, 362 "civilian technicians" arrived to begin construction of a base that would eventually include ship repair facilities, a radio station, barracks and administrative headquarters, plus ammunition and storage depots. The base was officially commissioned on 5 February 1942, and by May the number of

The "Newfyjohn" Solution

US personnel in Northern Ireland reached 37,000. Ultimately, the US spent five million dollars developing the facilities, the majority being targeted for the repair, maintenance and refuelling of convoy escorts.[251] The repair facilities were especially important to the RCN.

During the summer of 1942, there were seven British, one American and four Canadian escort groups operating out of Londonderry, but by March 1943 Canadian forces accounted for more than half the escort forces based there.[252] By this time, Londonderry had become the most important escort base in the North West Approaches[253] with 149 escorts, twice the number at the British bases at Liverpool and Greenock combined.[254] The RCN assumed almost sole responsibility for maintaining the MOEF after D-Day, and by the end of 1944 Canadian ships made up the majority of seaborne forces using Londonderry. In February 1945, 109 RCN warships were serviced at the Londonderry facilities.[255]

Londonderry was an important port for the RCN for a number of reasons. Possibly the most significant was training, and Londonderry was the operational anti-submarine training centre for all three navies based there. The RN provided most of the training facilities, and throughout the war these facilities played a vital role in providing instruction to the inadequately trained ships of the RCN. As the Battle of the Atlantic intensified, Londonderry became the main anti-submarine training base in the Eastern Atlantic.[256] "Tame" submarines were used to teach ships' crews the subtleties of tracking submerged U-boats, and the Night Escort Attack Teacher (NEAT) trained them in measures to battle the highly successful *Rudeltaktik* perfected by Dönitz's commanders. Until 1944, the instruction Canadian ships received in Londonderry was often the only organized training the crews experienced after accepting their ships from the builders in Canada despite the FONF's attempts to provide this at HMCS *Avalon*.

Another crucial aspect for the RCN was the repair facilities. While both the RN and USN had facilities at Londonderry, by the fall of 1942, most repair work on Canadian ships was undertaken by the Americans. By the end of 1943, sixty-eight Canadian ships had been repaired at the United States Navy Yard in Lisahally. The American repair facilities were not only well equipped but also efficiently organized to reduce paper work and avoid unnecessary delays. The work was completed with a speed and thoroughness that the Canadians appreciated, and it included not only running repairs but also refits. This was especially important to the RCN as many Canadian escorts came off the ways either lacking in important rig or with obsolescent fittings.

Londonderry was particularly well suited to this task from the RCN's point of view as British equipment was more readily available in Northern Ireland than at the bases and refit yards in North America. Considering the repair/modernization crisis that enveloped the RCN in 1943, it could be argued that Londonderry's major impact on the RCN's participation in the Battle of the Atlantic was its contribution to keeping Canadian warships at sea and reasonably well equipped.[257]

In the meantime, there were further developments ashore at St. John's in January 1942. Retired Lieutenant-Colonel Leonard Outerbridge became Director of Civil Defence (DCD), replacing Charles H. Hutchings, the former inspector general of police who had been appointed Director of Air Raid Precautions (ARP) in April 1940.[258] This was a welcome change because Hutchings had refused to co-ordinate his civil defence measures with the various fighting services. Outerbridge, on the other hand, took immediate steps to keep the services in the loop, and liaison officers from each service were appointed to his staff. Blackout was enforced starting in late January, and steps were taken to darken the naval establishment, including those facilities under construction. Captain of the Port Schwerdt was also concerned with the increased submarine activity. The temporary minefield and indicator loops at the approaches to St. John's harbour had worn out, and Schwerdt worried that a U-boat might try to force its way through the Narrows. Later events would justify his concern. Measures were underway by the end of the month to re-lay the loops and minefield with the arrival of Lt. B.G. Jemmett RCNVR, but in the interim, patrols were instituted using the few harbour craft available, putting a "severe strain" on their crews.[259]

Thanks to both the severe weather and U-boat activity, congestion in St. John's harbour again became a serious problem. During January, 140 merchant ships arrived at the port, many having to be berthed alongside four abreast. On one day alone there were fifty-three merchant ships taking refuge at St. John's in addition to the daily average of twenty-one NEF escorts. The Newfoundland government intended to lay additional moorings, but as this required the clearing of most of the harbour for a month, this measure was postponed until May, when authorities hoped congestion would be somewhat alleviated. In the meantime, some of the overflow was sent to Bay Bulls, the only available anchorage with adequate communication facilities within reasonable distance of St. John's. It could accommodate approximately ten ships but was exposed to U-boat attack from the sea. Patrols were instigated when forces were available, and the Department of National Defence promised to supply four Fairmile patrol boats as soon as possible.

The reorganization and renaming of the convoy escort system came into effect in February. The difficulty lay in maintaining the required strength. A large number of ships for the reconstituted Mid-Ocean Escort Force (MOEF), both destroyers and corvettes, had to come from the UK and had not yet arrived. This put considerable strain on Murray's resources, as maintaining a six- ship escort group "absorbed every single corvette at F.O.N.F's disposal." Ultimately, a conference with the commander of the newly re-designated Task Force 24 (TG.24), Admiral Bristol, decided that, by adhering to a tight schedule, Canadian or mixed Canadian/American (A/C) groups could adequately escort the first seven eastbound convoys, both HX and SC, as well as assist the escorts of ON convoys. Murray hoped that the situation would improve when the promised reinforcements arrived and the weather moderated.[260]

The MOEF also suffered its first casualties in February with the loss of the Free French Ship *Abysse* and HMCS *Spikenard*. *Abysse* was torpedoed the night of 8 February escorting ON-60, while *U-136* sank *Spikenard* two nights later in the mid-Atlantic, escorting SC-67. Unfortunately, Spikenard's group-mates did not discover its loss until the next day, by which time all except eight of its crew, including the captain, had perished.[261] Both losses were keenly felt in the Newfoundland Command.[262] On the brighter side, the first of the twenty-four anti-submarine trawlers promised by the British to help contain the slaughter along the American eastern seaboard arrived at St. John's. After a short layover for fuel and running repairs, the ten small warships proceeded to Halifax or New York. With coastal convoys having been instituted in response to the increased presence of U-boats in Newfoundland waters, Murray pressed these ships into service as escorts for these convoys. Regardless, despite the institution of coastal convoys, fear of attack prompted many Newfoundlanders to travel overland from St. John's rather than by coastal steamer as was the norm. This increase in traffic caused some strain on the Newfoundland Railway's already overloaded facilities, to the point where the manager requested that Capt. Schwerdt limit the number of naval personnel boarding any one train. Schwerdt recognized that the RCN accounted for sixty percent of Armed Forces personnel using Newfoundland Railway services, but as the Battle of the Atlantic, not necessarily the RCN, dictated naval travel requirements, Schwerdt could not comply. An additional weekly steamer service was added "to cope with the situation."[263]

There was also progress in base development despite typically bad winter weather. The wireless receiving and transmitting stations and the Cape Spear Port War Signal Station were finished and manned. The hospital, administration building and officers' accommodation block were all well advanced, and while construction of the naval barracks was well in hand, completion was being held up by the non-arrival of the heating system. Bad weather was also causing problems at the dockyard. Work at the site was retarded because conditions prevented the completion of the breastwork. Regardless, approximately 500 feet of wharf at the western end of the harbour was almost finished, and 200 feet at the west end of the Bowring Brothers' property were "sufficiently advanced to be usable." Despite this, congestion was such that ships were berthed three and four abreast along wharves that were still under construction. This issue was discussed at a meeting at the end of February attended by Sir Wilfred Woods in his capacity as Chairman of the Newfoundland Harbours Board, as well as other officials. The meeting recommended that a floating dock moored near Cahill Point and able to accommodate both destroyers and corvettes would greatly improve the situation in St. John's harbour.[264] To this end, meetings were held in London later in 1942 between the Minister of War Transport and the Canadian Minister of Munitions and Supply, C.D. Howe, in an effort to obtain a section of the Vicker's Floating Dock in Montreal. London argued that as Montreal's benefit to merchant shipping was severely limited by both the freezing of the St. Lawrence and the fear of U-boat attack, the Vicker's dock was of little use where it was.[265] Unfortunately, NSHQ did not share this view and could not support the scheme as it felt that not only would removal of the dock negatively impact new construction but also its presence at St. John's would actually add to the congestion problem.[266]

The month of March started out, quite literally, with a bang at HMCS *Avalon*. On 3 March, three large explosions were heard just outside St. John's harbour during the late afternoon. It took a couple of days before the cause could be determined, but U-boat attack was suspected.[267] The Americans had attacked a submerged contact the previous month in Placentia Bay, not far from their base at Argentia, and an Argentia-based aircraft sank *U-656* just south of Trepassey on 1 March and another northwest of the Virgin Rocks several days later.[268] Captain (D) immediately dispatched patrols to investigate but to no avail. However, torpedo fragments were recovered from the rocks below Fort Amherst a few days later which proved that torpedoes had been fired at St. John's harbour, probably from long range. However, authorities puzzled as to why a U-boat commander would waste valuable torpedoes firing at (and missing) the entrance to an obviously defended port.[269] The mouth of St. John's Harbour is called "The Narrows" for a reason, so

The "Newfyjohn" Solution

perhaps *Kapitänleutnant* Ulrich Borchcrdt in U-587 was attempting to seal it, or possibly compromise the harbour defences, but his motives will never be known as the U-boat was lost with all hands a few weeks later.[270] Possibly prompted by this attack, Murray received a request from the Newfoundland government to come up with a denial plan should the Germans mount some sort of landing at St. John's.

With the United States now an official belligerent, local commanders became very concerned about a German raid on Newfoundland. Indeed, evidence given at a 1944 US Congressional hearing suggested that Hitler actually did plan to attack Newfoundland as part of a campaign against the United States.[271] President Roosevelt had expressed his concerns to Prime Minister Churchill the previous April and proposed sending additional American forces, comprising a half battery of eight-inch guns, one squadron of three medium and three heavy bombers, and fifty-seven officers and 575 men to bolster defences.[272] Fortunately, the torpedo attack in March was the closest St. John's came to a direct assault, but by then the British government had already released its secret "Scorched Earth Policy" to the governments of its dominions and colonial dependencies.[273]

Faced with the very real possibility of invasion in 1940, the British planned to leave nothing of value for the Germans. The instructions called for the destruction of all naval, army and air force installations, plus cable and telegraph stations, oil and gasoline stocks, food and raw materials, transportation facilities (including harbour installations), mine workings and equipment, as well as all supplies of currency, stamps, securities and other valuable documents. Quite naturally, the British plan stressed total destruction without consideration for recovery after the enemy withdrew. Measures had to be "Rigorously Applied in Practice" and emphasized that the decision to implement them against private property "should not repeat not" be left to the individuals involved. Large property owners would be taken into the government's confidence and assured that such a plan was a worst-case scenario only and that their properties would be destroyed only as a last resort. On the subject of compensation, the instructions suggested that any sort of award would have to wait until after the war. On the other hand, in the event that small property owners were un-cooperative, provisions were made to requisition such properties before they were destroyed. This would allow payment without setting a precedent of immediate compensation.[274]

The Newfoundland government also received a copy of these instructions. In early March, Emerson sent duplicates of a condensed version of them to all military commanders in St. John's, plus the new Director of Civil Defence, and requested a meeting to discuss the formulation of a plan for Newfoundland.[275] This was ten days before the Canadian War Cabinet approved its own release of the plan. Indeed, instructions were not forwarded to the Joint Services Sub-Committee (JSC) Newfoundland, or any other JSC, until the following month.[276] In the event, Admiral Murray ordered his staff, under the chair of Captain (D) Capt. E.R. Mainguy, to draft a proposal for the destruction of the RCN facilities. In May, a committee comprising Lt.-Cmdr Heseltine, RN, the base Ordnance Officer, Lt. Cmdr. Thompson, RCNVR, Staff Officer (Intelligence) and Engineering Lt. Ross, RCNR, met in Captain (D)'s office to discuss a general scorched earth policy. They decided that because most of the RCN buildings in St. John's–the hospital, barracks, administration and officers' accommodation buildings–were made of wood, the quickest way of destroying them was by fire. Similarly, they proposed the use of fire for most of the wharves, machine shops, dockyard and buildings on the Southside of the harbour–all except the buildings on the Marine Agencies Ltd. wharf. The committee cautioned that if these buildings were still used as a magazine, the non-explosive material should be smashed because fire could result in "the whole of St. John's [being] flattened if the explosives were detonated." For the same reason, the underground magazines would just have their roofs blown in. The various fuel oil tanks on the Southside would have their valves opened or pipes smashed and would be burned. All naval stores, stock, vehicles and harbour craft would also be burned. The committee recommended that any merchant shipping that could not be evacuated would be scuttled or burned, "taking into cooperation any other authorities as necessary."[277]

The committee consulted throughout the summer, and in September Captain Mainguy, now acting as interim FONF, issued copies of "Denial Plans–Naval Installations, Equipment and Supplies" to the other service heads. The navy's plans were comprehensive and fraught with danger. Fire was still to be the main means of destruction. The RCN buildings in St. John's would be burned. The Newfoundland and Naval dockyards would be demolished using depth charges, naval vehicles would be driven off wharves, and the harbour entrance would be sealed with block ships. The authors repeated their concern as to how best to destroy the naval ordnance facilities on the Southside of the harbour. The proposal for the Imperial Oil fuel tanks was equally worrisome. The easiest and most effective means of destroying the fuel stocks was simply to open or smash the valves and ignite the leaking fuel. However, the authors cautioned that if this were done, it could "result in a fire, the extent of which cannot be gauged." Even if the fuel was not ignited and was simply contained behind the concrete retaining walls surrounding the tanks, the authors cautioned that the fire danger would still be great.[278]

Some in the military establishment doubted the need for a scorched earth policy at all. Rather, Eastern Air Command Chief of Staff Air Marshall F.V. Heakes, RCAF, felt that "while the present scales of attack warrant a Denial Scheme, they do not warrant a 'Scorched Earth Policy.'" He further advised that "the less said about 'Scorched Earth' on the east coast, the better, for morale reasons."[279] Captain Schwerdt thought that other than the really vital installations, such as the dockyards, workshops, and fuel and ordnance depots, there was really no "particular object in destroying the shore establishment." He recognized that confidential documents had to be destroyed but suggested that the "Naval Accommodation, Administration and other buildings might just as well be left." Indeed, Schwerdt opined that preventing an enemy landing and acts of sabotage by Fifth Columnists or others was "more important than the completion of an effective 'Scorched Earth Policy.'"[280] Perhaps at Schwerdt's suggestion, the RCN, RCAF, the Canadian Army, the United States Army, and Army Air Corps conducted combined manoeuvres during September, which also included members of the local ARP organization. The exercise took the form of a mock landing some distance outside St. John's and thoroughly tested the defence preparedness of the local command. Overall, the exercise was a success and afforded the opportunity to improve defence arrangements still further.[281] Regardless, the navy's denial plans remained in force until a month after D-Day when "the improved strategic situation" prompted the Chiefs of Staff Committee in Ottawa to cancel the scorched earth policy for both the Atlantic and Pacific coasts.[282]

In the meantime, Murray found that the new convoy escort system initiated the previous month was working reasonably well. All except the British groups, now based in Argentia under Commander D. Mcintyre, RN, were up to full strength, but even they never sailed with fewer than five ships. The difficulty lay with the WLEF, which used St. John's for refuelling and repair. In some cases, the turnaround time between assignments was only a few hours, a situation which put tremendous strain on both men and ships, especially the older ex-USN destroyers which required constant upkeep. Murray recommended at least two or three days for turnaround, but NSHQ still pushed the WOMP further east in March to 50 degrees West, thus extending the WLEF's duties even further. The minesweepers of the NDF were not spared either. Besides their minesweeping duties, these little ships were further drafted as local coastal convoy escorts. During the month, forty-four merchant ships were escorted in seventeen coastal convoys, many by minesweepers.[283]

Congestion was again a problem during March when the remainder of the A/S trawlers destined for the US arrived at St. John's. These were coaled and provisioned as quickly as possible, but the presence of these ships caused extreme congestion, necessitating their being berthed up to four on each side of a moored ship. Even though the trawlers were coal-fired, fuelling facilities at St. John's were also becoming a concern. Fuel storage for naval vessels was still afloat because the Imperial Oil facility was used exclusively by merchant ships. However, the MOEF was dependent on Imperial Oil for replenishing its stocks, and when the company did not import enough fuel at the beginning of the month to resupply the oilers *Clam* and *Teakwood*, stocks fell to 1800 tons. As daily consumption was roughly 725 tons, this caused Capt Schwerdt considerable concern.[284]

In the meantime, Lt. Jemmett's attempts to lay anti-submarine defences at the approaches to St. John's harbour met with failure for a number of reasons, including weather. As the commander of HMRT *Tenacity* observed, there was no transition period between the heavy seas of the North Atlantic and the calm waters of St. John's harbour. Ultimately, Lt. A.R. Turnbell, RCN, in charge of controlled mining at Halifax, arrived in St. John's and redesigned the outer detector loop and superintended the laying of the minefield. While this was not completed by the end of the month, construction of the control house and barracks did progress satisfactorily.[285]

At this time, the question of a secondary service facility was also investigated. Schwerdt nominated three candidates–Bay Bulls, Harbour Grace and Aquaforte, further along the Southern Shore. Bay Bulls was his first choice because it was more likely to be ice-free than the other two and thus more accessible during the winter. Schwerdt felt this aspect was most important since the majority of repairs would be from weather damage during the severe winter months. Schwerdt also thought that acquiring the needed sites would be less expensive at Bay Bulls than at Harbour Grace. The difficulty lay in protecting the anchorage, which he argued was "difficult to divorce from the question of the...Marine Dock." An anti-torpedo baffle would have to be installed along the wide mouth of the bay. Schwerdt's second choice, Harbour Grace, was more sheltered and easier to defend and was already used to a limited degree by the RCN. It was connected by the Newfoundland Railway and had accommodation and wharfage, including a small privately owned marine dock. On the downside, it was not as ice-free as either St. John's or Bay Bulls and was too far away to be considered an extension of the St. John's repair organization. Aquaforte came in a poor third due mainly to its isolation. It had a better harbour and could be defended more easily than Bay Bulls, but it was not connected to St. John's by either road or railway.[286]

Construction of the base at St. John's continued unabated during March despite the poor weather. Three of five magazine tunnels planned for the Southside Hills had been excavated, and approximately 150 feet of wharf was finished, or nearly so, and the cribbing for jetties 1-4 was completed. The Administration Building and the Officers' Accommodation block were complete except for equipment, including heating, as was the naval hospital, which had ten wings occupied and two still under construction. Unfortunately for the patients and staff, this facility was "being indifferently heated by temporary measures."[287]

Regardless, with the Battle of the Atlantic having moved mainly to the east coasts of Canada and the United States, April was a relatively quiet month for the MOEF. No MOEF- escorted convoys were attacked during the month, with Murray noting that all losses had been of unescorted vessels. This was fortunate because while Canadian groups were at full strength, the British groups were still inadequate with only one destroyer and four corvettes per group. Murray hoped that this would improve by the summer with each group containing two destroyers and four or five corvettes. In the meantime, the slack was taken up by US and RCAF aircraft which supplied at least some air cover to even coastal convoys. Fortuitously, many coastal convoys during April were sailing directly to Halifax and could avail of the continual stream of escort vessels travelling back and forth between St. John's and HMCS *Stadacona*. During the month, 175 merchant vessels arrived in St. John's,[288] and a total of twenty local convoys sailed. All in all, the Murray felt that the new convoy system was working well and, despite the extended MOMP, even his concerns over the turnaround of the WLEF were alleviated during the month, thanks mainly to the improved weather.[289]

One new cause for concern for Murray, however, was the increased number of incidents of drifting mines. Mines and mysterious explosions were reported from Bonavista, Musgrave Harbour, Notre Dame Bay and Cape Bauld. What was particularly troublesome to the FONF was that these appeared to be British mines;[290] consequently, an officer and a rating were sent to Halifax to undergo training in mine disposal. Captain Schwerdt thought that this was highly advisable under the circumstances, as local residents could not be "restrained from falling on any unknown and strange object in order to collect mementoes." He related one incident in which a salvaged mine was completely dismantled before any report was made of its discovery and its interior displayed to all and sundry by the "intrepid wreckers."[291]

Thanks to the improved weather, continued progress was made on base facilities. Probably most appreciated by the average sailor was the completion and opening of the naval canteen on 22 April. Schwerdt felt that this amenity would be of "outstanding benefit to Naval personnel" because it was on the streetcar route and not too far from the new YMCA hostel club, *The Red Triangle*. By this time, much of the hospital was finished and in full operation, and the Officers' Accommodation building was "to all intents and purposes complete." On the other hand, the dockyard garage still needed doors and a concrete floor, and the Administration Building and the naval barracks were held up by problems with completing the heating system.[292]

With the concentration of U-boat attacks further west during May, the threat to mid-Atlantic shipping decreased, and only one convoy (ON-92) was attacked during the month. As a result, Murray opened the convoy cycle to seven-day intervals from six and reduced the number of MOEF groups to twelve from fourteen. This allowed NSHQ to assign seven corvettes to the newly formed tanker convoys to the Caribbean.[293] Meanwhile, the Admiralty decided that eleven groups were adequate and released British Group 5 (B.5) for the same purpose. Unfortunately, this re-organization shortened the lay-over period for the ships of the remaining groups to only six days. This, in turn, led to congestion problems, especially considering that all WLEF groups were also turning around in St. John's.[294] On average, there were twenty-five escorts daily in St. John's harbour, in addition to the 263 merchant vessels that passed through the port during the month.[295] Of this number, ninety were escorted between St. John's and various other ports in twenty-eight different convoys. To help relieve the pressure, Murray attempted to "stagger" the A, B, and C Groups of the MOEF. This provided indifferent results because there were still periods when St. John's was overcrowded with ships and others when none arrived at all.[296] Nevertheless, the fuelling problems were lessened to some degree in the middle of the month with the arrival of *Scottish Heather* with 8500 tons of Admiralty fuel. At the same time, Major Dunsmore, representing the Fuel Controller, arrived in St. John's to access the fuelling situation.[297] Regardless of these difficulties, as well as frequent fog, bad weather and uncertainty over the position of convoys, Murray felt that the escort system in general "continued to work satisfactorily" with few delays in

The "Newfyjohn" Solution

escorts rendezvousing with their charges.[298] There was one concern, though: training.

As most ships needed their lay-over time for boiler cleaning and/or repairs, there was very little left for any training between convoy assignments. This was alleviated somewhat during turnaround at Londonderry, but Murray also tried to pull a few ships out of operation during May for group training. This was conducted at Harbour Grace under the discerning eye of Commander Prentice in HMCS *Chambly*, who had scored the NEF's first U-boat kill of the war. The ill-fated *P-514* arrived on 17 May and provided invaluable A/S training for ships of the MOEF. Until the arrival of a second submarine, the WWI-vintage British *L-27, P-514* alternated between Harbour Grace and training the B Groups in Argentia. It was on transit from Argentia the following month that the ex-USN R-class submarine was mistakenly sunk with all hands by the minesweeper HMCS *Georgian*. This was not only a human tragedy, for *P514*'s loss seriously hampered training for the MOEF.[299]

During the second week of May, a full-scale air raid drill was carried out in St. John's involving both the fighting services and the civil defence authorities. It revealed a number of serious deficiencies in both equipment and organization. Part of this could have been due to the absence of Lt.-Commander Feilman, RCNVR, who had been appointed ARP Officer at Halifax. His replacement, Lt.-Commander V.T. Elton, RCNVR, did not arrive in St. John's until 21 May. Regardless, the drill showed clearly that there was a serious lack of fire-fighting equipment, first aid stations, and gas masks and decontamination units for the civilian population. While some of the material deficiencies were being rectified, Capt. Schwerdt suggested that a series of exercises was needed to bring departmental organization up to scratch. Regrettably, so much time and manpower were being expended on base construction and maintenance of the escort forces that these exercises could only be conducted at their expense.[300] As the lull in U-boat activity in the mid-Atlantic would soon end, this was not an option.

May also saw the arrival of survivors of the convoy battles being waged offshore. As it was often the closest port of refuge, St. John's was a safe haven for survivors during the war, and had been since 1940.[301] Over a period of two days in May, the rescue ship HMS *Bury* and HMCS *Shediac* arrived at St. John's with 241 survivors from five torpedoed merchant ships on board. Two were off-loaded to hospital, and some were put in the care of Mona Wilson and the Canadian Red Cross, but the rest were kept aboard *Bury* and sailed for Halifax the next day.[302] Over the next year, 2976 survivors arrived at St. John's, and evidence suggests that twice this number were cared for in St. John's during the Second World War, many requiring medical care.[303] This brought another concern to the attention of the FONF. In early May, Dr. Mosdell, Secretary for Public Health and Welfare for the Newfoundland government, called on Admiral Murray with a serious problem. With the influx of service personnel and workers employed at military facilities around Newfoundland, medical care in the outports was suffering because doctors were moving to the larger centres. The government had built a number of cottage hospitals since 1934 to care for outport people, but these were now in jeopardy due to the lack of doctors to operate them.[304] In most cases, military doctors, both Canadian and American, offered free care to civilians living around the various bases and outports, but the cottage hospitals were an essential service for many isolated areas, and this was of grave concern to the Newfoundland government, especially in the event of some sort of epidemic or other medical emergency.[305]

Progress continued on construction of the base throughout May, but a number of projects were held up due to the non-arrival of central heating equipment. The naval hospital was still operating with a temporary system only, and the barracks were complete except for heating which arrived late in the month. This last job was especially pressing as the Royal Fleet Auxiliary *City of Dieppe*, which had been supplying accommodation alongside, left for Quebec early in May, and no doubt Lt.-Commander S.W. Davis, RCN, had his hands full sorting things out when he arrived mid-month to take over duties as executive officer of the naval barracks. The Administration Building was awaiting completion of the main plotting room and other operational areas, particularly communications facilities, before naval headquarters could be moved from the Newfoundland Hotel. The officers' quarters were being cleaned prior to being furnished, but they were awaiting the arrival of an adequate number of cooks and stewards to get the galley and other housekeeping equipment ready for the care of the officers of the command.[306]

Captain Schwerdt considered that the progress on the Naval Dockyard was "remarkable taking into account the difficulties with which the builders have had to contend." These difficulties included congestion caused by the backlog of stores and supplies which were still languishing ashore despite the promises of the Chairman of the Customs Board back in November 1941. Most of the buildings were more than half complete and some, such as the naval canteen, were in use. The Dockyard breastwork was ready for paving, and jetties 1, 3 and 4 required only the installation of bollards, some boat hooks and floating

The "Newfyjohn" Solution

fenders. Jetty 2 was about halfway complete. In the meantime, 180 feet of the Southside wharf was ready, and considerable progress was made on the piles and bracing for the remainder. Progress in this area was hampered by the depth of water, the need to splice the piles and the requirement of having all the bracing ready in advance of the pile-driving equipment.[307] Regardless, a remarkable amount of work had been accomplished since the previous summer.

With the base slowly but surely taking shape, naval authorities addressed the issue of the number and composition of personnel needed to support operations and adequately run HMCS *Avalon*. It takes a tremendous number of men (and women) to operate a naval base at war. Senior officers included, aside from FONF, the Chief of Staff (COS), the Chief Engineer, Newfoundland Command (CENC), the Staff Signal Officer (SSO), Staff Officer (Intelligence) (SO(I)), Staff Officer (Operations) (SO(O)), the Base Medical Officer (BMO), the Command Accountant Officer (CAO), Captain (D), the Naval Officer In Charge (NOIC), the Extended Defence Officer (XDO), Base Naval Stores Officer (BNSO), Accountant Officer (Supply) AO(S), the Superintendent Naval Armament Depot (SNAD) and the Fleet Mail Officer (FMO). In addition, there were numerous junior officers (Lieutenant and below) filling such positions as the Commanding Officer Tactical Training Centre (COTTC), the Staff Meteorological Officer (SO Met), the Chief Public Relations Officer (CPRO), the Flotilla Engineer Officer (FEO), the Central Coding and Cypher Officer (CCO) and the Physical and Recreational Training Officer (P & R TO), to name but a few. On Captain (D)'s staff alone, there was a Gunnery Officer (Staff G), Torpedo Officer (Staff T), Signal Officer (Staff S), A/S (Anti/Submarine) Officer (Staff A/S) and RDF (radar) Officer (Staff RDF). In addition to the officers, HMCS *Avalon* also needed Yeomen, Typists, Telegraphers, Coders, Sick-berth Attendants, Stokers, Sentries, and even Bandsmen.[308]

In consultation with Murray, the Naval Board divided *Avalon*'s requirements into five areas: FONF (Administrative), Capt.(D) (Operations), CENF (Force Maintenance), the Manning Pool and the Naval Barracks (including *Avalon II* which was alongside and used for office and accommodation space). It estimated that in addition to officers, FONF needed 304 ratings, Capt. (D) 23, the Chief Engineer's department 504, the Naval Barracks 669, and the Manning Pool 328, equalling 1828 ratings. Officer numbers would remain at current level with "a reasonable addition to allow for future developments."[309] Captain of the Port Schwerdt amended the estimates, advising Admiral Murray that two Master-at-Arms were required at the barracks and on board

Avalon II, seven additional Regulating Petty Officers were needed for the Military Embarkation Officer at Port-aux-Basques and the new Administration and Officers' Accommodation Building plus the barracks and *Avalon II*, and twenty-eight additional Chief Petty Officers (5) and Petty Officers were required for such duties as harbour patrol, bomb disposal, and berthing parties, among other duties. Furthermore, Schwerdt projected that the command needed an additional 278 Leading, Able, and Ordinary Seamen to fill such responsibilities as barracks maintenance, shore patrol, harbour craft, sentry, orderly and messenger duty. To this, Schwerdt suggested a Chief Yeoman for Murray's staff and another for the Signal Training Centre (STC), thirty-eight Signalmen and Ordinary Signalmen, as well as an increase in Leading Telegraphists, Telegraphists and Ordinary Telegraphists to handle the much increased message traffic, plus additional Motor Mechanics, Leading Stokers, Stokers, Electricians, Sick-berth Attendants and Writers. Murray concurred with Schwerdt's assessment of required personnel[310] and by the end of 1942, HMCS *Avalon* had a compliment of over 4400 men, not including the crews from the two dozen-odd warships that were alongside each day.[311] Even then, the newly appointed FONF, Commodore H. E. Reid, estimated that he needed 4629 officers and ratings to meet his manning commitments.[312]

As has been shown, establishing the base at St. John's was a lot more complicated than the Admiralty had anticipated. This was partly its own fault as it started the ball rolling before it had a clear idea of what was needed. Initially, the NEF was to be the North American component of a three-part convoy escort system that also included an Iceland Escort Force and the existing Clyde Escort Force. The complications arose when NSHQ offered to accept responsibility for the North American part, including establishing the base at St. John's. The Canadians had a number of reasons for wanting to do this, some not necessarily military in nature. For one, the RCN did not just want to be an adjunct to the RN. Having Canadian naval assets operating from a Canadian base under a Canadian officer in traditional Canadian waters was very attractive to both the RCN and the government of Prime Minister Mackenzie King. The other, equally important, consideration was the Americans. Thanks to the Anglo-American "Destroyers for Bases Deal" the Americans were building bases and outposts across Newfoundland. The Canadian government feared that Canada could find itself with an American protectorate on its front doorstep if it did not exert its "special interest" in Newfoundland. A major naval base at St. John's was "just the ticket." The problem was that the Newfoundland government was not very keen on having a larger Canadian *or* American presence in Newfoundland,

The "Newfyjohn" Solution

especially in St. John's harbour. The Commission of Government had a number of good reasons for this reluctance. Newfoundland and its government had been shown little consideration by either the American-Canadian PJBD or in the Anglo-American Leased Bases deal. If a naval base was going to be developed at St. John's, as far as the Commission of Government was concerned, it had to be British.

To add further confusion, the Admiralty decided to eliminate the Iceland leg of the convoy escort circuit and have the NEF escort convoys directly to a MOMP into the waiting arms of the RN. Of course, this would require a larger force and more substantial facilities at St, John's. With an estimated cost of ten million dollars, the Canadian government had second thoughts about shouldering the financial burden and withdrew its offer to underwrite the base. The Admiralty offered to cover half and thought that the Americans could be asked to construct the base under Lend-Lease. However, if the Newfoundland government did not want the Canadians to have ownership of a fair share of St. John's waterfront property, they did not want the Americans to have it either. The Admiralty realized that its best option was to revert back to its original plan and develop the base itself with whatever help it could get from both the Canadians and Americans.

By this time, however, a month had gone by, and the ships of the NEF were escorting convoys and being serviced by facilities afloat. Negotiations were underway to acquire shorefront land, but it was a slow process because most owners just wanted to be left alone. Added to this was the Admiralty's suspicion that the Newfoundland government, which was negotiating compensation, was not necessarily acting in their best interests. Further delays occurred due to labour troubles on the waterfront and problems obtaining needed building materials. Winter was approaching, and as much progress as possible had to be made before bad weather hampered construction. The United States' official entry into the war also complicated things for the Newfoundland Command. With the US a true belligerent and Newfoundland the site of two naval bases, five military and civilian aerodromes, two seaplane bases, five army bases and a variety of civilian assets important to the Allied war effort, not to mention its strategic location, local commanders were fearful of a German attack. Furthermore, in disregard of the provisions of the ABC-1 agreement under which the USN was supposed to take over convoy responsibilities in the Western Atlantic, the Americans hauled all but a token force out of the North Atlantic for duty in the Pacific, while retaining strategic control of the Western Atlantic, including Canadian forces. To add insult to injury, as a result of the slaughter of ships along the US eastern seaboard, Admiral Murray had to detail precious resources for convoy duty to the Caribbean. Still, a year after the first ships of the NEF sailed through the Narrows, HMCS *Avalon* was fully operational, and base facilities were slowly but surely nearing completion.

---

[112] Great Britain, National Archives (TNA/PRO), Admiralty (ADM) 116/4526, United Kingdom High Commissioner in Canada to Dominions Office, 11 June 1941.

[113] *Ibid.*, ADM 1/4387, H.N. Morrison, Head of Military Branch (M Branch), minute, 27 July 1941.

[114] *Ibid.*, Morrison, minute, 15 June 1941.

[115] Governor of Newfoundland to Dominions Secretary, 6 June 1941, in Paul Bridle (ed.), *Documents On Relations Between Canada and Newfoundland* (2 vols., Ottawa: Department of External Affairs, 1974-1984), I, 568.

[116] TNA/PRO, ADM 1/ 4387, M Branch, minute, 17 June 1941.

[117] *Ibid.*

[118] W.A.B. Douglas, *The Creation of a National Air Force: The Official History of the Royal Canadian Air Force* (2 vols., Toronto: University of Toronto Press, 1986), 383.

[119] TNA/PRO, ADM 116/4409, Government of Newfoundland to Dominions Office, 16 September 1940. See also Peter Neary, "Newfoundland and the Anglo-American Leased Bases Agreement of 27 March 1941," *Canadian Historical Review*, LXVII, No. 4 (December 1986), 491-519.

[120] The Lend-Lease Bill permitted the US government to provide war supplies to Great Britain without the British having to pay for them. Up to this point, Britain had to pay for any supplies on a "cash- and-carry" basis, and its foreign reserves were by now exhausted.

[121] In response to the slow pace of negotiations, Roosevelt suggested to the British Ambassador to Washington, Lord Halifax, that the pending Lend-Lease Bill might be jeopardized if agreement was not achieved soon. See Stetson Conn, Rose C. Engelman and Byron Fairchild, *Guarding the United States and Its Outposts* (Washington, DC: Office of the Chief of Military History, 1964; reprint, Washington, DC: US Government Printing Office, 2000), 373.

[122] Neary, "Newfoundland and the Anglo-American Leased Bases Agreement," 510.

[123] David MacKenzie, *Inside the Atlantic Triangle: Canada and the Entrance of Newfoundland into Confederation, 1939-1949* (Toronto: University of Toronto Press, 1986), 51.

[124] Library and Archives Canada (LAC), Record Group (RG) 24, Vol. 11,956, NFM 2-8, L.E. Emerson and J.G. Penson to Governor of Newfoundland, 19 March 1941.

[125] *Ibid.*, Governor of Newfoundland to Emerson and Pension, 17 March 1941.

[126] "Letter From Prime Minister to Commissioner of Defence," *Evening Telegram* (St. John's), 27 March 1941.

[127] Neary, "Newfoundland and the Anglo-American Leased Bases Agreement," 514.
[128] TNA/PRO, ADM 1/4387, M Branch, minute, 17 June 1941.
[129] *Ibid.*, M Branch, minute, 18 June 1941. As it was, the Americans did not completely pull out of Newfoundland until the 1990s.
[130] *Ibid.*, M Branch, minute, 17 June 1941.
[131] *Ibid.*
[132] TNA/PRO, ADM 116/4526, Government of Newfoundland to Dominions Office, 6 June 1941.
[133] *Ibid.*, ADM 1/4387, Base Planning Committee, Minutes of Twenty-sixth Meeting, 23 June 1941.
[134] *Ibid.*
[135] *Ibid.*
[136] *Ibid.*, M Branch, minute, 27 June 1941.
[137] *Ibid.*, British High Commissioner to Canada to Admiralty, 23 July 1941.
[138] *Ibid.*, ADM 1/4388, British Admiralty Delegation to Washington to Admiralty, 5 August 1941.
[139] *Ibid.*, ADM 1/4387, Dominions Office to British High Commissioner to Canada, 26 June 1947.
[140] *Ibid.*, British High Commissioner to Canada to Admiralty, 23 July 1941.
[141] *Ibid.*, M Branch, minute, 27 June 1941.
[142] *Ibid.*, Admiralty to Chief of Naval Staff (CNS), Ottawa, 29 June 1941.
[143] *Ibid.*, British High Commissioner to Canada to Dominions Office, 5 July 1941.
[144] Marc Milner, *North Atlantic Run: The Royal Canadian Navy and the Battle for the Convoys* (Toronto: University of Toronto Press, 1985), 47. Jürgen Rohwer and Gerhard Hummelchen, *Chronology of the War At Sea, 1939-1945: The Naval History of World War Two* (London: Ian Allan, 1972; 3rd rev. ed., London: Chatham Publishing, 1992), 65.
[145] LAC, RG 24, Flag Officer, Newfoundland Force (FONF), Vol. 11,953, file 1-1-1, vol. 1, Commodore Commanding, Newfoundland Force (CCNF) to Naval Service Headquarters, Ottawa (NSHQ), monthly report, June 1941. "Commodore" is really as much of a title as an actual rank and was usually conferred upon a Captain in a position normally occupied by an Admiral. Murray was promoted to Rear Admiral in September.
[146] Marc Milner, "Rear-Admiral Leonard Warren Murray: Canada's Most Important Operational Commander," in Michael Whitby, Richard H. Gimblett and Peter Haydon (eds.), *The Admirals: Canada's Senior Naval Leadership in the Twentieth Century* (Toronto: Dundurn Press, 2006), 96-123. See also Roger Sarty, "Rear-Admiral L.W. Murray and the Battle of the Atlantic: The Professional Who Led Canada's Citizen Sailors," in Bernd Horn and Stephen J. Harris (eds.), *Warrior Chiefs: Perspectives on Senior Canadian*

Military Leaders (Toronto: Dundurn Press, 2001), 165-186.

[147] Schwerdt's staff at the time consisted of himself and three other officers plus three typists and one writer. LAC, RG 24, FONF, Vol. 11,953, file 1-1-1, vol. 1, CCNF to NSHQ, monthly report, June 1941.

[148] *Ibid.*, CCNF, monthly Report, July 1941.

[149] *Ibid.*, CCNF, monthly report, August 1941.

[150] *Ibid.*

[151] *Ibid.*

[152] TNA/PRO, ADM 1/4387, memorandum, St. John's, Newfoundland Naval Base, 8 July 1941.

[153] *Ibid.*

[154] *Ibid.*

[155] *Ibid.*

[156] *Ibid.*

[157] Provincial Archives of Newfoundland and Labrador (PANL), GN 38, S4-2-4, file 2, memorandum for Commission of Government, 10 July 1941.

[158] *Ibid.*

[159] *Ibid.*

[160] *Ibid.*, GN 38, S4-2-3.3, file 4, Secretary of State for Dominion Affairs to Governor of Newfoundland, 8 September 1941. London agreed to cover the total cost of this scheme in December 1941. See *Ibid.*, Secretary of State for Dominion Affairs to Governor of Newfoundland, 20 December 1941.

[161] *Ibid.*, GN38, S4-2-3.3, file 4, Secretary of State for Dominion Affairs to Governor of Newfoundland, 13 September 1941. See also "Mechanics to Train at Local Dockyards," *Evening Telegram* (St. John's), 22 August 1941.

[162] PANL, GN38, S4-2-3.3, file 4, Governor of Newfoundland to Secretary of State for Dominion Affairs, 14 November 1941.

[163] LAC, RG 24, FONF, Vol. 11,953, file 1-1-1, vol. 1, CCNF, monthly report, August 1941.

[164] *Ibid.*, Ranger B. Gill to Chief Ranger, 16 August 1941, in CCNF, monthly report, October 1941.

[165] *Ibid.*, CCNF, monthly report, August 1941. The Atlantic Charter was the proclamation made by Churchill and Roosevelt at the conclusion of their meeting in Placentia Bay and promised a return to freedom and democracy for all mankind. It is somewhat ironic that this historic meeting took place in Newfoundland, which at the time was under the governance of a non-elected commission appointed by Britain, and the United States was a neutral nation. See Peter Neary, *Newfoundland in the North Atlantic World, 1929-1949* (Montreal: McGill-Queen's University Press, 1988; 2nd ed., Montreal: McGill-Queen's University Press, 1996), 162; Samuel Eliot Morison, *History of United States Naval Operations in World War II. Vol. I: The Battle of the Atlantic, September 1939-May 1943* (Boston: Little, Brown, and Co. 1947; reprint, Urbana: University of Illinois Press, 2002), 69-70; and Sandor S. Klein, "Would Disarm Aggressors and Restore Self-Rule to All," *New York World-Telegram*, 14 August 1941.

[166] PANL, GN 38, S4-2-4, file 5, CCNF to Sir Wilfred Woods, 25 August 1941.

[167] LAC, RG 24, FONF, Vol. 11,949, file 1-1-1, Department of National Defence (DND) to CCNF, 25 November 25 1941; and DND to CCNF, 6 December 1941. This was not the only instance of tension between the city administration and the Canadian government. The City of St. John's felt that the Canadians should pay property taxes on their facilities and share the cost of road maintenance due to the increased traffic and damage caused by the various services. In one instance, a Canadian contractor was accused of driving his tractor home for his midday meal, leaving a trail of torn pavement in his wake. The Canadian government felt it was exempt from paying taxes and accepted no liability for the extra wear and tear on the city's roads. However, it did agree to a one-time lump sum payment to help repair the roads and promised to instruct its contractors to practice due diligence with city property and services. City of St. John's Archives. See, for example, City of St. John's Archive, MG40, Jackman Collection, 2-2-2, file 38, J.J. Mahoney to Charles Burchell, 6 October 1943; Burchell to Mahoney, 25 November 1943; Mahoney to Major-General J.B. Brooks, 14 April 1943; Mahoney to Commodore C.R.H. Taylor, 10 June 1944; and Mahoney to E.G.M. Cape and Co. Ltd., 7 June 1944.

[168] *Ibid.*, 953, CCNF, monthly report, September 1941.

[169] *Ibid.*, CCNF, monthly report, September 1941.

[170] *Ibid.*

[171] *Ibid.*

[172] *Ibid.*

[173] *Ibid.*

[174] *Ibid.*, RG 24, FONF, RG 24, Vol. 11,953, file 1-1-1, vol. 1, Report of Proceedings by the Maintenance Captain, Captain of the Port, in CCNF, monthly report, September 1941.

[175] *Ibid.*, Report of Proceedings for the Month of November, Captain of the Port, in CCNF, monthly report, November 1941.

[176] *Ibid.*, Edgar Gilbert to Captain of Port, 23 October 1941, in CCNF, monthly report, October 1941.

[177] *Ibid.*, Gilbert to Capt. C.M.R. Schwerdt, 29 October 1941, in CCNF, monthly report, October 1941.

[178] *Ibid.*, Gilbert to Schwerdt, 23 October 1941.

[179] *Ibid.*, Vol. 11,951, Murray to Woods, 10 July 1941.

[180] In an attempt to contain inflation and protect local business from having to match the wages paid by American and Canadian contractors, the Commission of Government brought in a maximum wage scale for local labour. This caused considerable dissent because if two men were doing the same job but one was from outside Newfoundland, the local man would be paid less than his American or Canadian co-worker. For a full discussion, see Steven High, *Base Colonies in the Western Hemisphere, 1940-1967* (New York: Palgrave Macmillan, 2009).

[181] LAC, RG 24, FONF, Vol. 11,949, Woods to Murray, 1 October

1941.

[182] *Ibid.*, FONF to NSHQ, 1 October 1941.
[183] High, *Base Colonies*, 141-146. See also Neary, *Newfoundland in the North Atlantic World*, 152.
[184] TNA/PRO, ADM 116/4388, British Admiralty Delegation (BAD) to Admiralty, 5 August 1941.
[185] *Ibid.*, BAD to Admiralty, 15 March 1942.
[186] Christopher A. Sharpe and A.J. Shawyer, "Building a Wartime Landscape," in Steven High (ed.), *Occupied St. John's: A Social History of a City at War, 1939-1945* (Montreal: McGill-Queen's University Press, 2010), 44-46. See also High, *Base Colonies*, 141-146.
[187] LAC, RG 24, FONF, Vol. 11,953, file 1-1-1, vol. 1, Report of Proceedings by Maintenance Captain, Captain of the Port, in FONF, monthly report, August 1942.
[188] *Ibid.*, 953, FONF, monthly report, November 1941.
[189] *Ibid.*, Gilbert to Schwerdt, 29 October 1941, in FONF, monthly report, November 1941.
[190] *Ibid.*, Report of Proceedings for the Month of November, in CCNF, monthly report, November 1941.
[191] *Ibid.*
[192] Governor Walwyn observed that many of these fires occurred on Saturday nights when these places would have been full of service personnel. PANL, DO 35/1359, Governor's Report, 30 June 1945.
[193] "Arena and Curling Rink Completely Destroyed in Spectacular Blaze, *Evening Telegram* (St. John's), 29 November 1941; and LAC, RG 24, FONF, Vol. 11,953, file 1-1-1, vol. 1, Report of Proceedings, in FONF, monthly report, November 1941.
[194] LAC, RG 24, FONF, Vol. 11,953, file 1-1-1, vol. 1, Report of Proceedings for the Month of November, in FONF, monthly report, November 1941.
[195] *Ibid.*
[196] *Ibid.*, FONF, monthly report, December 1941.
[197] *Ibid.*, RG 24, FONF, Vol. 11,505, MS 1550-14636-1, Secretary of the Navy, Washington, to FONF, 7 December 1941.
[198] *Ibid.*, FONF to Naval Secretary, NSHQ, 8 December 1941.
[199] *Ibid.*, FONF to Naval Secretary, NSHQ, 31 December 1941.
[200] TNA/PRO, ADM 116/4540, Governor of Newfoundland to Admiralty, 31 March 1942.
[201] LAC, RG 24, FONF, Vol. 11,505, MS 1550-14636-1, FONF to Naval Secretary, NSHQ, 31 December 1941.
[202] *Ibid.*, Vol. 11,951, Brant to Admiral Commanding, Newfoundland, 24 December 1941.
[203] PANL, GN 38, S4-1-6, file 8, Civil Defence Meeting, minutes, 15 December 1941.
[204] LAC, RG 24, FONF, Vol. 11,951, Murray to General G.C. Brant, 6

January 1942.

[205] Indeed, a book published in 1940 in Britain entitled *101 Things To Do In War Time* included, among other useful advice, instructions on protection from splintering window glass, blacking-out windows and basic first aid. See Lillie B. Horth and Arthur C. Horth, *101 Things to Do in War Time 1940: A Practical Handbook for the Home* (London: B.T. Batsford, 1940; reprint, London: B.T. Batsford, 2007).

[206] PANL, GN 38, S4-1-6, file 8, Civil Defence Meeting, minutes, 15 December 1941.

[207] *Ibid.*

[208] *Ibid.*

[209] LAC, RG 24, FONF, Vol. 11,953, file 1-1-1, vol. 1, Report of Proceedings for the Month of December 1941, in FONF, monthly report, December 1941.

[210] *Ibid.*

[211] LAC, RG 24, FONF, Vol. 11,953, file 1-1-1, vol. 1, Report of Proceedings for the Month of December 1941, in FONF, monthly report, December 1941.

[212] Günther Hessler, *The U-Boat War in the Atlantic 1930-1945* (3 vols., London: HMSO, 1989), II, 1.

[213] Karl Dönitz, *Memoirs: Ten Years and Twenty Day*, (Annapolis: Naval Institute Press, 1990), 183.

[214] Nathan Miller, *War at Sea: A Naval History of World War II* (New York: Scribner, 1995; reprint, New York: Oxford University Press, 1997), 291.

[215] Michael Gannon, *Operation Drumbeat: The Dramatic True Story of Germany's First U-boat Attacks along the American Coast in World War II* (New York: Harper and Row, 1990), xviii.

[216] Dan van der Vat, *The Atlantic Campaign: The Great Struggle at Sea, 1939-1945* (New York: Harper and Row, 1988), 242.

[217] Clay Blair, *Hitler's U-Boat War: The Hunters, 1939-1942* (New York: Random House, 1996), 461. See also David Jordan, *Wolfpack: The U-Boat War and the Allied Counter-Attack, 1939-1945*. (Staplehurst: Spellmount, 2002), 103-105.

[218] *Ibid.*, 465-466.

[219] Hadley, *U-Boats against Canada*, 57.

[220] Jordan, *Wolfpack*, 106. See also Van der Vat, *Atlantic Campaign*, 264-265.

[221] *Ibid.*, 239.

[222] *Ibid.*, 264-266. See also Thomas Parrish, *The Submarine: A History* (New York: Viking Penguin, 2004), 260-261.

[223] Jordan, Wolfpack, 106.

[224] Van der Vat, *Atlantic Campaign*, 265-266.

[225] From the first arrival of the U-boats in mid-January 1942 until the American campaign ended at the end of July, 360 ships were sunk off the US eastern seaboard. See Eric J. Grove (ed.), *The Defeat of the Enemy Attack on*

Shipping, 1939-1945 (Aldershot: Ashgate Publishing, 1997), 84. See also V.E. Tarrant, *The U-Boat Offensive 1914-1945* (Annapolis: Naval Institute Press, 1989), 104; and van der Vat, *Atlantic Campaign*, 265-266.

[226] Hessler, *U-Boat War*, II, 4.

[227] Spencer Dunmore, *In Great Waters: The Epic Story of the Battle of the Atlantic, 1939-45* (Toronto: McClelland and Stewart, 1999), 144.

[228] Gannon, *Operation Drumbeat*, 205.

[229] Hessler, *U-Boat War*, II, 4.

[230] Hadley, *U-Boats against Canada*, 63.

[231] Jurgen Rohwer, *Axis Submarine Successes, 1939-1945* (Cambridge: Patrick Stephens, 1983), 73-77.

[232] Hadley, *U-boats against Canada*, 71.

[233] *Ibid.*, 71. Rowher, *Axis Submarine Successes*, 89, says that Topp used torpedoes.

[234] Hadley, *U-boats against Canada*, 73.

[235] Blair, *The Hunters*, 512.

[236] Hadley, *U-boats Against Canada*, 79.

[237] Blair, *The Hunters*, 771.

[238] Strange would be a major figure in the equipment scandal that enveloped the RCN in 1943.

[239] Hadley, *U-boats Against Canada*, 81.

[240] Rohwer, *Axis Submarine Successes*, 95.

[241] Hadley, *U-boats against Canada*, 93.

[242] LAC, RG 24, FONF, Vol. 11,953, File 1-1-1, vol. 1, monthly report, January 1942.

[243] *Ibid.* See also van Der Vat, *Atlantic Campaign*, 262.

[244] Joseph T. Carroll, *Ireland in the War Years, 1939-1945* (Newton Abbot: David and Charles, 1975), 25.

[245] *Ibid.*

[246] Winston S. Churchill, *The Gathering Storm* (18th ed., New York: Bantam Books, 1961), 248.

[247] John W. Blake, *Northern Ireland in the Second World War* (Belfast: HMSO, 1956; reprint, Belfast: Blackstaff Press, 2000), 316-317.

[248] Gilbert Tucker, *The Naval Service of Canada* (2 vols., Ottawa: King's Printer, 1952), II, 205.

[249] *Ibid.*

[250] As quoted in Jonathan Barton, *A History of Ulster* (Belfast: Blackstaff Press, 1992; rev. ed., Belfast: Blackstaff Press, 2005), 559.

[251] *Ibid.*, 574-575. See also Derrick Gibson-Harris, *Life-Line to Freedom: Ulster in the Second World War* (Lurgan: Ulster Society, 1990), 16-30.

[252] Tucker, *Naval Service of Canada*, II, 207. As previously noted, the Canadian groups had been pulled out of the North Atlantic for training and duty on the UK-Gibraltar run.

[253] John W. Blake, as quoted in Barton, *History of Ulster*, 575.

254 Brian Lacy, *Seige City: The Story of Derry and Londonderry* (Belfast: Blackstaff Press, 1990), 240.

255 Tucker, *Naval Service of Canada*, II, 208.

256 Samuel Eliot Morison, *The Two-Ocean War: A Short History of the United States Navy in the Second World War* (Boston: Little, Brown, 1963; reprint, Annapolis: Naval Institute Press, 2007), 104.

257 Tucker, *Naval Service of Canada*, II, 208.

258 LAC, RG 24, FONF, Vol. 11,953, file 1-1-1, vol. 1, monthly Report, January 1942. See also Neary, *Newfoundland in the North Atlantic World*, 126.

259 LAC, RG 24, FONF, Vol. 11,953, file 1-1-1, vol. 1, Report of Proceedings, St. John's Naval Base, monthly report, January 1942.

260 *Ibid.*, monthly report, February 1942.

261 One can still see "Spikenard's Spike" proudly displayed at the *Seagoing Officers Club*, better known as "The Crow's Nest" in St. John's, founded by Capt. (D) E.R. Mainguy in 1942. Hadley, *U-Boats against Canada*, 256.

262 LAC, RG 24, FONF, Vol. 11,953, file 1-1-1, vol. 1, Monthly Report, February 1942.

263 *Ibid.*, Report of Proceedings by Maintenance Captain, Captain of the Port, in FONF, monthly report, February 1942.

264 *Ibid.*

265 TNA/PRO, ADM 116/4526, Dominions Office to Newfoundland Government, 16 October 1942.

266 *Ibid.*, NSHQ to Admiralty, 26 October 1942.

267 This incident was not reported in the newspapers and, indeed, many people did not learn of the source of the explosions until after the war. Training and test firing of guns were regular occurrences and the explosions would probably have, at least initially, been dismissed as such. There is also some question as to whether two or three torpedoes were fired at the Narrows. Rowher claims that only two were fired, while the FONF in his report wrote that three explosions were heard. It is possible that the third explosion was actually an echo from the first hit under Fort Amherst. Authorities puzzled as to why a U-boat commander would waste valuable torpedoes firing at (and missing) the entrance of an obviously defended port. The perpetrator, *Kapitänleutnant* Ulrich Borcherdt in U-587, was sunk three weeks later. Jürgen Rowher, *Axis Submarine Successes, 1939-1945* (Cambridge: Patrick Stephens, 1983), 82. LAC, FONF, RG 24, Vol. 11,953, file 1-1-1, Vol. 1, Report of Proceedings by Maintenance Captain, Captain of the Port, in FONF, monthly report, March 1942. See also LAC, RG 24, FONF, Vol. 6901, file 8910-166/25 vol. 1., FONF to NSHQ, 5 March, 1942. Kenneth Wynn, *U-Boat Operations of the Second World War, Vol. 2: Career Histories U511-UIT25* (London: Chatham Publishing, 1998), 58-9.

268 LAC, RG 24, FONF, Vol. 11,951, CTF 24 to FONF, 3 February 1942.

269 LAC, FONF, RG 24, Vol. 11,953, file 1-1-1, Vol. 1, Report of

Proceedings by Maintenance Captain, Captain of the Port, in FONF, monthly report, March 1942.

[270] Kenneth Wynn, *U-Boat Operations of the Second World War, Vol. 2: Career Histories U511-UIT25* (London: Chatham Publishinbg, 1998, 58-9.

[271] "Says Newfoundland Was Included in Hitler's Plans," *Evening Telegram* (St. John's), 13 July 1944.

[272] LAC, RG 24, FONF, Vol. 11,956, Secretary of State for Dominion Affairs to Governor, 8 April 1941.

[273] *Ibid.*, RG24, Vol. 11,927, MS 1400-4, vol. 1, "Instructions Issued To Certain Colonial Dependencies on 'Scorched Earth Policy.'" See also Paul Collins, "'Canada's Plan to Torch St. John's' during the Second World War: Upper Canadian Arrogance or Tabloid Journalism?" *Newfoundland and Labrador Studies*, XXIV, No. 2 (Fall 2009), 261-270; and Kerry Badgley, "'Rigorously Applied in Practice': A Scorched Earth Policy for Canada and Newfoundland during the Second World War," *The Archivist*, No. 446 (1998), 38-43.

[274] LAC, RG24, Vol. 11,927, MS 1400-4, vol. 1, "Instructions Issued To Certain Colonial Dependencies on 'Scorched Earth Policy.'"

[275] *Ibid.*, Emerson to FONF, 11 March 1942.

[276] *Ibid.*, RG 24, FONF, Vol. 5256, file HQS-22-1-13, memo to CGS on "Scorched Earth Policy," 22 June 1944.

[277] *Ibid.*, Vol. 11,927, MS 1400-4, vol. 1, Draft copy of Minutes of Meeting on "Scorched Earth Policy, 22 May 1942.

[278] *Ibid.*, Denial Plans—Naval Installations, Equipment and Supplies, 23 September 1942.

[279] *Ibid.*, Vol. 5256, file HQS-22-1-13, Acting/Air Member for Air Staff to Chief of Air Staff, 8 October 1942.

[280] *Ibid.*, Vol. 11,927, MS 1400-4, vol. 1, Schwerdt to FONF, *et al.*, "'Scorched Earth' Policy, Newfoundland, 14 March 1942.

[281] *Ibid.*, RG24, FONF, Vol. 11,953, file 1-1-1, vol. 1, Report of Proceedings by Maintenance Captain, Captain of the Port, in FONF, monthly report, September 1942.

[282] *Ibid.*, Vol. 5256, file HQS-22-13, "Extract From Minutes Of Meeting Of Defence Council Held on 7 July 1944."

[283] *Ibid.*, RG 24, FONF, Vol. 11,953, file 1-1-1, vol. 1, FONF, monthly report, March 1942.

[284] *Ibid.*, Report of Proceedings by Maintenance Captain, Captain of the Port, in FONF, monthly report, March 1942.

[285] *Ibid.*

[286] *Ibid.*

[287] *Ibid.*

[288] *Ibid.*, RG 24, FONF, Vol. 11,953, file 1-1-1, vol. 1,Report of Proceedings by Maintenance Captain, Captain of the Port, in FONF, monthly report, April 1942.

[289] *Ibid.*, FONF, monthly report, April 1942.

[290] *Ibid.*
[291] *Ibid.*, Report of Proceedings by Maintenance Captain, Captain of the Port, in FONF, monthly report, April 1942.
[292] *Ibid.*
[293] In an attempt to stem the tremendous losses in tankers in the Caribbean and along the US eastern seaboard, NSHQ decided to initiate its own tanker convoys to and from the Caribbean. For a discussion of these new convoys, see W.A.B. Douglas, et al)., *No Higher Purpose: The Official Operational History of the Royal Canadian Navy in the Second World War, 1939-1945,* Volume II, Part 1 (St. Catherines: Vanwell, 2002) 412, and Robert C. Fisher, "'We'll Get Our Own:' Canada and the Oil Shipping Crisis of 1942," *The Northern Mariner/Le Marin du Nord,* III, No. 2 (April 1993), 33-39.
[294] LAC, RG 24, FONF, Vol. 11,953, file 1-1-1, vol. 1, FONF, monthly report, May 1942.
[295] *Ibid.*, Report of Proceedings by Maintenance Captain, Captain of the Port, in FONF, monthly report, May 1942.
[296] *Ibid.*, FONF, monthly report, May 1942.
[297] *Ibid.*, Report of Proceedings by Maintenance Captain, Captain of the Port, in FONF, monthly report, May 1942. One remedy suggested for the fuelling difficulties was to construct reserve storage tanks at Holyrood, Conception Bay. However, before these measures were started the strategic situation had changed in the Allies' favour and the plans were shelved. See Tucker, *The Naval Service of Canada,* II , 528-9.
[298] *Ibid.*, FONF, monthly report, May 1942.
[299] *Ibid.*, See also Hadley, *U-Boats against Canada,* 98-99.
[300] LAC, RG 24, FONF, Vol. 11,953, file 1-1-1, vol. 1, Report of Proceedings by Maintenance Captain, Captain of the Port, in FONF, monthly report, May 1942.
[301] PANL, DO 35/725, Reel B-5012, Governor's Quarterly Report for the period ending 30 September 1940.
[302] LAC, RG 24, FONF, Vol. 11,953, file 1-1-1, vol. 1, Report of Proceedings by Maintenance Captain, Captain of the Port, in FONF, monthly report, May 1942. See also Gillian Poulter and Douglas O. Baldwin, "'Never a Dull Moment in this Port:' Mona Wilson and the Canadian Red Cross in Wartime St. John's," in High (ed.), *Occupied St. John's,* 220-250.
[303] DND, Directorate of History and Heritage (DHH), NHS 8000, 25, Lt. Stuart Keats, "The Royal Canadian Navy in Newfoundland, 1940-1944," October 1944.
[304] For the most recent study of the Newfoundland Cottage Hospital system see Edward F. J. Lake, *Capturing an Era: History of the Newfoundland Cottage Hospital System* (St. John's, NL: Argentia Pilgrim, 2010).
[305] LAC, RG 24, FONF, Vol. 11,953, file 1-1-1, vol. 1, Report of Proceedings by Maintenance Captain, Captain of the Port, in FONF, monthly report, May 1942. This request might have been prompted by the USS *Truxton*/USS *Pollux* disaster in February 1942 whereby the two ships went

aground off the Burin Peninsula in a storm on their way to the Argentia Naval/Air Station and the survivors were rescued and cared for by the people of St. Lawrence. It took days for the news to get out and proper medical care sent.

[306] *Ibid.*

[307] *Ibid.*

[308] *St. John's Naval Book*, DC Miller, ed. (St. John's: Robinson & Co. Ltd., 1942, 5-6.

[309] LAC, RG 24, Vol. 11,949, No. 30-1-1, Vol. 1, Secretary, Naval Board to Flag Officer, Newfoundland Force, 26 March 1942.

[310] *Ibid.*, RG 24, Vol. 11,949, No. 30-1-1, Vol. 1, Captain of the Port to Flag Officer Newfoundland Force, 23 May 1942.

[311] This figure includes the 786 officers and men required to administer and maintain the Halifax-based Western Support Force which used St. John's for turnaround.

[312] LAC, RG 24, Vol. 11,949, No. 30-1-1, Vol. 2, Flag Officer, Newfoundland Force to Secretary, Naval Board , 16 December 1942.

Chapter 4
Holding the Line: June 1942 to May 1943

While the Americans were getting some sort of handle on the situation off their eastern seaboard, things were heating up again off the east coast of Canada. The "Battle of the St. Lawrence," a term coined by the *Ottawa Journal*, was not actually a battle but a series of effective U-boat sorties that accounted for the heaviest Canadian losses in the inshore zone.[313] Recognizing the Gulf of St. Lawrence as a hub of both local and trans-Atlantic shipping, Dönitz sent six U-boats over a six-month period to attack seven convoys, sinking twenty merchantmen, a loaded troopship and two Royal Canadian Navy (RCN) warships.[314] The pièce de résistance, as far as domestic impact was concerned, was the sinking of the Sydney to Port-Aux-Basque passenger ferry SS *Caribou* with the loss of 136 people, including ten children.

On 30 June 1942, *U-132* under the command of *Kapitänleutnant* Ernst Vogelsang penetrated the Cabot Strait and entered the Gulf of St. Lawrence. For the first few days, he reconnoitred the area, but despite the presence of targets, mist and/or distance frustrated his efforts. But in the early hours of 6 July, Vogelsang sighted and tracked the Quebec-Sydney convoy QS-15. Shortly thereafter, he initiated an attack which Eastern Air Command would later describe as "the greatest loss that was sustained in any one locality" off the east coast of Canada.[315] In the space of a few minutes, Vogelsang sank the Belgian *Hianaut*, the Greek *Anastassios Pateras* and the British-registered *Dinaric*.[316] This attack, however, was not without consequences for *U-132*. The Bangor minesweeper HMCS *Drummondville* (Lt. J.P. Fraser, RCNVR) sighted the U-boat and gave it a severe pounding. The attack exacerbated previous battle damage, most notably the main ballast pump which controlled the boat's trim. Slowly *U-132* sank to 180 metres. With only eighty kilograms of compressed air left to blow the ballast tanks, Vogelsang decided to surface and put his faith in the darkness, the U-boat's speed and its manoeuvrability. Although spotted by one of the escorts, now two miles distant, *U-132* eluded him in the darkness. When Vogelsang finally reached the 100-metre sounding, he submerged and lay on the bottom to make repairs.[317]

For the next week, *U-132* patrolled the Strait of Belle Isle but sighted no tempting targets. Vogelsang therefore deemed this area to be "unfavourable" and headed back to the mouth of the St. Lawrence River where he had enjoyed his previous successes.[318] He arrived off Cap de la Madeleine on 20 July and sighted the Quebec-Sydney convoy QS-19 escorted by HMCS *Weyburn*, HMCS *Chedebucto* and the two Fairmile patrol boats, *Q-074* and *Q-059*. In a daring daylight attack, Vogelsang penetrated the convoy at periscope depth and fired two torpedoes. One hit SS *Frederick Lensen*, damaging it so that when towed to Grand Vallée Bay it broke in half and sank. *U-132* made its escape in the resulting confusion and, traversing the Cabot Strait unmolested, sent a lengthy situation report on 24 July. *U-132* arrived home safely after a patrol of sixty-eight days, having steamed 10,000 miles. With its score of five ships sunk, the patrol was considered "a fine success."[319]

Things were fairly quiet for the next month. There were no sinkings in the Gulf itself, but there was some activity to the east of Nova Scotia. The east coast of North America was no longer the "happy hunting ground" it had been for the previous six months. Few ships now travelled alone, and the last seven U-boats to operate off the coast found few valuable targets. *U-458* (Diggins) claimed a 4870-ton merchantman, but *U-89*'s (Lohmann) bag was only the fifty-four-ton schooner *Lucille M*, and *U-754*'s(Oestermann) the 260-ton American fishing vessel *Ebb* 120 miles south of Halifax.[320]

With Dönitz concentrating his efforts further south, June was fairly quiet for the Newfoundland Command. Only two convoys were attacked–ON-100 and ON-102–with the loss of just one straggler from ON-100. However, the command did suffer two "severe and painful losses" during the month. *P-514* was sunk by mistake off the southern Avalon Peninsula, as previously noted, and the Free French corvette *Mimosa* was torpedoed with only four survivors while escorting ON-100. In spite of these tragic losses, ninety ships in twenty-six local convoys arrived at their destinations unscathed. Still, Murray knew that this lull in U-boat attacks in the mid-Atlantic would not last much longer. With the increasing strength of both surface and air escorts in the Caribbean and Gulf of Mexico, he knew it was only a matter of time before the U-boats, emboldened by their successes in the Western Hemisphere, moved back into their familiar hunting grounds in the mid-Atlantic. Nevertheless, a meeting in Washington in early June attended by Murray's Chief of Staff, Capt. Bidwell, decided to further reinforce the escort forces in the Caribbean at the expense of the Mid-Ocean Escort Force (MOEF). This forced Murray to reduce the size of each group to six vessels, with two being destroyers whenever possible. This move released eight corvettes for duty in the Caribbean theatre. The redeployment of these ships, along with the loss of *P-514*, effectively halted any local training for the MOEF.[321]

While not of major impact on the war effort, but indicative of a growing problem in St. John's, two naval ratings were court marshalled during the month for theft.[322] While the presence of the various armed forces allayed local fears of German assault, it also created other difficulties worth noting. With so many young men in St. John's, many away from home for the first time and with money in their pockets, it was almost inevitable that some would end up in trouble with the police. Indeed, statistics indicate that during 1941, a year from the arrival of the Americans and six months after the creation of the NEF, there were 3417 criminal prosecutions, an increase of 1203 over 1940 and almost double the number in 1939.[323] By 1943 there were 8000 cases, 1000 more than 1942.[324] A large portion of these were liquor-related, and many involved the men of the RCN. Possibly the most notorious incident occurred on Christmas night in 1941 when 150 naval ratings destroyed the Imperial Café on Water Street.[325] Popular memory has it that the Americans were much better behaved than the Canadians, and a review of the Magistrate's Court section of the *Evening Telegram* during the war seems to bear this out. Seldom did a day go by that a Canadian naval rating or soldier did not appear before the magistrate.[326] Yet in truth, the infrequency with which American servicemen appeared before the bench resulted as much from an agreement between the Newfoundland government and US authorities as from better behaviour.[327] Some American military personnel did appear before local courts, but the majority were transferred to the US military. While the punishments handed out by military courts were often harsher than those of the civilian courts, this special treatment raised the ire of some in the community. In the case of the two RCN ratings, the accused were acquitted due to lack of evidence.[328]

June was also marked by an air raid scare. Early in the month the mayor of St. John's, Andrew Carnell, phoned Commissioner for Defence Emerson from Montreal with supposedly reliable information from a prominent citizen that a number of enemy aircraft would attack St. John's on 10 June. A "yellow" alert was issued, and all air raid measures were instigated for the nights of both 9 and 10 June, although only the fighting services stayed on high alert on the 10th. Fortunately, no raid occurred. Another bit of excitement took place in the middle of the month, although this was more a celebration than a threat. The first

United Nations Day was held in St. John's. Fifteen hundred service personnel and eight hundred civil defence members took part in a parade through St. John's with honours given to His Excellency the Governor, Admiral Walwyn, and the senior military commanders in front of Government House. Unfortunately or fortunately, depending on your point of view, the majority of the MOEF were on duty in the North Atlantic, but Murray was able to scrape together a naval contingent comprising roughly 100 seamen.[329]

Progress on the base continued, but Canadian bureaucracy was causing delays. Despite approval from Naval Services Headquarters (NSHQ), the Supervising Engineer still required approval from his own department to proceed with certain items. To save time, Schwerdt suggested that approval from NSHQ and the Engineer's departmental head should be issued concurrently. Nevertheless, construction was advancing at a satisfactory rate. Tunnels 3, 4 and 5 of the Southside magazine were well in hand, the latter two being more than 400 feet deep. Number 1 fuel tank was erected and was being tested with water for leaks, and the site for tank Number 6 was being cleared. Contractors had nearly completed the Southside wharf for its full length from Job Brothers property westward, and progress was underway at the Newfoundland Fuel and Engineering and the Marine Agencies wharves. At the Naval Dockyard, all of the cribwork west of the haul-up slip was finished, and work on the slip itself had begun. Most of the buildings were nearly finished, although Building 7 would be delayed for upwards of six months due to the difficulty in obtaining heating and other equipment. The heating plant finally arrived for the hospital and was being installed, and both the administration building and the officers' accommodation building were just about ready for occupancy. All the naval barracks, with a few exceptions, were ready for habitation. Thus, by the end of June 1942, after a year of delays, negotiations, setbacks and changes in jurisdiction, Murray was finally seeing HMCS *Avalon* nearing completion.[330] This was fortunate, because the next six months were going to bring trying times for the Flag Officer Newfoundland Force (FONF) and the rest of the MOEF.

By the beginning of the summer of 1942, when the Americans had stemmed the tide of slaughter along their eastern seaboard and in the Caribbean and Gulf of Mexico, Dönitz again turned his sights on the North Atlantic. As a result, the FONF noted an increase in U-boat sightings in the waters patrolled by the MOEF during July. One outward-bound convoy–ON-113–was attacked on 23 July with the loss of three merchantmen, and another–ON-115–was shadowed by U-boats. HMCS

St. Croix, one of the ex United States Navy (USN) Town-class destroyers from the "destroyers for bases" deal, sank *U-90* while escorting ON-113, and HMC Ships *Skeena* and *Wetaskiwin* escorting ON-115 sank *U-588*. Both sinkings were confirmed by large amounts of wreckage and human remains.[331] While Murray had difficulty finding escorts due to refits and repairs, none of the 124 ships escorted in twenty-four local convoys was molested, despite being only lightly escorted by Bangor minesweepers which lacked radar.[332]

In July, Captain C.M.R. Schwerdt, Captain of the Port and until June 1941 the Naval Officer in Charge (NOIC) of St. John's, departed. Schwerdt had come to St. John's as Governor Walwyn's private secretary and took on the responsibilities of NOIC when war was declared. With only a skeleton staff, Schwerdt had arranged for the defence of St. John's, set up an examination service, installed signal stations at Cape Spear and Signal Hill and been the Admiralty's point man in establishing HMCS *Avalon*. No doubt these accomplishments led to his appointment as NOIC at Sydney, Cape Breton. Commander G.B. Hope, RCN, arrived as Schwerdt's replacement along with his assistant, Acting/Lt-Commander J.O. Merchant, RCNVR. Until the arrival of Acting/Captain W.L.B. Holms, Hope also served as Commanding Officer of the naval barracks.[333]

In the meantime, all of the naval offices except that of Extended Defence Officer (XDO) Captain Langston moved from the Newfoundland Hotel to the new administration building. This included FONF and his staff, Captain (D) and his staff, the Base CB Office, the NOIC and his staff, and the Staff Signals Officer (SSO) and his staff.[334] The building also accommodated the Naval Control Service Officer (NCSO), the Maintenance Officer Rescue Tugs (MORT) and the Ministry of War Transport (MWT) as well as numerous Royal Canadian Air Force (RCAF) offices. Shortly thereafter, the Captain's Office for HMCS *Avalon* moved to the newly completed barracks at Buckmasters' Field along with the Leave and Transportation Office. With the barracks finished, a meeting was held in Commander Hope's office to discuss moving Captain(D) as well as some selected maintenance personnel to the now somewhat redundant HMCS *Avalon II* (the former *SS Georgian*), and towards the end of July a representative of the Chief Engineer's staff flew to Ottawa to discuss these plans with NSHQ. Meanwhile, the rest of HMCS *Avalon* was nearing completion. The various shops and stores at the dockyard were "substantially complete," as was the garage, and contractors had almost finished the excavation of the magazines, albeit delayed somewhat by rock falls. The fuel tanks were progressing satisfactorily with Number 1 ready to be connected to the wharf and Number 2 erected except for the roof. Numbers 3-5 were in various stages of preparation.[335]

The month of August was a busy time for HMCS *Avalon* as a number of VIPs arrived in St. John's. The first was Captain C.N.E. Currey, RN, who arrived by Trans-Canada Airlines on 2 August to inspect the torpedoed tanker *British Merit* which was being towed into St. John's. The ship was equipped with an anti-torpedo "Admiralty Net Device" (AND), and Captain Currey, one of the originators, was ferried out to the stricken ship. Next to arrive was the Chief of the Naval Staff (CNS), Vice-Admiral Percy Nelles, who arrived on 4 August on an inspection tour. He visited the Combined Operations Room (COR) and was briefed by Murray and Air Commodore C.M. McEwen on combined RCN/RCAF operations in the western Atlantic. He also inspected the rest of the facilities of HMCS *Avalon* as well as several of the ships in port. On 9 August Paymaster Director General Commander R.W. Wright, RCN, arrived to complete a detailed survey of accountant personnel at HMCS *Avalon*. Limping into port at the same time was HMCS *Assiniboine*, which had been severely damaged in its encounter with U-210 in defence of SC-94. Interestingly, on board *Assiniboine* at the time was Dr. Gilbert Tucker, who after the war would write two volumes of the official history of the RCN. R.W. Rankin arrived towards the middle of the month to replace Major Lyon, who had been handling the selection and acquisition of the various base sites for the Canadian government and had been reporting on the workings of the arbitration board.[336] Newfoundland Commissioner Woods probably welcomed Rankin's arrival as he had not found Lyon's performance satisfactory.[337]

A.B. Manarey, Transport Supervisor from NSHQ, also arrived in mid-August to inspect and report on motor transport facilities in St. John's. While in the city, he was instrumental in arranging the hiring of a civilian dispatcher and also recommended that NSHQ provide additional vehicles and a central garage. Captain H.N. Lay, RCN, Director of Operations (DOD), and Captain W.H. Creery, RCN, Chief of Staff (COS) to the Commanding Officer Atlantic Coast (COAC), arrived a week later for a joint operations conference with American authorities. They met with Commander Woolridge, USN, who was representing Admiral Bristol, and Captain Bidwell at Naval Headquarters in St. John's to discuss problems with the new trans-Atlantic convoy schedule.[338] They agreed upon a schedule that provided a balanced time at sea for all MOEF groups and equal layover time at both the eastern and western terminals. In addition, the committee decided that a more efficient repair service could be provided for the B Groups at Argentia by staggering their arrivals, and a sailing schedule was established that could be opened

The "Newfyjohn" Solution

out to eight days when necessitated by winter operating conditions.[339] Later that day Creery, accompanied by Major Dunamore, real estate advisor Rankin, Maintenance Officer in Charge (MOIC) Lt.-Commander R.U. Langston and E.V. Gilbert, Engineer of Docks and Dredging, went to Botwood to look at the oil tank site chosen earlier by Captain Bidwell and Commander Hope. They decided to use that site for the Naval Headquarters, Barracks and Stores, and chose another one for the oil tanks. The paperwork was drawn up by Rankin and forwarded to Ottawa.[340] The same day, Commander G.R. Weymouth, RN, arrived from England en route to Argentia. While in St. John's he briefed Murray and his staff on the latest developments and policy concerning Type 271 radar, High Frequency Direction Finding (HF/DF) and Very High Frequency (VHF) radio transmission. At the invitation of Captain Lay, Weymouth accompanied him to Ottawa by air upon his return from Argentia.[341]

The last VIP to visit St. John's during August was the Governor General of Canada, Major-General Alexander Cambridge, First Earl of Athlone, and his wife Princess Alice, both of whom arrived on 25 August. After a flurry of public appearances, luncheons and inspections of the newly constructed naval facilities–some in less than perfect weather–the Vice-Regal couple departed on 29 August. Two other interesting visitors to St. John's during the month were the British S-Class submarine *Seawolf*, veteran of the North Sea campaign, en route to a refit in Philadelphia, and the training submarine *L-27* on its way to the UK after a refit in the US.

While Murray was dealing with all this activity ashore during August, Dönitz's U-boats continued to concentrate their activities on the mid-ocean convoys. The battle for ON-115, during which HMC Ships *Skeena* and *Wetaskiwin* sank *U-588* on 31 July, continued into the first week of August, resulting in three more ships being sunk and two U-boats severely damaged.[342] SC-94, escorted by group C.1, was attacked on 6 August and lost eleven ships over five days, the worst losses on the northern convoy routes in almost a year. In return, Dönitz lost two U-boats–*U-210* (HMCS *Assiniboine*) and *U-379* (HMS *Dianthus*)–plus several damaged, some seriously. The sinking of *U-210* by *Assiniboine* on the first night of the battle for SC-94 was something right out of a war novel. *Assiniboine*, under the command of Lt.-Commander John Stubbs, RCN (who later became Staff Officer Operations at St. John's and went down with HMCS *Athabaskan* off the French coast in 1944), sighted *U-210* early in the evening on 6 August and closed at full speed. After a thirty-minute gun battle in which the combatants wove in and out of a fog bank hurling shells at each other, Stubbs eventually managed to manoeuvre his ship into a favourable position and rammed the U-boat abaft the conning tower while dropping a pattern of shallow-set depth charges at the same time. The blow was fatal for *U-210*, and the crew scuttled the boat and abandoned ship. Thirty-eight survivors were recovered, but the U-boat's captain, *Kaptänleutnant* Rudolf Lemcke, was killed with all the bridge crew late in the battle when one of *Assiniboine*'s shells hit the conning tower. *Assiniboine* suffered fourteen casualties, including one killed. The destroyer was damaged so severely in the action that it limped home to St. John's for repairs, arriving on 9 August. The next MOEF convoy to be attacked was ON-122, which was escorted by the British B.1 group. It was stalked by ten U-boats over a span of twenty hours and lost four merchantmen for two U-boats damaged. It is no wonder that during August, 120 survivors, including three RAF/RCAF aircrew and sixteen German POWs from *U-210*, were landed in St. John's.[343]

Meanwhile, work on HMCS *Avalon* continued apace. Most of the administration, medical, accommodation and mess buildings were finished and occupied, with the remainder nearing completion. All of the dockyard buildings had been turned over by the contractor other than the machine and shipwright shops, the guardhouse and the central heating plant, all of which were well advanced. Most of the wharves and jetties were being completed or were in use, which was welcome news because 276 vessels passed through St. John's during August, not including the twenty-four naval vessels that were on hand on any given day.[344] There was also a change in command of the MOEF when Admiral Murray was promoted to Commanding Officer Atlantic Coast (COAC), taking over his duties on 18 September, with Capt. (D) E.R. Mainguy commanding in the interim until Murray's replacement, Commodore H.E. Reid, RCN, assumed his duties as FONF at the end of October.[345]

By September, it was clear that Dönitz's U-boats were back in northern waters, including those around Newfoundland, in force. Several convoys were badly mauled, and a total of 479 survivors were landed at St. John's during the month, including sixty-eight crew from HMCS *Ottawa*–sunk in the defence of ON-127–and forty-nine DEMS (Defensively Equipped Merchant Ships) personnel[346] Closer to home, on the night of 4 September *U-513*, under the command of Rolf Ruggeberg, followed the ore carrier *Evelyn B* into the Wabana anchorage in Conception Bay. Spending the night submerged in seventy feet of water, Ruggeberg rose to periscope depth the next morning and sank two ships, SS *Saganaga* and SS *Lord Strathcona*. Damaged by a collision with *Strathcona*, *U-513* left the scene, once again trailing *Evelyn B*. Twenty-nine men were killed in the attack, all aboard *Saganaga*.[347] Nothing

The "Newfyjohn" Solution

appeared in the press about this incident, no doubt the result of the strict censorship regime in place, but news quickly spread.[348] The public was shaken because the attack had occurred in broad daylight, in an inshore protected anchorage. Captain Mainguy complained that while losses in convoys were accepted as the "fortunes of war," sinkings so close to St. John's were harder to explain to the public, which considered them the result of "dereliction of duty on the part of the Navy." Mainguy rightly saw such events as being the result of too few resources, suggesting that the scarcity of escorts for local convoys was being "keenly felt." The number of such escorts available depended largely on the numbers required for the more important trans-Atlantic convoys, and the FONF quite simply had to make a choice. Mainguy was concerned, however, that if the U-boats decided to make "resolute attacks" in coastal waters, Newfoundland's trade could be brought to "a virtual standstill." [349]

The local defence force received some relief in mid-month with the arrival from the UK of the 30th Motor Launch Flotilla (MLF) under the command of Lt.-Commander Daish, RNVR, and HMCS *Preserver*. The 30th MLF, based out of St. John's, would provide protection for Bay Bulls, and *Preserver*, which was based in Harbour Grace, would act as mother ship to the 71st and 73rd MLFs. This allowed the FONF to establish a permanent patrol at Wabana using the 71st and two boats from the 73rd and a regular schedule of ore convoys between Wabana and Sydney. By the end of September, eleven ore carriers, along with eighteen other vessels, had been successfully convoyed between the two ports.[350]

Similar to his predecessor, Mainguy had to contend with a number of distinguished guests during September. The Right Honourable Clement Attlee, British Secretary of State for Dominion Affairs and Deputy Prime Minister, arrived on 14 September on a fact-finding tour and inspected the new administration building.[351] The Joint Defence Committee, including Captain H.G. deWolf, RCN, Director of Plans (DOP) at NSHQ, and Mayor Fiorello La Guardia of New York, made a flying one-day visit to St. John's on the 27th. Also arriving in St. John's in September was Colonel P.F. Clarke, the Property Commissioner, who met with the manager of the Newfoundland Fuel and Engineering Company to negotiate for the site of a proposed power house on the Southside of the harbour. Clarke reached an agreement with Newfoundland Fuel and Engineering to lease the required site for $1.00 per annum in exchange for the navy straightening the road through the property by removing approximately 600 cubic yards of rock at a cost of $1500. This was a typical arrangement between the RCN and property owners on the Southside of the harbour. In most cases, the RCN received the use of a site for the cost of improvements which were turned over to property owners at the end of the war.[352]

Construction of HMCS *Avalon* neared completion by the end of September with most main buildings fully occupied. Some areas of the barracks were yet to be finished, however, due mainly to the non-arrival of equipment. The same could be said for the dockyard, where most buildings were finished, although the central heating plant was still not operational due to delays in receiving equipment. Also awaiting completion were the sickbay, yard water and sewer installation and fencing. The magazines were having their interiors timbered, and the two-story office building on the site was complete except for heating, plumbing and painting. The six fuel tanks were at various stages of construction; most were well advanced, but only Tank 1 was ready to receive oil. The remaining buildings–the Port War Signal Stations at Fort Amherst and Cape Spear and the Mobile Training Unit garage–were fully operational, and the Gunnery School was complete except for minor items. Work had begun on the new boom defence gate at the Narrows, with completion expected by the end of October.[353] The command arrangements at the naval barracks were also finalized in September when Lt.-Commander Davis assumed command from Captain Holms, with Lt.-Commander H.W. Balfour, RCNVR, taking over from Davis as Executive Officer (XO). Lt. R.S. Astbury, RCNVR, assumed command of *Avalon II*, which was used as office and living accommodation afloat.[354]

The base chaplaincy was also established during the month under the command of the Chaplain-in-Charge, J.M. Armstrong. Church services were held both at the base and on board the ships of the MOEF, and wardrooms and messes of thirty warships were visited. Three marriage ceremonies were conducted. Interestingly, the chaplains were also responsible for censoring ratings' mail, and "four to five hundred letters" were handled a day. The chaplains also had the sad duty of writing to next-of-kin, and did so to the families of those lost on HMCS *Ottawa*.[355] Sailors' religious needs were likewise well met outside the naval establishment. The Church of England Cathedral on Church Hill, and St. Mary's, St. Michael's and the historic St. Thomas churches held services for those men of that faith every Sunday at 11 AM and 6:30 PM. So did the United Church at the Gower St., Cochrane St., George St. and Wesley United churches. Roman Catholics could attend mass every hour from 7 to 11 AM on Sundays, and at 7:30 and 8:30 AM on Wednesdays, and confession was scheduled at convenient times every Wednesday, Friday and Saturday. Presbyterians were welcomed at St. Andrew's Church on Queen's Road, and the Salvation Army held services at its

The "Newfyjohn" Solution

halls on Springdale, Adelaide and Duckworth streets every Sunday at 11 AM and 6:30 PM. Christian Scientists gathered at the Crosbie Hotel on Sunday mornings and Wednesday evenings.[356]

As with the previous month, U-boats remained concentrated in the North Atlantic and off the east coast of Canada during October 1942. However, Mainguy reported that the month had been "very largely free of instances of a major character," although ON-139 was attacked on 22 October and HMCS *Morden* landed 192 survivors, including seniors, women and children, in St. John's a few days later. Despite the loss of the 30th MLF to Sydney in the middle of the month, the FONF still maintained the regular schedule of Wabana/Sydney convoys, a total of sixteen being run each way during October. He also inaugurated defensive patrols for Botwood and Lewisporte with the transfer of HMCS *Preserver* and four of its brood to Botwood early in the month. But the big news for October was the sinking of the Port-aux-Basques to North Sydney passenger ferry SS *Caribou* in the early hours of 14 October, some 35 miles west of Port-aux-Basques.[357] *Caribou* was the last casualty of the Battle of the St. Lawrence.

As we have seen, the Battle of the St. Lawrence was actually a series of highly successful U-boat incursions into Canadian waters that started in June with *Kapitänleutnant* Vogelsang's attack on QS-15 in early July. The next stage of the Battle commenced at the end of August when *Kapitänleutnant* Paul Hartwig, in command of *U-517*, attacked the American troop ship SS *Chatham* in the Strait of Belle Isle. It was the first US troop ship sunk during the war, but fortunately loss of life was slight. *U-517* escaped on the surface unseen while Hartwig's packmate, *U-165* (Hoffmann), attacked the 3304-ton SS *Arlyn* and the 7253-ton tanker *SS Laramie*. *Laramie* survived with five casualties, but *Arlyn* sank an hour later with the loss of thirteen passengers and crew.[358]

Hartwig continued further south into the Strait and decided to investigate Forteau Bay, Labrador, which *Sailing Directions*[359] suggested might be an anchorage for merchantmen in the western end of the Strait of Belle Isle. In the dark hours of 1 September, Hartwig entered the bay and ventured within sixty-five feet of the main jetty in search of targets. Finding none, he departed unscathed and undetected. Continuing along the Labrador coast, Hartwig sighted not one but two convoys: the inbound NL-6 and outbound LN-7. With the escorts occupied with preventing the two convoys from mixing, *U-517* was able to get in position to fire at the 1781-ton laker SS *Donald Stewart*. Just at the moment of firing, one of the escorts HMCS *Weyburn* spotted Hartwig and turned to ram. Unable to overtake *U-517* as it submerged, *Weyburn* opened up with its four-inch gun but missed. *Donald Stewart* sank with the loss of three of its crew, and *U-517* escaped.[360]

Meanwhile, *U-165* had been tracking the Quebec-Sydney convoy QS-33 comprising eight merchantmen with five escorts, including the converted yacht HMCS *Racoon*. In the darkness on 6 September, *U-165* fired a salvo at the 2988-ton Greek *Aeas* and sank it. Two of the torpedoes missed the target, and shortly thereafter *Racoon* reported being attacked by two torpedoes, one of which went right underneath it. It then apparently ran up the torpedo track for 6000 yards, dropping depth charges. About two and a half hours later two explosions in rapid succession were heard. It was assumed that *Racoon* was attacking a contact, but despite a search and calls for it to report its position it was never seen again. Two weeks later, wreckage identified as from the yacht washed up on Anticosti Island, and a month after the sinking, the badly decomposed body of one of its officers was found. A board of inquiry concluded that the sinking was due to enemy action, but this could not be confirmed because *U-165* was sunk along with its log book on the way back to France after this patrol.[361]

Shortly after the loss of HMCS *Racoon*, the RCN lost another of its warships to the enemy. HMCS *Charlottetown*, in company with two other corvettes, was sunk off Cap Chat on 11 September 1942 by *U-517*. Its loss dominated newspapers for a week after the news was released.[362] As Commodore Mainguy observed the previous month about the Wabana sinkings, people were prepared to hear of losses in the dangerous wastes of the Atlantic Ocean but not in Canada's *"mare nostrum,"* the Gulf of St. Lawrence. But the real tragedy of *Charlottetown* was that most of the casualties were caused by the ship's own depth charges. None had been set to safe, and they exploded when the sinking hull reached their preset depth. Of its entire crew of close to a hundred men, only fifty-seven survivors were rescued, three of whom later died ashore. The perpetrator of the attack, the redoubtable Paul Hartwig, escaped retribution at the hands of *Charlottetown*'s associates and sank two more ships before heading home. In total, *U-517* accounted for eight vessels, including *Charlottetown*.[363]

Public outcry over the sinkings in the Gulf and pressure from the British Ministry of War Transport (MWT) forced Ottawa to close the St. Lawrence River to all but local convoys. Trans-Atlantic shipping was re-routed to ports in Nova Scotia, New Brunswick and the US.[364] As a result, when *Kapitänleutnant* Ulrich Gräf and the crew of *U-69* entered the Gulf on 30 September, they found no targets. Gräf retraced *U-132*'s track up the St. Lawrence, and on the night of 8/9 October sighted the

The "Newfyjohn" Solution

homeward-bound convoy NL-9. Despite the presence of three escorting corvettes, Gräf sank the 2245-ton steamship SS *Carolus* with the loss of twelve of its crew. This sinking, less than 200 miles from Quebec City–the furthest penetration of the river to date–caused an uproar in both Quebec and Ottawa.[365] Still, this was nothing compared to the public reaction to Gräf's next victim.

The Sydney to Port-aux-Basque ferry SS *Caribou* left Sydney for its last trip at approximately 9:30 PM on 13 October. According to its escort, the Bangor minesweeper HMCS *Grandmere*, the night was very dark with no moon. *Grandmere's* skipper, Lt. James Cuthbert, RCN, was unhappy about both the amount of smoke *Caribou* was emitting and his screening position. In his mind the best place for him to be was in front of *Caribou*, not behind as the Western Approaches Convoy Instructions (WACI) advised. He felt he would be better able to detect the sound of a lurking U-boat if he had a clear field in front to probe.[366] He was correct, for in *Caribou*'s path lay *U-69*.

At 3:21 AM *U-69* spotted *Caribou* "belching heavy smoke." Gräf misidentified both the 2222-ton *Caribou* and 600-ton *Grandmere* as a 6500-ton passenger freighter and a "two-stack destroyer." At 3:40 AM, according to *Grandmere's* log, a lone torpedo hit *Caribou* on its starboard side. Pandemonium ensued as passengers, thrown from their bunks by the explosion, rushed topside to the lifeboat stations. For some reason, several families had been accommodated in separate cabins and now sought each other in the confusion. To make matters worse, several lifeboats and rafts had either been destroyed in the explosion or could not be launched.[367]

Meanwhile, *Grandmere* spotted *U-69* in the dark and turned to ram it. Gräf, still under the impression he was facing a "destroyer" rather than a minesweeper, crash dived. As *Grandmere* passed over the swirl left by the submerged submarine, Lt. Cuthbert fired a diamond pattern of six depth charges. Evading the barrage, Gräf headed for the sounds of *Caribou* sinking to the bottom, knowing that the survivors floating on the surface would inhibit *Grandmere* from launching another attack. *U-69*'s manoeuvre went unnoticed by *Grandmere*, and Cuthbert dropped another pattern of three charges set for 500 feet. Gräf fired a "Bold," an ASDIC decoy the British referred to as a "Submarine Bubble Target" (SBT), and slowly left the area. At 6:30 AM *Grandmere* gave up the hunt and began to pick up survivors. Unfortunately, they were too few: of the 237 people aboard, only 103 were found alive and two died shortly thereafter.[368] Of the forty-six-man crew, mostly Newfoundlanders, only fifteen remained. Five families were decimated: the Tappers (five dead), Toppers (four),

Allens (three), Skinners (three), and Tavernors (the captain and his two sons). The press truthfully reported that "Many Families [were] Wiped Out."[369] The St. John's *Evening Telegram* reported that the disaster left twenty-one widows and fifty-one orphans in the Channel/Port-aux-Basques area of Newfoundland.[370]

Among the casualties were also twenty-two naval personnel, including Nursing Sister A.W. Wilkie. RCN, and W.H. Hathway and Preston H. Cawley of the Naval Stores Department. Sister Wilkie was buried in St. John's on 20 October with full military honours. Mr. Cawley's body was sent to Edmonton for burial, but Mr. Hathway's was not recovered. HMCS *Avalon* suffered another severe loss during the month with the death due to surgical complications of Lt.-Commander R.U. Langston, the NOIC at Botwood. Langston served as the Command Executive Officer (CXO), MOIC, and XDO in St. John's before being appointed to Botwood in July 1942. He was buried with full military honours in the Church of England Cemetery on Forest Road in St. John's. Commander B.L. Johnson, captain of HMCS *Preserver*, took over as the acting NOIC at Botwood.[371]

While the construction on almost all of the buildings at HMCS *Avalon* was complete, the occupancy of many was still delayed by the non-arrival of equipment. This was the case with the laundry and bakery facilities at the naval barracks, and even the electrical services at the dockyard were jury-rigged because "a considerable amount of the necessary equipment [had] not been received by the Contractors." Such delays had plagued the base at St. John's since its inception. To try to remedy this, NSHQ sent Construction Liaison Officer (CLO) Sub-Lt. W.A. Ramsay, RCNVR (Special Branch), to survey the construction projects. Commander Hope felt that Ramsay was of considerable assistance and strongly recommended that such an officer be appointed at St. John's as soon as possible. He felt that a local CLO could expedite construction and guarantee that a building was ready for occupation when handed over to the RCN.[372] One bright spot was the opening of the third ratings' block at the naval barracks, which brought the total number of men accommodated at the barracks to 890.[373] Governor Walwyn felt that the barracks were well equipped, but worried about the lack of fire equipment.[374]

U-boat activities continued to be prevalent in the northwest Atlantic, including Newfoundland waters, during November. Three ocean convoys–SC-107, ON-144 and ON-145–were attacked, all with serious losses. The most serious was SC-107 which lost fifteen of forty-two merchant ships over three days during the first week of November.

The "Newfyjohn" Solution

ON-144 lost six merchant ships, as well as the Norwegian corvette *Montbretia* in mid-month, and ON-145 lost one, although another two were torpedoed but survived.[375] A total of 109 survivors were landed at St. John's.[376] Shortly after these attacks, A/Capt. F.L. Houghton, COS to the FONF, travelled to Ottawa to meet with USN, Royal Navy (RN) and Canadian authorities to discuss recent developments in the northwest Atlantic. As a result, the Western Support Force (WSF) was created by withdrawing all the destroyers from the Western Local Escort Force (WLEF) and forming them into groups to provide support to both eastbound and westbound convoys. At additional meetings in Argentia between Houghton and Commander TF 24's staff, it was decided that CTF 24 would be the operating authority with the FONF as his deputy. The support groups would be based in St. John's and travel back and forth between 35 degrees West. When the force became operational later in the month, it consisted of eight ships operating in four groups, each containing two destroyers.[377]

Possibly the biggest upset for the command on the local level in November was the second attack in two months on shipping at anchor at Wabana. At approximately 3 AM on 2 November *U-518*, under the command of *Kapitänleutnant* Friedrich Wissmann, rounded the southern end of Bell Island and entered the sheltered Wabana anchorage, locally known as "The Tickle." There, silhouetted in the light of a searchlight, he found several ore carriers at anchor. At approximately 0330 he fired one torpedo at the 3000-ton *Anna T*. It missed, passed under the bow of SS *Flyingdale*, and exploded ashore at the loading dock. Wissmann then fired two torpedoes at SS *Rose Castle*. It is interesting to note that the previous month *U-69*, having just sunk *Caribou*, fired a torpedo at *Rose Castle* southeast of Ferryland on the Southern Shore of the Avalon Peninsula. Fortunately for the ship, it was a dud. It was not as lucky this time, and *Rose Castle* sank, taking twenty-eight of its crew with it, five of whom were Newfoundlanders. The next target was the Free French vessel *PLM 27*, which sank almost immediately after being hit with the loss of twelve men. In the ensuing confusion, and despite the presence of a corvette and two Fairmile patrol boats, *U-518* escaped on the surface in the darkness. In a ten-minute attack, two ships, along with forty men, had been lost.[378]

There was something else notable about *U-518*'s foray into Conception Bay. Sinking shipping was not its only mission. On board the U-boat was Werner von Janowski, a spy for the *Abwehr*, the German military intelligence organization. Evading patrols in Conception Bay and surviving a surprise attack by a Digby bomber just south of Cape Race, *U-518* made its way through the Cabot Strait and into the Gulf of

St. Lawrence. Initially, the plan was to land von Janowski at a point in the St. Lawrence River. This was discarded in favour of the Baie des Chaleurs, between New Brunswick and the Gaspé Peninsula. On the morning of 8 November, *U-518* entered the mouth of the bay submerged. With no shoals and a depth of more than 200 feet, the bay offered clear passage for the U-boat. Surfacing that night, Wissmann beached the U-boat on a sandbar not far from shore, and Janowski was transported by dingy. All went well, and at 0120 on 9 November the dingy returned, and *U-518* lifted its bows and departed the bay. Wissmann was well satisfied and considered the mission a success. Unknown to *Kapitänleutnant* Wissmann, however, his passenger was caught within twenty-four hours.[379]

The Governor of Newfoundland, Admiral Walwyn, was outraged at the sinkings off Bell Island. The previous day, he had been on a hillside overlooking the anchorage and was horrified to see two ore ships at anchor awaiting a loading berth. Upon his return to St. John's, Walwyn called COS Capt. F.L. Houghton and told him that he thought "it was madness to let ships lie unprotected" at the anchorage. Walwyn felt it was wiser to leave them in St. John's until a berth was vacant.[380] Indeed, Capt. Schwerdt had suggested a similar scheme several months earlier which was apparently received "somewhat casually by the Canadian Naval authorities." The Dominions Office also criticized local naval authorities, unfairly charging that despite the sinkings in September, nothing had been done to protect the anchorage and concluded that the incident "reflect[ed] little credit on those in charge."[381] In truth, the newly appointed FONF, Commodore H.E. Reid, knew the risk and that anti-submarine protection at Wabana was inadequate. However, he had little choice but to do the best he could with what he had if the vital ore shipments to Sydney were to continue before the ice set in for the winter. The greater threat was while the ore carriers were at sea, and despite the strain on his resources, Reid had maintained the regular schedule of Wabana/Sydney convoys, a total of sixteen being run each way during October.[382] Besides, with 250 merchant vessels passing through St. John's during November, and with an average of twenty-seven naval vessels in port on any given day, there was very little room left to spare.[383] In the end, net protection was installed off the loading piers, and provisions were made to allow only two ships to load at a time while being protected by an escort vessel and a Fairmile patrol boat.[384] These measures must have worked because no other attacks occurred in the anchorage for the rest of the war.

In the meantime, construction at HMCS *Avalon* wound down as buildings were completed or construction stalled due to the non-delivery of necessary equipment. The hospital and dockyard were still on temporary electrical services, the wireless receiving station still awaited the installation of a generator, and the laundry, bakery and central heating plants were all awaiting equipment. Nonetheless, the magazines and fuel tanks were nearing completion, one being in use and two finished except for fittings.

December 1942 was a rough month for the Newfoundland command for a number of reasons. Weather conditions were terrible and many ships, both naval and merchant, suffered some degree of storm damage. Necessary repairs strained the facilities of both the depot ship, HMS *Greenwich*, and the dockyard to the utmost during the month. Possibly the worst example was HMS *Beverley*, which arrived in St. John's missing a funnel, necessitating a five-day stay at the dockyard. Convoys were also hard hit by the enemy during December. Eight of them reported U-boat contacts and four were attacked, with ON-154 losing sixteen ships. With the extreme bad weather, refuelling at sea was impossible, and the escorts often had to detach to refuel at the Azores or to return to St. John's. Fortunately, the newly formed WSF was able to fill the breach along with USN ships from Argentia and escorts from the WLEF out of Halifax. Regardless, four ships were lost from HX-217, the first convoy to avail of the WSF, and three merchant ships and HMS *Firedrake* were sunk from ON-153. U-boats also got a straggler from ON-152.[385] No wonder sixty-six survivors were landed at St. John's during the month.[386] Admiral Bristol, CTF 24, decided during December that all MOEF groups, whether Canadian, British or American, should depart from St. John's. This had a number of advantages. Each ship would meet its assigned convoy with a full allotment of fuel, and it would also give the RN and USN crews some rest-and-relaxation time in St. John's. This reassignment, of course, placed still more pressure on FONF's staff, but Reid felt that after eighteen months in operation the arranging of rendezvous, fuelling and provisions had been sufficiently perfected to stand the strain.[387]

The ships of the Newfoundland Force also felt the pressure of meeting the requirements of the local convoy system, many containing twelve to eighteen vessels. In addition, escorts were needed to screen ore carriers both en route and while loading at Wabana, as well as on the return voyage.[388] In spite of the severe weather, the installation of the anti-torpedo net at Wabana progressed well during December. Even rescue tugs were used as escorts during this time, in between their other duties.[389] HMRT *Frisky* towed targets for firing practice at both Harbour Grace and St. John's, searched for several vessels in distress, offered assistance to HMS *Caldwell* and attempted to salvage the tug *Champlain* off Lawn Bay on the Burin Peninsula. HMRT *Tenacity* was similarly employed during the month assisting four disabled ships, including HM Ships *Caldwell* and *Broadway*.[390]

Winter weather and the non-arrival of equipment continued to delay completion of some work at HMCS *Avalon*. The hospital and dockyard remained on temporary electrical services, and the laundry, bakery and wireless receiving station were still awaiting necessary equipment. Various other buildings required minor work, although the magazines and fuel tanks were progressing on schedule, with two of each already completed. Also during December, E.V. Chambers, a real estate advisor, arrived to negotiate the exclusion rights on the Hickman property to the east of the naval dockyard and to investigate the possibility of acquiring land west of the dockyard for berthing additional naval vessels. Chambers was unsuccessful in his negotiations with the Great Eastern Oil and Import Company for a site on the Southside of the harbour to construct a YMCA building and a wet canteen.[391] This became a more significant setback a few days later when the Knights of Columbus hall burned with tremendous loss of life, including twenty-five naval personnel.

War is a young man's game, and this was certainly true of the RCN during the Second World War. The average ages of RCN and RCNVR officers during the war were twenty-nine and twenty-eight years, respectively. The average lower-deck age was even lower at twenty-two years, with many of the men being just over eighteen.[392] Surrounded by such youth, recreation and entertainment were major factors in crew morale. Whereas the Americans provided facilities for their personnel on the various bases, the Canadian services relied heavily on local facilities.[393] While barely more than a good-sized town, St. John's did its utmost to meet this challenge.[394]

Sports, of course, were major features of any recreation program, and there was no shortage of competitive and recreational opportunities in the city, all available to RCN personnel. Rugby, soccer, baseball, softball and cricket were played at the Feildian and Ayre Athletic Grounds, and at the St. George's and Memorial Fields, and aside from the various service and open leagues, hockey was played almost daily at the St. Bon's Forum and the Prince of Wales Arena. Tennis was offered at Government House (officers only), Bowring Park and the Riverdale Tennis Club. Swimming, golf, squash and bowling were available to officers and men alike at various facilities throughout the city, and bicycles could be rented at Martin's Cycle Shop on Duckworth Street. The navy provided badminton and gymnasium facilities at the naval barracks at Buckmasters' Field, and hunting, fishing and "spending a few days under canvas" were all attractions of the Naval Camp at Donovan's, just outside St. John's.[395]

Of course, "liquid refreshment" was a requirement for any successful run ashore, and officers had the pick of the more "civilized" establishments, including their own Seagoing Officers' Club, better known as "The Crow's Nest." Officers were also expected to attend Captain (D)'s cocktail party every Friday. While the young officers were charged a one-dollar cover, the invitation guaranteed that their female companions were "admitted free of charge." From there, the happy couples could proceed to the City Club, Bally Haly Golf Club or the Bella Vista Country Club. Both officers and men frequented the Old Colony Club and the Terra Nova Club. Ships' crews had naval canteens at the naval dockyard on Water Street and at the naval barracks. In addition, those of the lower deck had their pick of dozens of cafés and taverns that catered to the ordinary soldier and sailor. Some of these were considered less than respectable. Two of the most notorious were the Green Lantern on Water Street and the Queen Tavern on Queen Street, both of which caused the Chief of Police concern because they were often "frequented by disorderly persons."[396]

Nor was there a shortage of places to eat, although the military had to put a number of them "off limits" due to health concerns. Officers could also get a meal for forty cents at the Fort William Officers Mess and the Naval Barracks Officers Mess, and both officers and men were welcome at the United Services Overseas (USO) Club at the corner of Bonaventure Avenue and Merrymeeting Road. There were a variety of restaurants and lunch counters on Water and Duckworth streets, and tearooms on Henry Street and at Rawlins Cross. For a town of just over 40,000 civilians, St. John's boasted a total of five cinemas–the Paramount, Capitol, Nickel, Star and York–all of which featured the latest Hollywood films.

To get to the various attractions, the men of the Royal Canadian Navy could choose a number of forms of transportation, all at reasonable prices. Street cars cost twenty cents, buses ten. Taxis charged seventy cents during the daytime and one dollar at night, but as the 1943 *Naval Guide Book* pointed out, most were "very loathe to carry passengers to and from the South Side." Transportation to and from a ship by way of "bum boats" cost twenty cents "if obtainable," but the authorities had to bring in regulations governing these harbour craft after a couple of near disasters.[397] The more studious could avail of reading material from a number of places, including the Gosling Memorial Library on

Duckworth Street, the RCN's Magazine Exchange and the Canadian Legion at the corner of Bannerman Street and Military Road which offered material to "officers, ratings and their families."

Shopping was offered by four main department stores, all located on Water Street: Bowring Brothers, Ayre and Sons, James Baird and the Royal Stores, and there were no fewer than six drycleaners, including Soon Lee's near Rawlins Cross, the site of the only traffic lights in the city. Two locations of the Commercial Cable Company and the Water Street office of the Anglo-American Cable Company ("Just Ask for 'Anglo'") provided telegraph facilities, and telephone service was the responsibility of the Avalon Telephone Company.

Possibly the most heavily utilized service facilities in St. John's during the Second World War were the three hostels. *The Caribou Hut* was likely the most famous of the three. During the 1637 days it operated, "The Hut" rented 253,551 beds, served 1,545,766 meals, and hosted 1518 movies, 459 dances, 395 shows and 205 Sunday night sing-songs with a total attendance in excess of 700,000 people.[398] Canada's High Commissioner to Newfoundland, Charles Burchell, officially opened the *Red Triangle*, the YMCA hostel on Water Street West, on 8 January 1942. Built at a cost of $100,000, the facility boasted a social hall for dances and concerts, a lounge, an 1100-person dining room and sleeping accommodation for fifty men.[399] The Knights of Columbus hostel on Harvey Road opened in December 1941. The horseshoe-shaped building featured an auditorium, recreation room, restaurant and dormitories, and could accommodate approximately 400 men. All of the hostels were famous for their hospitality, but unfortunately the latter became infamous for a tragedy.

On 12 December 1942 a fire broke out in the attic of the Knights of Columbus hostel. The building had been built to provide a recreation facility for military and merchant marine personnel, and dances, concerts and other entertainments were held frequently. All were well attended, and the event held that cold December night was no different. *Uncle Tom's Barn Dance* played to a packed audience, and the show was broadcast over radio station VOCM. Suddenly there was a cry of "Fire!" and the broadcast ended. Within forty-five minutes ninety-nine people were dead, including twenty-five naval personnel (only seventeen of whom were identified), and 100 were injured.[400] The inquiry into the fire, headed by retired Chief Justice Sir Brian Dunfield, concluded that many of the victims died from smoke inhalation rather than from the fire itself. Most had been trapped in the auditorium because the exits opened inward and did not have "panic bars," and the windows were shuttered

The "Newfyjohn" Solution

because of blackout regulations. In his February 1943 report, Justice Dunfield concluded that while the fire was the work of an arsonist, there was no evidence that enemy agents had started it.[401]

Regardless, suspicion of enemy action persisted, and not without some justification. There had been other fires in buildings frequented by military personnel during the same period. *The Old Colony Club* had burned with the loss of four lives, and fires had been set at the USO Club on Merrymeeting Road and the *Red Triangle* hostel on Water Street. Much was made of the fact that someone had torched the Knights of Columbus hostel in Halifax shortly before. However, what really fuelled alarm was the rumour that only ninety-eight bodies of the ninety-nine people reported killed were recovered. No one was ever charged with the crime.

Overall, the year 1942 was difficult for the Allies. During the first six months, the Japanese had advanced almost unchecked throughout the western Pacific. Rommel had the British on the ropes in North Africa, and Admiral Dönitz's U-boats had moved across the Atlantic and decimated shipping within sight of land from the Gulf of St. Lawrence to the Gulf of Mexico. Whereas the Americans stopped the Japanese advance at the Battle of Midway, and the British halted Rommel at El Alamein, Dönitz's U-boats continued to exact a terrible toll on Allied shipping. When the United States belatedly commenced convoying along its eastern seaboard in the spring, the U-boats simply moved further south into the Caribbean. As this theatre became untenable, Dönitz moved his forces back into the North Atlantic, including the waters around Newfoundland. If there had been any doubt among Newfoundlanders that they were at the front lines of the Atlantic war, these were washed away with the torpedo attack on St. John's, the sinkings at Bell Island and the tragic loss of *Caribou* in the Gulf. The fire at the Knights of Columbus which claimed so many lives seemed just a culmination of a year of disasters both at home and abroad. Yet as Winston Churchill announced to the House of Commons in London, 1942 was not the beginning of the end, but perhaps it was the end of the beginning. The NEF had been re-designated the MOEF and now provided continuous protection to both eastbound and westbound convoys, and support groups based out of St. John's came to the aid of endangered convoys. Ashore, most of the facilities at HMCS *Avalon* were complete and occupied, and despite many challenges, the RCN was meeting its ever-increasing responsibilities. But a reckoning was coming, and the RCN would pay the price.

The winter of 1943 was something of a watershed for the RCN.

By the end of 1942, it provided upwards of forty percent of the escort groups in the North Atlantic, yet suffered fully eighty percent of the shipping losses. The Admiralty blamed this disparity on the RCN's lack of training and poor leadership.[402] NSHQ more correctly blamed it on outdated equipment and the continual increases in responsibilities. Regardless, Ottawa eventually bowed to Admiralty pressure and transferred the Canadian C Groups at St. John's to Western Approaches Command in January 1943. Ostensibly, this was to fill the vacuum left by the deployment of RN escorts to the newly formed tanker convoys in the central Atlantic, but it also afforded Canadian escorts the opportunity to avail of the modern training facilities at RN bases. Considering that most senior Canadian officers felt the RCN had been doing the best it could against tremendous odds and ever-increasing responsibilities, many looked at the withdrawal of Canadian forces from the main theatre of operations as a betrayal.[403]

Despite what the future held for both the RCN and the Battle of the Atlantic, enemy action was conspicuous by its absence during the first month of 1943. Commodore Reid found that January was "notable for the lack of U-boat sightings and attacks on convoys." Some of this good fortune was a result of evasive routing (Bletchly Park was making inroads in the new German Triton code by this time after a year's blackout), but it was also in large measure due to the atrocious weather that started in the new year. Even though several convoys were shadowed and reported by U-boats, only one, HX-222, was actually attacked with the loss of one ship. Still, many convoys became badly scattered, and while one straggler was torpedoed, many more foundered or were so badly damaged by weather that they were abandoned. The North Atlantic gales did not spare the MOEF either. Only four of the twelve destroyers assigned to the WSF based at St. John's were kept running during the month, with HMS *Roxborough* suffering the worst damage when stormy seas stove in its bridge, killing its captain and first lieutenant and washing another man overboard.[404] The weather also played havoc with the newly inaugurated JH-HJ convoys between St. John's and Halifax. Not only did ships leaving St. John's have to contend with monstrous seas and high winds, but often their mooring lines froze to the buoys and had to be chopped off with axes. Reid complained that this often delayed departures by several hours and on occasion led to ships having to wait for the next outbound convoy.[405] This had the expected effect on congestion in the harbour, with 154 merchant ships passing through the port and thirty-five warships alongside daily. The bad weather, however, did stabilize the number of men accommodated in the barracks at 980 as men on leave and newly drafted personnel were

The "Newfyjohn" Solution

stranded at their departure points.[406]

Perhaps wanting to assess Admiralty complaints about the efficiency and training of the RCN, Naval Minister Macdonald arrived in St. John's for a brief tour at the end of the month.[407] He found that most facilities were completed and fully occupied. Some buildings, however, such as the hospital, bakery and various dockyard facilities, still awaited equipment. The NOIC complained that it was unfortunate that whole systems were not shipped together as often one part would arrive but could not be installed until the rest were delivered. An example was the asphalt tiles for flooring two of the magazines: the tiles had arrived but not the glue to hold them in place. Indeed, the NOIC wondered if some of the missing equipment had even been ordered. The tank farm on the Southside of the harbour was a pressing concern. Only one tank was in operation, with several more finished or nearly so, but contractors had completed none of the piping to the wharf.[408] Until it was fully operational, the RCN had to depend on base oilers afloat and/or the Imperial Oil facilities which were shared with civilian vessels.

If weather was the greatest enemy in the North Atlantic in January, by the following month, Dönitz's U-boats usurped the honour. Reid noted "a considerable increase" in U-boat activity during the month, and a total of twenty-four ships were sunk in the six convoys attacked. ON-166, escorted by the American A.3 Group, was the worst hit, losing eleven ships over four days. One of the problems Commodore Reid faced was a shortage of escorts. With the C Groups leaving for the UK during January and February, plus enemy action and weather damage taking a toll on the remainder, the FONF was having a hard time meeting commitments. Again in February, only four of the remaining eleven WSF destroyers were available for duty, and then mainly thanks to the tireless efforts of the base engineering staff and USS *Prairie* in Argentia. The US Coast Guard cutter *Campbell* was damaged after ramming a U-boat attacking ON-166, and HMCS *Assiniboine* arrived in St. John's with a damaged A/S suite and had to be sent on to Halifax for repairs. Actually, the weather was playing havoc with ASDIC domes. Only one ship of C.3, HMS *Burnham*, arrived in St. John's after escorting ON-163 with its ASDIC dome fully functional. Such wear and tear on both the ships and their crews was further exacerbated by the drastically reduced turnaround time resulting from the shortage of escorts. This also led to tremendous congestion in St. John's harbour; while there were actually fewer warships, they passed through St. John's with greater frequency. Consequently, while only 112 merchant vessels arrived at the port, almost 200 arrivals of naval vessels were recorded, not including Fairmile patrol boats and harbour craft. The local defence forces were also fully stretched trying to maintain the JH-HJ convoy schedule along with the local convoys, and at mid-month a patrol by Fairmiles was initiated along the approaches to St. John's.[409] Considering the duration (forty-eight hours) and the amount of fuel these little ships consumed during such patrols (2500 gallons), Governor Walwyn wondered whether they were worth the expense.[410] To add to the strain, the NOIC lost one of his harbour defence craft to fire early in the month, with three of its crew suffering first- or second-degree burns. Unfortunately, bad weather prevented the slack from being picked up by aircraft patrols, and Reid complained that he was still waiting for the long-range Liberator bombers to arrive from the UK. He could not believe that with hundreds of these aircraft arriving in Britain weekly, a few squadrons could not be released to the Newfoundland command. He grumbled that the authorities did not fully appreciate the difference these aircraft could make to the Battle of the Atlantic, "where the threat to our trade convoys and consequently to our whole war effort is at its highest."[411] This became especially acute the next month.

Much has been made of how close the Germans came to winning the Battle of the Atlantic. Churchill is often quoted as saying that U-boat attacks were "the true evil" and that the Nazis should have invested everything in the U-boat campaign.[412] March 1943 is often pinpointed as the pivotal month when a total of 120 ships were sunk totalling 630,000 tons, the fifth highest month of losses in the entire war.[413] The official historian of the RN in World War II, Captain Stephen W. Roskill, RN, wrote that it was at this point that the Anti-U-Boat Division of the Admiralty started to doubt the effectiveness of the convoy system, and he asserted that Britain was on the brink of defeat in the Atlantic.[414] A number of historians have argued more recently, however, that while the losses in the winter of 1943 were significant, especially on top of the enormous losses of 1942, the Germans never came close to winning the Battle of the Atlantic.

Clay Blair has suggested that in their rush to describe the "massacre" of ships in the fall of 1942 (which was used as justification for pulling the St. John's-based RCN out of the Atlantic for training in early 1943), historians have seldom examined German casualties (sinkings and aborted patrols due to battle damage). U-boats were able to mount attacks on only six of the thirty-five convoys that crossed the Atlantic during this period. These assaults accounted for a total of fifty-seven merchant ships out of a total of approximately 1700, plus two destroyers totalling 343,535 tons. At the same time, Allied forces sank sixteen U-boats, an intolerable exchange rate for the Germans. Further, this actually represented a decrease in sinkings per U-boat per patrol

The "Newfyjohn" Solution

from the previous two months. During July/August 1942, U-boats sank .92 ships per patrol, whereas during September/October this decreased to .78.[415] The loss rate continued to drop in the next two months.

During November/December 1942, U-boats sank thirty-four merchantmen in the North Atlantic. But this needs to be put in perspective: only forty-three of the eighty-four U-boats that went to sea during this period sank anything, producing a sinkings per boat rate of .63 for November and .75 for December. In return, the Allies sank twelve U-boats. In the meantime, 1159 of the 1218 ships convoyed across the Atlantic reached their destinations unscathed. During the first four months of 1943, the Allies sailed approximately 2400 merchant ships across the Atlantic: 1320 in eastbound convoys to Britain and 1081 in westbound convoys. Of these, U-boats sank 111 vessels, representing a mere five percent of the total. Moreover, this included thirty-eight vessels on their way back to North America in ballast, and therefore their loss had no effect on British imports. From the point of view of the British ability to wage war, 1247 out of 1320 (94.5 percent) of eastbound ships laden with war supplies reached their destinations.[416]

Jak Mallmann Showell's research reveals that the U-boat war in the Atlantic actually started to go against the Germans as early as 1940 when the number of ships sunk per U-boat at sea began to decline.[417] During the first "Happy Time" in the autumn of 1940, U-boats were sinking 5.5 ships per month per U-boat. But there were only ten U-boats at sea at any one time, and only half of these were ever in a position to attack. By the time the second "Happy Time" peaked in May 1942, U-boats were only sinking two ships per boat even though there were upwards of sixty-one boats at sea. Up to 1941, it was possible for most U-boats to make multiple attacks on the same convoy. From 1941 onwards, thanks to Allied anti-submarine measures, they could not get into a shooting position more than once. Furthermore, the high number of sinkings during the first part of 1942 occurred along the American eastern seaboard and was more a consequence of the United States' failure to protect its shipping than the skill of the U-boat commanders. As a matter of fact, the diversion of the limited number of available U-boats along the eastern seaboard of the United States was actually a strategic blunder for the Germans.[418]

By 1941, the Allies already had "the winning hand that would ultimately defeat the U-boats." By removing boats from the North Atlantic battle in 1942 for easier hunting in the western Atlantic and Caribbean, Admiral Dönitz gave the Allies the breathing space needed to perfect that winning hand. The Allies were able to refine technology, increase the number of escorts, and improve training in time for the crucial convoy battles of the winter of 1943. By that time, U-boat numbers had risen to 116 boats at sea, but the sinking rate per boat had dropped to often less than a half a ship sunk per U-boat. Consequently, the rate of sinkings fell from over five ships per U-boat per month in 1940 to two U-boats per sinking by the winter of 1943.[419]

The centrepiece of the crisis theory were four convoy battles during the first twenty days of March–HX-228 and 229, and SC-121 and 122.[420] In these four convoys, over half the March sinkings in the Atlantic were accomplished (thirty-nine ships). Regardless of the fact that these losses accounted for approximately twenty percent of the convoys involved, eleven other convoys got through without incident, and a twelfth only lost one vessel. Such losses were serious, but do they constituted the "crisis of crises" depicted by Roskill in his official history?[421] Michael Gannon completely dismisses Roskill's apocalyptic statement that "defeat...stared [the Allies] in the face." Indeed, American shipyards were producing more than enough Liberty ships to replace the losses, and ninety percent of all ships in convoys attacked by U-boats during this period arrived safely. Even the hard hit HX-228/229 and SC-121/122 safely arrived with eighty-two percent of their ships.[422] Roger Winn and Patrick Beesly of the Special Branch of the Admiralty's Operation Intelligence Centre were actually convinced that the battle was going Britain's way. During the period heralded as the "darkest hour" of the Battle of the Atlantic, 270 more merchant ships arrived safely in port than in the previous three months, more U-boats were sunk in February than in any previous month of the war, and during the "March Crisis," ship construction exceeded sinkings by over 300,000 tons.[423]

Canadian historians quite rightly have a special interest in the "crisis myth." By March, the four Canadian escort groups were no longer in the North Atlantic. Accused of being poorly trained and led, the C Groups were undergoing training in Londonderry, Northern Ireland, and Tobermorry, Scotland, and escorting Gibraltar and African convoys. That the superior British escort groups experienced similar difficulties as had the RCN in 1942 demonstrates the unfairness of the British attitude towards the RCN. Indeed, Marc Milner suggests that the only way the Germans could have won the Battle of the Atlantic was if the Allies had made such "colossal errors as to defeat themselves." Thanks to a correct defensive strategy at the beginning of the war, which included the RCN "holding the line" from May 1941 to early 1943, the British had the time needed to marshal their available resources. Furthermore, the Germans greatly underestimated the industrial power of the United States which, as previously noted, was replacing shipping faster than the Germans

The "Newfyjohn" Solution

could sink it. Milner claims that the Allies won the Battle of the Atlantic on all fronts—industrial production, intelligence, research and command and control—and while Dönitz's U-boat campaign greatly complicated the Allied war effort, in the end it had no major influence on the Allies' ultimate victory over the Third Reich.[424]

British historian Geoffrey Till doubts whether the Germans ever could have won the Battle of the Atlantic. He suggests that the campaign has to be viewed on three levels: the macro-industrial, the grand strategic and operational-and-tactical levels. From the macro-industrial point of view, there are several reasons why the Germans could not have won the Battle of the Atlantic. The British reduction of imports from sixty to twenty-six million tons a year and the effective management of shipping were two factors, but it was the industrial capacity of the United States that really made the biggest difference. Between 1940 and 1945, the US built twice as much shipping as the Germans sank. Even accounting for the "crisis" of early 1943, by that summer the Allies had a "generous amount of shipping."[425]

At the grand strategic level, a number of reasons explain why the Germans could not have won in the Atlantic. First, they did not concentrate on U-boats early enough in the war—up until the spring of 1941, there were never more than a dozen U-boats in the Atlantic at any one time. As a result, Dönitz's wolfpack attacks "developed slowly enough for the British to take effective countermeasures."[426] This was compounded by Dönitz's error in emphasizing quantity rather than quality when it came to his U-boats. As a number of historians have pointed out, Second World War U-boats "were only marginally better than their World War I predecessors."[427] German strategy was also too continental. U-boat construction did not become a priority until Dönitz became head of the *Kriegsmarine* in 1943. Furthermore, Hitler continually diverted U-boats from what Dönitz correctly considered the main battleground—the North Atlantic—to support army operations in other theatres. As a maritime power, Britain recognized that the North Atlantic battle was vital to the war effort and acknowledged its "fundamental strategic vulnerability." The German command, other than perhaps Dönitz, did not seem to realize that it was the sea that tied the Allied powers together, and if they could keep the sea lanes open, they would win the war.[428]

The final mistake the Germans made was that they built the wrong kind of navy, relying too much on a single weapons system—the U-boat. On the other hand, Till argues that the Germans probably would not have had any better luck with the balanced fleet envisioned in

Admiral Eric Raeder's pre-war Z-Plan. Even early in the battle, when the RN was scrambling to maintain all its commitments and the *Kriegsmarine* roamed both the North and South Atlantic, German surface forces were not handled aggressively, often avoiding encounters even with inferior forces. It was this timidity that led to Raeder's resignation as head of the German Navy in 1943. As it turned out, mines were actually a bigger threat than the surface fleet and, in fact, sank more ships than did Dönitz's U-boats.[429]

Whether or not the Germans came close to winning the Atlantic war or not, March 1943 was a difficult month for the Allies in general and the Newfoundland command in particular. U-boats sank forty ships in six MOEF convoys, not including HMS *Harvester*, an almost thirty percent increase in losses over February. Three U-boats were claimed in return. The worst hit convoy was HX-229, escorted by B.4, which lost thirteen ships. There were a number of mitigating factors involved with this catastrophe, all of which demonstrate that the British and American escort groups suffered the same difficulties as their Canadian brethren resulting in similar results. The group arrived late from escorting ON-169 and had a very short turnaround before rendezvousing with HX-229. The senior officer in HMS *Highlander* was delayed for two days with defects and was unable to catch up with the convoy until after the engagement. In addition, three more escorts were held up, which left a gap of four ships in the group. HMS *Volunteer* was transferred from B.4 to help out, but this left a hole in that group's ranks, contributing to SC-122 losing five ships to U-boats. HX-228 was also heavily attacked, losing seven ships plus *Harvester*, despite the presence of the new American escort carrier USS *Bogue*.[430] With the battles raging in the Atlantic, a steady stream of survivors were landed in St. John's during the month. Over three hundred arrived in various conditions, including five German POWs on board the severely damaged USGC *Campbell* that limped into harbour early in the month.[431]

As disastrous as March was, Winn and Beesly's optimism was not off the mark. Despite Dönitz's U-boats being "extremely active" in the Atlantic in April, losses in convoys were relatively small. U-boats torpedoed fifteen ships, including HMS *Beverley*, in eight convoys but Allied forces destroyed seven U-boats in return.[432] This resulted in 203 survivors landing at St. John's, including forty-three German U-boat POWs.[433] Reid attributed this change in fortunes to C-in-C WA's formation of five new support groups which had "saved convoy after convoy" during the month and the basing of fifteen USAF Liberators at Gander. Maintaining group strength remained a problem as weather damage and defects caused delays and substitutions, both of which

The "Newfyjohn" Solution

affected group cohesion. HX-233 illustrates the difficulties faced by the FONF. The convoy was escorted by the American A.3, which arrived in St. John's three days late after escorting ON-175. Of the six escorts, three were removed for refit and replaced by one American and two Canadian ships. Of the three remaining, two had defects which could not be repaired in the forty-eight-hour turnaround, and Reid was forced to reassign HMCS *Skeena* en route to join C.3 in the UK, and he took two ships from B.4 to make up the numbers. Consequently, A.3 basically constituted a completely new group that had never worked together. Luckily, only one ship was sunk–in exchange for one U-boat destroyed by USCG *Spencer*–before EG.3 joined the convoy and the U-boats backed off.[434]

With over 300 naval vessels passing through St. John's during the month, it is no wonder that expansion plans were under consideration.[435] Sub-Lieutenant W.A. Ramsay, RCN, had visited St. John's in early January to survey possible sites on the Southside of the harbour, as well as at Buckmasters' Field, and NOIC Capt. Hope had travelled to Ottawa in March to meet with senior officers at NSHQ. During April a number of high- ranking officials arrived to inspect the facilities at St. John's and to meet with Reid and other base officers. W.G. Mills, Deputy Minister of Naval Service, and Capt. E. Johnston, RCN, Director of Organization (DOO), arrived on 1 April, followed shortly thereafter by Engineering Commander J.W. Keohane, RCN, Surgeon Lt-Commander J.E. DeBolle, RCNVR, Sub-Lt. Ramsay and E.A. Seal and R. Hunter of the British Admiralty Delegation (BAD) to Washington. The Chief of Naval Equipment and Supply (CNES), Captain G.M. Hibbard, RCN, arrived last, and a series of conferences produced plans to greatly expand existing facilities.[436] To maintain the build-up of forces in Britain for an invasion of Fortress Europe, St. John's needed to be able to service the maximum number of escorts with minimal turnaround time. This figure was set at fifty and required "major new construction and reorganization of the base repair capacity." In his report, Seal recommended that a new machine shop complex be constructed on the Southside of the harbour to provide heavy engineering plant, smithy and foundry facilities, and that a new naval stores building be installed on an adjacent piece of land. The current dockyard storehouse would then be converted to a light engineering/electronic shop to handle electronic, navigational and ASW equipment repairs. The plan also called for a new, 11,000 square foot harbour craft/boat repair shop with haul-out, plus an eighty-vehicle garage for the existing barracks complex.[437] Seal's report estimated that the new facilities necessitated increasing personnel at St. John's by adding 1500 ratings (mainly tradesmen) and 850 servicewomen. This increase prompted the inclusion of a new 250-bed hospital and new barracks on the Southside of the harbour in the plan.[438]

Training was also on the agenda. HMCS *Avalon* provided for the working-up and refresher training of many of the RCN's recently commissioned ships.[439] From the summer of 1941, Mobile Anti-Submarine Training Unit No. 11, under the direction of Commander G.A. Harrison, RN, provided almost all onshore training. In its first year of operation, 120 ships received 496 periods of training totalling 1144 hours and forty-five minutes.[440] The 1943 plans envisioned a considerable expansion of training facilities including DEMS (Defensively Equipped Merchant Ship) training at Cape Spear, and anti-submarine and signal training space provided by an annex to the Southside barracks. Elaborate simulator trainers, including an anti-aircraft dome teacher and tactical anti-submarine attack teacher, would also be installed on an adjacent site.[441] By the end of hostilities, the Tactical Training Centre (TTC) in St. John's contained the Anti-Submarine, Gunnery, Radar and Loran[442] schools, plus a Night Escort Teacher (NET). A report issued in mid-1945 indicates that on one day alone, fifty-one classes were taught between 0900 and 1730. These consisted of thirty-five Gunnery, eleven A/S, one Radar, two Loran and two NET classes, which included the use of the Depth Charge Driller (DCD). The DEMS training range on the cliffs at Cape Spear mounted both anti-aircraft and larger calibre practice artillery pieces.[443] Harbour defences were also beefed up, with the controlled minefield in the Narrows upgraded and enlarged and a fully-equipped boom defence depot built at the Admiralty's wharfage on the Southside.[444] The cost of the expansion program was $7 million, which brought the total Canadian investment in the base, albeit on Britain's account, to $16 million.[445]

The plan also provided for a floating dock. The latter had been under discussion long before the meetings in April, but the BAD had little luck in finding a floating dock in Canada throughout 1942. The closest they came was the smaller section of the Vickers Montreal Dock, which they felt would be better utilized at St. John's.[446] Nevertheless, NSHQ considered new construction the overriding priority[447] and did not think there was enough room for it at St. John's anyway.[448] The Admiralty Delegation was also hesitant to ask the Americans for one without assurances that the Newfoundland Dockyard was working on a twenty-four-hour basis.[449] The High Commissioner for Canada, Charles Burchell, complained that the dockyard was only working one shift per day and was closed on Sundays and holidays. He pointed out that despite the extreme pressure on repair facilities at St. John's, the dockyard was

The "Newfyjohn" Solution

actually "idle" for a total of ninety-five days per year. Burchell argued that it should operate two, if not three, shifts per day during the entire year and work all except a few holidays.[450] Unfortunately, there was a severe shortage of skilled labour in Newfoundland despite the dockyard hiring 170 apprentice mechanics in the fall of 1941.[451] These were fully employed, and Governor Walwyn felt that the only way to increase usage to twenty-four hours was to import men from the UK. At a minimum, Walwyn figured that the dockyard needed sixty-six fully trained and experienced craftsmen. He also warned that, even with these extra men, twenty-four-hour operation was dependent upon getting a floating dock because the delays caused by docking and undocking naval vessels meant these extra men could not be fully employed.[452] In the end, it was not until September 1943 that the USN was able to provide an 1800-ton lifting capacity floating dock from Perth Amboy, New Jersey.[453] In the meantime, Bay Bulls was being developed as an overflow facility. Engineer-in-Chief Captain G.L. Stephens' original nominee for an overflow site, Harbour Grace, was rejected by NSHQ as being too costly to develop.[454] In its stead, Bay Bulls was chosen, and in July 1942 the Canadian War Cabinet approved the project at a total cost of $3 million dollars. ($2 million for the haul-out and support facilities and $1 million for harbour protection).[455] The Newfoundland Commission of Government committed to a contribution of $300,000, part of which was the acquisition cost of the site itself. General construction contracts were let in the fall of 1942, but final completion was not anticipated before the end of 1943.[456]

Meanwhile, most of the remaining work at HMCS *Avalon* was completing. The hospital was finally getting permanent electrical service, but the dockyard still had to rely on a temporary generator as the diesel generator and DC rectifiers for the standby power plant had not arrived. The magazines were mostly complete and in use, as were most of the fuel tanks, but only Tank No. 1 was operational. The newly re-designated Commander-in-Chief, Canadian Northwest Atlantic (CNC, CNA),[457] Admiral Murray, was probably reasonably pleased with the situation when he and Commander P. Bliss, RCN, Staff Officer, Anti-Submarine (SO (A/S)), arrived at St. John's for a short inspection tour.[458] The situation at sea must also have given him some satisfaction.

Most historians point to May 1943 as the turning point in the Battle of the Atlantic. During the month, no fewer than thirty-eight U-boats were sunk by Allied forces, bringing the total number of losses since September 1939 to 251, with 150 of those from August 1942.[459] The Allies' innovations in tactics and technology–radar, asdic, Leigh Lights, ahead-throwing depth charges, escort carriers and support groups, to name but a few—finally intersected with resources and spelled the long but irreversible decline of Dönitz's war in the Atlantic. One other major factor was signals intelligence, and the Newfoundland Command both contributed and benefited from its success.[460]

The Allies used several methods to gather signals intelligence during the Battle of the Atlantic. The main two were passive monitoring of radio transmissions and Ultra. With passive monitoring, the Allies ascertained as much information as they could from the transmissions themselves without actually reading them. Dönitz orchestrated his U-boat battles from his headquarters in France and eventually Berlin. He arranged patrol lines straddling known shipping lanes hoping that a U-boat would detect a convoy. That boat then informed Dönitz by radio and started to trail the convoy, sending out a regular radio beacon for the rest of the U-boats to home in on. U-boat headquarters also sent signals to all the U-boats in the vicinity that a convoy had been spotted at a certain grid-square on the specially prepared plotting map all U-boats carried. All those boats acknowledged that they had received the message and were on their way. Once they arrived at the convoy they all radioed Dönitz again that they were in contact and then waited for the order to attack. Dönitz waited until the maximum number of U-boats was in contact before he gave the order. When he did, all boats acknowledged receipt and went in on the convoy at the same time on the surface from different directions and overwhelmed the convoy escorts. All of this radio traffic was picked up by shore stations that determined that a convoy had been sighted and was in danger, but with dozens of convoys travelling in several directions at the same time, the problem was identifying which convoy was threatened.

The solution was Huff Duff–High Frequency Direction Finding. Both just before and during the war, the Allies set up radio receiving stations, including in Newfoundland (Cape Spear, the most easterly point in North America), that ringed the North Atlantic, and these stations determined the location of a transmitting U-boat by triangulating the location and strength of its transmission with other stations. This information was sent to the Operational Intelligence Centre (OIC) at the Admiralty, and if a convoy was in the vicinity it altered its course to try to avoid the U-boat. The same was true for a wolfpack attack. If radio signals were intercepted all in the same area at roughly the same time, the intelligence people knew that a wolfpack was gathering around a convoy and just how big it was. As a result, they alerted the convoy escort and either sent reinforcements or diverted escorts from a convoy that was not threatened. Huff Duff was also useful on a smaller scale. As the war progressed, Huff Duff equipment, like radar, became much more portable, and as a result more of the escort ships carried direction-finding equipment. Consequently, when a signal was picked up by one of the escorts, it was triangulated by using two or three of the other escorts, thus giving the Senior Office, Escort (SOE) the location of the transmitter. If this was the shadowing U-boat, using the co-ordinates obtained by Huff Duff an escort "ran down the track of the U-boat"– meaning it headed towards the spot where Huff Duff indicated the U-boat to be–and attacked it, while the convoy performed evasive manoeuvres. Huff Duff proved to be very useful during the Battle of the Atlantic because it could not only tell which convoys were in danger but also the ones that were not, so that their escorts could be diverted to help the threatened convoys.[461]

The other way the Allies used signals intelligence was Ultra.[462] Ultra stood for Ultra-Secret and was the information that was obtained from the decryption of actual signals. It was so secret that it was not revealed to the public until the 1970s. In the early 1930s, the Germans had developed the Enigma machine mainly to prevent industrial espionage, but it was so complex it was thought to be impenetrable. The Enigma machine basically consisted of a typewriter and several rotors. When an operator pressed a key, the rotors turned a set number of times and a letter would light up on top of the machine. To decode a message, the person receiving it had to know the setting of the rotor, otherwise the message would just come out as gibberish. Because there were millions of possibilities, depending on the number of rotors and the number of times they were set to turn, breaking the code was thought to be impossible. It may well have been except for a number of fortuitous events. The first occurred with the fall of Poland in September 1939. Just before Poland surrendered, that country's intelligence service managed to smuggle an Enigma machine out of the country. However, British intelligence needed the codes and rotors before they could read the German coded transmissions. Consequently, the British set out to capture everything they could on the Enigma machines. In February 1940, some rotors were recovered from the *U-33*, which was sunk while on a mine-laying mission, with further material being recovered from *U-13* in May. The following March, further intelligence was obtained from a captured German trawler, with more taken from a weather ship boarded the same month and another captured in June. But the real break came with the seizure of a full naval Enigma machine, including rotors and codebooks, from *U-110* in June 1941. From then until January 1942, the Allies were able to read German naval transmissions. Unfortunately, in February the German navy added a fourth rotor called "Triton" (codenamed "Shark" by the British), and for the next year–the most disastrous for Allied shipping in the Atlantic–German transmissions were unreadable. This Ultra blackout was particularly catastrophic for the St. John's-based MOEF, as without this intelligence, the Admiralty could not divert the slow RCN-escorted SC convoys around U-boat concentrations or call in re-enforcements before the U-boats set upon them. As a result, the MOEF faced the full force of Dönitz's U-boat arm. This fourth rotor was finally broken in December 1942, and for the rest of the war, the Allies knew everything that went into every naval transmission, but by then the decision had been made to pull the RCN out of the Atlantic.[463]

All of this code breaking was done in Hut 8 at the Government Code and Cipher School at Bletchley Park, just outside London, using large computers called "Bombes" developed by mathematician Alan Turing. After the messages had been decoded, the information was teletyped to the Submarine Tracking Room (STR) at the OIC in London where Commander Roger Winn, RN, and his staff combined it with all the other intelligence–Huff Duff, spy reports, sightings, attacks, etc.–to produce the whole picture of the Battle of the Atlantic. As a result of this, convoys were re-routed or re-enforced, and escorts warned of the imminence of an attack. This information was also disseminated to similar submarine tracking rooms in Ottawa and Washington and then on to the various local commands, including HMCS *Avalon*.[464]

The Germans never seriously entertained the idea that the Enigma code could be broken, and investigation after investigation suggested no reason why the Allies were so uncanny in tracking down and killing U-boats while convoys successfully avoided them. The authorities suspected spies at U-Boat headquarters, infra-red detection, equipment emissions, everything other than that the Enigma code had been broken. Some historians suggest that breaking the Enigma codes won the Battle of the Atlantic for the Allies, but realistically it was just one of many factors that turned the tide against the Germans in May 1943.

That May 1943 was the turning point in the Battle of the Atlantic was not lost on those in the front lines. Commodore Reid made just such an observation in his Operational War Diary for the month. He pointed to two actions in particular which illustrated the change in fortunes. Early in the month, ON-5 lost nine ships (plus one straggler) but at a cost to the Germans of eight U-boats plus several others severely damaged. SC-130, on the other hand, fought a three-day battle with a large concentration of U-boats without losing a single vessel. Reid attributed this reversal of fortunes to the introduction of support groups, escort carriers and the "steadily increasing efficiency of the men and material in Mid-Ocean

Escorts."[465] Unfortunately, all credit for this success went to British rather than Canadian groups, even though most of the RCN ships were back in the North Atlantic by May. Although fresh from training cruises, they were used only as "close escorts" and were always accompanied by support groups and, thus, did not participate in the carnage. The one exception was HMCS *Drumheller*, which, as a member of the predominantly British C.2 Group, shared a kill with HM ships *Broadway* and *Lagan*.[466] Reid did not note it, but the arrival of Very Long Range (VLR) Liberator bombers in Newfoundland and Iceland at the end of April also played a major role in the defeat of the wolfpacks in May.

On average, there were twenty-three merchant vessels and thirty-seven warships in St. John's harbour on a daily basis during the month, and despite the victory, survivors still arrived in a steady stream. In total, 619 people were landed in St. John's in May, including twenty-five German POWs who arrived on board HMCS *St. Laurent*. Waiting on the wharf for the latter was Lieutenant J.P. Lunger, sent from NSHQ to interrogate them. He must not have had too much luck with them because all except one wounded prisoner left with him the next day for Boston on board HMCS *St. Francis*. All the same, things were fairly quiet at HMCS *Avalon*. There was some reshuffling of office accommodation during the month as the offices of the Naval Control Service Officer (NCSO) and the MWT moved to the officers' accommodation building at Fort William, and those of Captain (D) were relocated to the Administration Building in their stead. Naval Laundry finally opened at the RCN barracks, and the anti-torpedo net at Wabana was completed. Really, the most notable event at the base during May was the first large dance held at the drill hall of the barracks. It was sponsored by the St. John's Naval Canteen Committee and attracted approximately 2500 attendees.[467]

If 1942 was a rough year for HMCS *Avalon*, the first month of 1943 seemed to promise more of the same. While the enemy was conspicuous by his absence, the atrocious weather put an incredible strain on the men and ships of the MOEF. Many suffered severe storm damage, and the FONF was hard put to meet all his commitments. While monstrous seas and high winds played their parts, some of his difficulty lay with the departure of the first of the C Groups for the UK. This became even more of a problem as enemy activity increased dramatically over the next couple of months and the American A Groups and the British B Groups tried to pick up the slack while suffering the same difficulties as the Canadian Groups the year before. Breakdowns, late arrivals, weather and storm damage, and crew exhaustion due to short turnarounds in port all contributed to the March crisis in which thirty-two ships, including an escort, were sunk in six MOEF-escorted convoys, a thirty percent increase over the previous month. Fortunately, the tide was starting to turn as support groups appeared to bolster threatened convoys and Very Long Range (VLR) aircraft began closing the mid-Atlantic air gap. May 1943 turned out to the month where all of these factors came together and the initiative in the Atlantic war passed to Allied forces.

At the same time, plans were in the works to expand the base at St. John's, including the addition of a floating dock, improved training facilities and expansion of the dockyard workforce. Existing work was being completed, although some areas, such as the dockyard, were still waiting for needed equipment. Nevertheless, with the improved spring weather and the war at sea reaching a new phase, HMCS *Avalon* continued its pivotal role as all the C Groups returned from the eastern Atlantic, and Support and Hunter-Killer Groups used the facilities at HMCS *Avalon* for turnaround.

Unfortunately, while the spring of 1943 was a triumph for the Allies, it was a humiliation for the RCN. After two years of "holding the line" in the Atlantic, it was denied participation in the climax of the battle. Although sold to the Canadian government as part of a larger effort to ready convoy escorts for the planned offensive against the U-boats, the withdrawal of the C Groups from the Atlantic in January and February was felt by many Canadian naval officers to be a betrayal. To add insult to injury, even when it returned to the fray in April, the RCN was relegated to its old role of close escort, a vital albeit inglorious responsibility, while the RN and USN Support and Hunter-Killer Groups racked up U-boat kills. This would have serious repercussions for the RCN and in particular for the CNS, Admiral Percy Nelles.

---

[313] Michael L. Hadley, *U-boats against Canada: German Submarines in Canadian Waters* (Kingston: McGill-Queen's University Press, 1985), 82.

[314] Günther Hessler, *The U-Boat War in the Atlantic, 1939 -1945* (3 vols., London: HMSO, 1989), II, 37.

[315] Hadley, *U-boats against Canada*, 101.

[316] Jürgen Rohwer, *Axis Submarine Successes, 1939-1945* (Cambridge: Patrick Stephens, 1983), 117.

[317] Hadley, *U-boats against Canada*, 103.

[318] *Ibid.*

[319] Tony German, *The Sea Is at Our Gates: The History of the Canadian Navy* (Toronto: McClelland and Stewart, 1990), 7.

[320] Hadley, *U-boats against Canada*, 117.

[321] Library and Archives Canada (LAC), Record Group (RG 24), Flag Officer Newfoundland Force (FONF), Vol. 11,953, file 1-1-1, vol 1., FONF, monthly report, June 1942.

[322] *Ibid.*, Report of Proceedings by Maintenance Captain, Captain of the Port, in FONF, monthly report, May 1942.

[323] "Criminal Cases Show Increase over 940," *Evening Telegram* (St. John's), 31 December 1941.

[324] "Very Busy Year In Magistrate's Court," *Evening Telegram* (St. John's), 31 December 1943.

[325] "Chinese Café Gutted By Naval Ratings," *Evening Telegram* (St. John's), 27 December 1941.

[326] For an official view of the behaviour of Canadian personnel and the disparity between Canadian recreational facilities and those of the Americans in St. John's, see Memorandum from Director of External Operations, Wartime Information Board [G.W. McCracken] to General Executive Manager, Wartime Information Board [A.D. Dunton], in Paul Bridle (ed.), *Documents on Relations between Canada and Newfoundland* (2 vols., Ottawa: Department of External Affairs, 1974-1984), I, 871.

[327] The so-called "Welty Agreement" between the general in command of American forces in Newfoundland and Newfoundland Justice and Defence Commissioner Emerson provided that American servicemen would be transferred to American authorities for punishment. Provincial Archives of Newfoundland and Labrador (PANL), GN 38, S4-2-4, file 3, Welty to L.E. Emerson, 4 October 94; and GN 38, S4-2-7, file 6, Emerson to Welty, 7 October 1941.

[328] LAC, RG 24, FONF, Vol.,1953, file 1-1-1, vol., Report of Proceedings by Maintenance Captain, Captain of the Port, in FONF, monthly report, June 1942. "Are Any Exempt," *Evening Telegram* (St. John's), 5 December 1941.

[329] *Ibid.*

[330] *Ibid.*

[331] About the only evidence the Admiralty would accept as proof of an RCN kill. *Ibid.*, FONF, monthly report, July 1942. See also W.A.B. Douglas, *et al.*, *No Higher Purpose: The Official Operational History of the Royal Canadian Navy in the Second World War, 1939-1945*, II part 2 (St. Catharines: Vanwell Publishing, 2002), 492-496.

[332] LAC, RG 24, FONF, Vol. 11,953, file 1-1-1, vol.1, FONF, monthly report, July 1942.

[333] *Ibid.*, Report of Proceedings by Maintenance Captain, Captain of the Port, in FONF, monthly report, July 1942.

[334] *Ibid.*

[335] *Ibid.*, Report of Proceedings by Maintenance Captain, Captain of the Port, in FONF, monthly report, August 1942.

[336] *Ibid.*, Vol. 11,949, Woods to Murray, 1 October 1941.

[337] *Ibid.*, Vol. 11,953, file 1-1-1, vol.1 , Report of Proceedings by Maintenance Captain, Captain of the Port, in FONF, monthly report, August 1942.

[338] *Ibid.*

[339] *Ibid.*
[340] *Ibid.*
[341] *Ibid.*
[342] Douglas, et al., *No Higher Purpose*, 503.
[343] LAC, RG 24, FONF, Vol. 11,953, file 1-1-1, vol.1 , FONF, monthly report, August 1942. See also Douglas, *et al., No Higher Purpose*, 506-507 and 525.
[344] LAC, RG 24, FONF, Vol. 11,953, file 1-1-1, vol. , FONF, monthly report, August 1942.
[345] Douglas, et al., *No Higher Purpose*, 641-643.
[346] LAC, RG 24, FONF, Vol. 11,953, file 1-1-1, vol.1 , Report of Proceedings by Maintenance Captain, Captain of the Port, in FONF, monthly report, September 1942.
[347] Jak Mallman Showell, *U-Boats at War: Landings on Hostile* Shores (London, Ian Allan, 1973; 2nd ed., Annapolis: Naval Institute Press, 2000), 38-39; and Hadley, *U-Boats against Canada*, 6. See also Steve Neary, T*he Enemy on Our Doorstep: The German Attacks at Bell Island, Newfoundland, 1942* (St. John's: Jespersen Press, 1994), 7-34.
[348] It would have been impossible to contain the news of the attack as many of the survivors had been rescued and cared for by the local residents and then transported to St. John's. For a discussion of censorship measures undertaken in Newfoundland, see Jeff A. Webb, *The Voice of Newfoundland: A Social History of the Broadcasting Corporation of Newfoundland, 1939-1949* (Toronto: University of Toronto Press, 2008), 124-125.
[349] LAC, RG 24, FONF, Vol. 11,953, file 1-1-1, vol.1, FONF, monthly report, September 1942.
[350] *Ibid.*
[351] For a review of Attlee's visit to Newfoundland and his conclusions, see Peter Neary, "Clement Attlee's Visit to Newfoundland, September 1942," *Acadiensis*, XIII, No. 2 (Spring, 1984), 101-109. A further parliamentary mission comprised of three British MPs travelled to Newfoundland in June 1943. It was not a formal Commission of Enquiry but an informal "goodwill" tour; it did however, submit its findings to the Dominions Office in November 1943 and issue a more formal report in December 1943. See Great Britain. National Archives (TNA/PRO), Premier 4/44/3, "Memorandum by Secretary of State for Dominion Affairs to the War Cabinet," November 1943; and "Newfoundland Past and Present: Addresses by Members of the Parliamentary Mission to Newfoundland," 2 December 1943.
[352] LAC, RG 24, FONF, Vol.11,953, file 1-1-1, vol.1, Report of Proceedings by Maintenance Captain, Captain of the Port, in FONF, monthly report, September 1942.
[353] *Ibid.*
[354] *Ibid.*, Report of Proceedings by Commanding Officer, HMCS *Avalon*, in FONF, monthly report, September 1942.
[355] *Ibid.*, Report by the Chaplain-in-Charge, HMCS *Avalon*, in FONF,

monthly report, September 1942.

[356] D.C. Miller (ed.), *St. John's Naval Guide Book* (St. John's: Robinson Blackmore, 1943), 20-21.

[357] LAC, RG 24, FONF, Vol. 11,953, file 1-1-1, vol.1 , FONF, monthly report, October 1942.

[358] Hadley, *U-boats against Canada*, 2-4.

[359] A manual issued to mariners giving information on harbours, currents, navigational beacons, etc.

[360] Hadley, *U-boats against Canada*, 5.

[361] *Ibid.*, 117-118 and 131.

[362] Marc Milner, *Canada's Navy: The First Century* (Toronto: University of Toronto Press, 1999), 107.

[363] Rohwer, *Axis Submarine Successes*, 119-126.

[364] Milner, *Canada's Navy*, 108.

[365] Hadley, *U-boats against Canada*, 132.

[366] Douglas How, *Night of the Caribou* (Hantsport, NS: Lancelot Press, 1988), 46-47.

[367] *Ibid.*, 73.

[368] *Ibid.*, 72 and 85.

[369] Hadley, *U-boats against Canada*, 38.

[370] "The Town Cast Down in Grief Caribou Disaster Leaves Twenty-on Widows and Fifty-one Orphans in Port aux Basques and Channel: Funeral of Six Victims Is Held," *Evening Telegram* (St. John's), 23 October 1942.

[371] LAC, RG 24, FONF, Vol. 11,953, file 1-1-1, vol.1, FONF, monthly report, October 1942.

[372] *Ibid.*, Report of Proceedings by Maintenance Captain, Captain of the Port, in FONF, monthly report, October. 1942.

[373] *Ibid.*, Report of Proceedings by Commanding Officer, HMCS *Avalon*, in FONF, monthly report, October 1942.

[374] TNA/PRO, Dominions Office (DO) 35/1354, Governor of Newfoundland to Secretary of State for Dominion Affairs, quarterly report, 3 December 1942.

[375] LAC, RG 24, FONF, Vol. 11,953, file 1-1-1, fol. , FONF, monthly report, November 1942. See also Douglas, *et al.*, *No Higher Purpose*, 534; and Arnold Hague, *The Allied Convoy System, 1939-1945: Its Organization, Defence and Operation* (St. Catharines: Vanwell Publishing, 2000), 137 and 116.

[376] LAC, RG 24, FONF, Vol. 11,953, file 1-1-1, vol. 1, Report of Proceedings by Maintenance Captain, Captain of the Port, in FONF, monthly report, November 1942.

[377] *Ibid.* See also Marc Milner, *North Atlantic Run: The Royal Canadian Navy and the Battle for the Convoys* (Toronto: University of Toronto Press, 1985), 188-189.

[378] Mallman Showell, *U-Boats at War*, 37-38; and Hadley, *U-Boats against Canada*, 152. See also Neary, *Enemy on Our Doorstep*, 49-94.

[379] Dean Beeby, *Cargo of Lies: The True Story of a Nazi Double Agent in Canada* (Toronto: University of Toronto Press, 1996); and Mallman Showell, *U-Boats at War*, 37-38. See also Hadley, *U-Boats against Canada*, 151-164.

[380] TNA/PRO, DO 35/1354, Governor of Newfoundland to Secretary of State for Dominion Affairs, quarterly report, 3 December 1942.

[381] *Ibid.*, Dominion Affairs Office, memorandum, 28 January 1943.

[382] LAC, RG 24, FONF, Vol. 11,953, file 1-1-1, vol. 1, FONF, monthly report, October 1942.

[383] *Ibid.*, Report of Proceedings by Maintenance Captain, Captain of the Port, in FONF, monthly report, November 1942.

[384] *Ibid.*

[385] *Ibid.*, FONF, monthly report, December 1942.

[386] *Ibid.*, Report of Proceedings by Maintenance Captain, Captain of the Port, in FONF, monthly report, December 1942.</

[387] *Ibid.*, Report of Proceedings by Maintenance Captain, Captain of the Port, in FONF, monthly report, December 1942.

[388] *Ibid.*, FONF, monthly report, December 1942.

[389] *Ibid.*

[390] *Ibid.*, Report of Proceedings by Maintenance Captain, Captain of the Port, in FONF, monthly report, December 1942.

[391] *Ibid.*

[392] David Zimmerman, "The Social Background of the Wartime Navy: Some Statistical Data," in Michael L. Hadley, Rob Huebert and Fred W. Crickard (eds.), *A Nation's Navy: In Quest of Canadian Naval Identity* (Montreal: McGill-Queen's University Press,1 996), 275. RCNR officers were mostly older, re-commissioned former RN and RCN officers. Most of them held senior administrative positions in Ottawa, Halifax or overseas.

[393] Evidence suggests that it was this reliance on public facilities (or the lack thereof) that was the root cause of the VE Day riots at Halifax in 1945. See R.H. Caldwell, "The VE Day Riots in Halifax, 7-8 May 1945," *The Northern Mariner/Le Marin du nord*, X, No. (January 2000), 3-20. Indeed, some argue that it was the lack of established naval recreational facilities rather than outdated equipment that was at the heart of the RCN's morale problem. See Richard O. Mayne, *Betrayed: Scandal, Politics, and Canadian Naval Leadership* (Vancouver: UBC Press, 2006), 82.

[394] Unless otherwise noted, all information concerning facilities available to naval personnel comes from Miller (ed.), *St. John's Naval Guide Book*.

[395] The St. John's Naval Rest Camp was officially opened by Capt. (D) Newfoundland, Capt. J.M. Rowland, in July 1943. LAC, RG 24, FONF, Vol. 11,505, Report of Proceedings by Naval Officer in Charge (NOIC), Administrative War Diaries, 1445-102-3, sub.1 , vol. 1, July 1943.

[396] "Police Ask Order against Beer Parlours," *Evening Telegram* (St. John's), 30 January 1941.

[397] "Two Motor Boats Collide in Harbour," *Evening Telegram* (St.

John's), 10 January 1941. See also "Harbour Regulations," *Evening Telegram* (St. John's), 27 June 1941. Public Archives of Newfoundland and Labrador (PANL), Government of Newfoundland, Department of Public Utilities, GN 38:S5-1-2, File 9, P.U. 38(a)-41,"Regulations for the Control of Small Boats Plying for Hire or Reward in the Harbour of St. John's," 17 June 1942.

[398] Margaret Duley, *The CaribouHut* (Toronto: Ryerson Press, 1949), 28.

[399] "Official Opening of St. John's 'Y' Hostel," *Evening Telegram* (St. John's), 10 January 1942.

[400] Darrin McGrath, *Last Dance: The Knights of Columbus Fire* (St. John's: Flanker Press, 2002), 5-16.

[401] *Ibid.*, 2-45. See also Gerhard P. Bassler, *Vikings to U-Boats: The German Experience in Newfoundland and Labrador* (Montreal: McGill-Queen's University Press, 2006), 287-290.

[402] While the complaints about training were certainly valid and not denied by Canadian naval authorities, there was a certain amount of British snobbery in the criticism of leadership. The British did not train their officers in leadership because the majority, especially senior officers, were products of the public (read private) school system which, by definition, was supposed to imbue them with leadership qualities. As officer appointments in the RCN were based on criteria other than old school ties, the British naturally assumed that Canadians were inferior leaders. Nonetheless, the Royal Navy did produce a number of officers' pamphlets to aid RN officers. The first, entitled "The Officers Aide Memoire" and issued in 1943 actually included rather paternalistic instructions on the subtleties of leadership. See Brian Lavery (comp. and intro.), *The Royal Navy Officer's Pocket-Book 1944* (London: Conway Maritime Books, 2007).

[403] For a full account of Admiralty efforts to transfer RCN forces to the eastern Atlantic in the fall of 942, see Milner, *North Atlantic Run*, 189-213. See also Milner, "Squaring Some of the Corners," in Timothy J. Runyan and Jan M. Copes (eds.). *To Die Gallantly: The Battle of the Atlantic* (Boulder, CO: Westview Press, 1994), 32; and Mayne, *Betrayed*, 96-98.

[404] LAC, RG 24, FONF, Vol. 11,505, FONF, monthly report, January 1943; and Report of Proceedings by NOIC, Administrative War Diaries, 1445-1023, sub. 1, vol. 1, January 1943.

[405] *Ibid.*, FONF, monthly report, January 1943.

[406] *Ibid.*, Report of Proceedings by NOIC, Administrative War Diaries, January 1943.

[407] *Ibid.*

[408] *Ibid.*

[409] *Ibid.*, RG 24, FONF, Vol. 11,505, FONF, monthly report, February 1943; and Report of Proceedings by NOIC, Administrative War Diaries, 1445-102-3, sub. 1, vol. 1, February 1943.

[410] TNA/PRO, DO35/1355, Governor's Report for the Yearly Quarter ending 30 June 1943.

[411] LAC, RG 24, FONF, Vol. 11,505, FONF, monthly report, February 1943; and Report of Proceedings by NOIC, Administrative War Diaries, 1445-102-3, sub. 1, vol. 1, February 1943.

[412] Winston S. Churchill, *The Second World War: The Hinge of Fate* (11th ed., New York: Bantam Books, 1962), 109.

[413] From all causes. Definitive figures for this period are difficult to find. Some sources included losses from all areas, while others included vessels that made it to port but were total losses nonetheless. See V.E. Tarrant, *The U-Boat Offensive,1 914-1945* (Annapolis: Naval Institute Press, 1989), 116; Andrew Williams, *The Battle of the Atlantic: The Allies' Submarine Fight against Hitler's Gray Wolves of the Sea* (London: BBC Worldwide., 2002), 247; and Nathan Miller, *War at Sea: A Naval History of World War II* (New York: Scribner, 1995; reprint, New York: Oxford University Press, 1997), 343-344.

[414] Stephen W. Roskill, *The War At Sea. Vol. II: The Period of Balance* (London: HMSO, 1956), 367. See also Jürgen Rohwer, *The Critical Convoy Battles of March 1943* (London: Ian Allan, 1977), 187; and TNA/PRO, ADM 199/2096, Review of the U-Boat War for the Year 1943 (as given in the Anti-Submarine Report, December 1943).

[415] Clay Blair, *Hitler's U-Boat War: The Hunted, 1942-1945* (New York: Random House, 1998), 47-49.

[416] *Ibid.*, 134-135.

[417] Indeed, Captain (D) Newfoundland, Captain E. Rollo Mainguy scored the RCN's first U-boat kill in 1940 while in command of HMCS *Ottawa*. Unfortunately, but in typical fashion, the Admiralty did not credit it to him and it was forty-two years after the war that he was finally awarded the kill. Wilfred G.D.Lund, "Vice-Admiral E. Rollo Mainguy: Sailors' Sailor," in Michael Whitby, Richard H. Gimblett and Peter Haydon (eds.), *The Admirals: Canada's Senior Naval Leadership in the Twentieth Century* (Toronto: Dundurn Press, 2006), 186-212.

[418] Jak P. Mallmann Showell, *U-Boats under the Swastika: An Introduction to German Submarines, 1935-1945* (London: Ian Allan, 1973; 2nd ed., Annapolis: Naval Institute Press, 2000), 21-22.

[419] *Ibid.*

[420] By this time all the St. John's-based C Groups had been transferred to the eastern Atlantic for training.

[421] Blair, *The Hunted*, 167-168.

[422] Michael Gannon, "Black May: The Epic Story of the Allies" Defeat of the German U-boats in May 1943 (New York: Harper Collins, 1998), xx-xxii

[423] *Ibid.*

[424] Marc Milner, *The Battle of the Atlantic* (St. Catharines: Vanwell Publishing, 2003), 235-236.

[425] Geoffrey Till, "The Battle of the Atlantic as History," in Stephen Howarth and Derek Law (eds.), *The Battle of the Atlantic, 1939-1945: The 50th Anniversary International Naval Conference* (Annapolis: Naval Institute Press, 1994), 584-595.

[426] Marc Milner, as quoted in Till, "Battle of the Atlantic," 589. See also Marc Milner, "The Battle of the Atlantic," *Journal of Strategic Studies*, XIII, No. 1 (1990), 450-466.

[427] Mallmann Showell, *U-Boats under the Swastika*, 98. See also David Syrett, *The Defeat of the German U-Boats: The Battle of the Atlantic* (Columbia: University of South Carolina Press, 1994), 261.

[428] Till, "Battle of the Atlantic," 584-595.

[429] *Ibid.*

[430] LAC, RG 24, FONF, Vol.11,505, FONF, monthly report, March 1943.

[431] *Ibid.*, Report of Proceedings by NOIC, Administrative War Diaries, 1445-102-3, sub. 1, vol. 1, March 1943.

[432] Tarrant, *U-Boat Offensive*, 118-119.

[433] LAC, RG 24, FONF, Vol. 11,505, Report of Proceedings by NOIC, Administrative War Diaries, 1445-102-3, sub. 1, vol. 1, April 1943.

[434] *Ibid.*, FONF, monthly report, April 1943.

[435] *Ibid.*, Report of Proceedings by NOIC, Administrative War Diaries, 1445-102-3, sub. 1, vol. 1, April 1943. See also TNA/PRO, ADM 116/4701, British Admiralty Delegation (BAD) to Admiralty, 5 February 1943.

[436] LAC, RG 24, FONF, Vol. ,505, FONF, monthly report, April 1943.

[437] Canada, Department of National Defence (DND), Directorate of History and Heritage (DHH) 81/520/1440-166/25, II (1), E.A. Seal to Admiralty, Report on Repair Facilities, 7 April 1943. See also TNA/PRO, DO 35/1368, FONF to Admiralty, 14 April 1943.

[438] *Ibid.*

[439] Working-up practices were discontinued in late 1942 when Pictou and St. Margaret's Bay, Nova Scotia, came into use. Refresher training continued to the end of the war. See DND, DHH, NHS 8000, 1-6, "Harbour Training in St. John's—Summary of General Development," 28 June 1945.

[440] LAC, RG 24, Vol. 11,505, 335.41., Vol.1, "Commanding Officer H.M. M.A/S. T. U. No. 11 to FONF, September 1942.

[441] DND, DHH 81/520/1440-166/25 II (1), Seal to Admiralty, Report on Repair Facilities, 7 April 1943. See also TNA, Kew, UK, DO35/1368, FONF to Admiralty, 4 April 1943.

[442] Long Range Navigation. The Loran system utilized radio signals to aid in navigation.

[443] DND, DHH, NHS 8000, 1-6, "Harbour Training in St. John's—Summary of General Development," 28 June 1945.

[444] *Ibid.*, DHH 81/520/1440-166/25, II (1), Seal to Admiralty, Report on Repair Facilities, 7 April 1943. See also TNA/PRO, DO 35/1368, FONF to Admiralty, 4 April 1943.

[445] "Minutes of a Meeting of Cabinet War Committee," 6 April 943 in Bridle (ed.), *Documents*, II, 616-617.

[446] PANL, GN 38, S4-2-1.1, file 9, 578-42, Secretary of State for Dominion Affairs to Governor of Newfoundland, 6 October 1942. See also

TNA/PRO, ADM 116/4540, minute series M 12672/42.

[447] TNA/PRO ADM 116/4540, Minute Series M 12672/42.

[448] *Ibid.*, ADM 116/4941, British Merchant Shipping Mission, Washington, to Shipminder, London, 8 February 1943.

[449] PANL, GN 38, S4-2-4, file 2, Governor of Newfoundland to Secretary of State for Dominion Affairs, 28 April 1943.

[450] LAC, RG 25, Series 62, Vol. 3198, file 5206-40, C.J. Burchell, High Commissioner for Canada, St. John's, to Scott MacDonald, Department of External Affairs, Ottawa, 6 April 1943.

[451] "Mechanics to Train at Local Dockyards," *Evening Telegram* (St. John's), 22 August 1941.

[452] PANL, GN 38, S4-2-4, file 2, Governor of Newfoundland to Secretary of State for Dominion Affairs, 28 April 1943.

[453] TNA/PRO, DO 35/1368, FONF to Admiralty, 14 April 1943; and ADM116/4701, BAD to Admiralty, August 1943. See also LAC, RG 24, FONF, Vol. 11,505, Administrative War Diaries, NOIC, monthly report, September 1943; and TNA/PRO, ADM 16/4941, Naval Service Headquarters, Ottawa (NSHQ) to Admiralty, 27 July 1943; and Ministry of War Transport Representative to Shipminder, London (Ministry of War Transport), 4 September 1943.

[454] DND, DHH, FOMR, NSS-1000-5-20, vol. I., Commodore Commanding Newfoundland Force (CCNF) to NSHQ, 30 June 1941.

[455] High Commissioner in Newfoundland to Commissioner for Public Utilities, 18 August 1942, in Bridle (ed.), *Documents on Relations*, II, 603-604.

[456] High Commissioner in Newfoundland to Commissioner for Public Utilities, 18 August 1942 in Bridle (ed.), *Documents on Relations*, II, 606. See also TNA/PRO, ADM 116/4941, Comments on extract from letter from Sir Wilfred Woods to Mr. Clutterbuck, Dominions Office, August 1943.

[457] The change of jurisdiction from the USN to RCN and Murray's assumption of the position of C-in-C CNA became effective April 1943, but Murray did not take over from US Task Force 24 until 30 April 1943.

[458] LAC, RG 24, FONF, Vol. 11,505, Report of Proceedings by NOIC, Administrative War Diaries, 1445-102-3, sub. 1, vol. 1, April 1943.

[459] Tarrant, U-Boat Offensive, 119.

[460] For a detailed account of how SigInt was acquired and used by the Government Code and Cipher School at Bletchley Park, London, see F.H. Hinsley, *et al.*, *British Intelligence in the Second World War: Its Influence on Strategy and Operations* (4 vols., London: HMSO, 1970-1990).

[461] Gannon, *Black May*, 64-68.

[462] For a detailed account of how Ultra directly impacted on the Battle of the Atlantic, see Syrett, *Defeat of the German U-Boats*.

[463] Signals Intelligence also played a crucial role in the early operations of the NEF. By being able to pinpoint possible areas of U-boat concentrations in 1941, the Admiralty could detour threatened NEF-escorted convoys out of danger which helped compensate for the inferior numbers, training and

equipment of the Canadian escorts. Jürgen Rohwer, "The Wireless War," in Howarth and Law (eds.), *Battle of the Atlantic*, 408-417. See also *Type IX U-Boats: German Type IX Submarine, German Submarine U-110, German Submarine U-155, German Submarine U-505, German Submarine U-862* (Memphis, TN: Books LLC, 2010).

[464] *Ibid.*

[465] LAC, RG 24, FONF, Vol. 11,505, FONF, monthly report, May 1943. See also Harrison Salisbury, "U-Boats' Defeat Total This Month—Churchill," *New York World-Telegram*, 30 June 1943.

[466] Milner, *North Atlantic Run*, 240.

[467] LAC, RG 24, FONF, Vol. 11,505, War Diary of NOIC, Administrative War Diaries, 1445-1023, sub. 1, vol. 1, May 1943.

Chapter 5

All Over but the Shouting: June 1943 to May 1945

Thinking that the reversal at sea was only a temporary setback, Dönitz suspended operations against North Atlantic convoys on 24 May. He moved his surviving boats to the Caribbean and West African coasts where he felt they would be less vulnerable to air attack but still capable of successes. Single boats were left in the North Atlantic so the Allies would not catch on, at least for a time, to this change in strategy. Regardless, it soon became obvious to all that the "U-boats had nearly all abandoned the North Atlantic convoy routes." Convoy cycles were opened up, and flotillas of up to ninety vessels sailed between North America and the United Kingdom.[468] At the same time, U-boat losses soared, averaging thirty a month worldwide over the summer of 1943.[469] Many of these were in the Bay of Biscay, and with the lull in the North Atlantic, mid-ocean groups were reduced to six ships with the surplus being sent to the eastern Atlantic to form support groups.[470] One of these was Canadian Escort Group 9, which unfortunately gained the distinction of being the only support group destroyed by U-boats.[471]

    Meanwhile, work on the expansion of HMCS *Avalon* commenced. As with the initial base development, the question of post-war ownership was raised again. The Canadians worried that the British might turn the facilities over to the Americans after the end of hostilities,[472] and the Newfoundland government feared that further Canadian encroachment would give that country intolerable control over St. John's harbour and hence the fisheries.[473] Ownership of the facilities would again have to rest with the Admiralty, but as the funds for further development would come from the Canadian Mutual Aid Fund, and since the Canadians felt that the future defence of Newfoundland was a Canadian responsibility, both the Admiralty and the Newfoundland government fretted that this would provide Canada with a case for claiming the facilities at war's end.[474] The Commission of Government was already troubled about the "ultimate effect on Newfoundland's political and economic independence [as a result] of the Canadian (and American) 'invasion.'" Moreover, it worried that the public might not remember how happy they were about the arrival of the forces from both countries during "the hour of danger" should there be further encroachments by either country.[475] Ultimately, the British provided assurances that no determination would be made about the disposal of the facilities at St. John's without full consultation with both the Canadian and Newfoundland governments.[476]

While these negotiations were taking place, the authorities were also trying to remedy the repair situation not only at St. John's but throughout eastern Canada. In April, Malcolm MacDonald, the British High Commissioner to Ottawa, suggested the establishment of a combined Canadian, British and American committee "to examine repair problems for warships and merchant ships" in the northwest Atlantic. Recognizing Newfoundland's importance, MacDonald recommended that representatives of the Newfoundland government be included.[477] To this end, the principal members of the Allied Anti-Submarine Survey Board–Rear Admiral J.M. Mansfield, RN (former Chief of Staff [COS] to the Commander-in-Chief Western Approaches [C-in-C, WA) and Rear Admiral J.L. Kaufman, USN (former Commander, Caribbean Sea Frontier)–arrived in St. John's to meet with senior RCN staff and to inspect repair facilities.[478] In their report to the Chief of the Naval Staff (CNS), the board pointed out that the RCN's maintenance facilities at St. John's (and at Halifax) had long "passed the saturation point" and that all of the repair facilities on the east coast of Canada needed extensive upgrading, including a much enlarged workforce. Of particular urgency, escorts needed to be given priority over merchant ship repair or new construction, and in agreement with the report of the British Admiralty Delegation (BAD), the board recommended a floating dock at St. John's for the exclusive use of the escorts.[479] During the summer, on average there were thirty-five warships and sixteen merchant vessels moored in St. John's harbour at any one time, and 1100 men were accommodated daily at the naval barracks during July and August.[480]

The Combined Canadian, United Kingdom and United States Committee to Examine Repair Problems for Warships and Merchant Vessels on the East Coast of Canada and Newfoundland met in Ottawa in August under the chairmanship of (now) Rear-Admiral G.L. Stephens, with Sir Wilfred Woods representing the government of Newfoundland. During the discussions, Woods stressed the necessity of reserving the Newfoundland Dockyard for the repair of merchant vessels because its close proximity to the convoy routes made it "the natural port of refuge for damaged and defective ships." Despite this argument, the committee reiterated the position of the Allied Anti-Submarine Survey Board that naval vessels had to take precedence. As it was, only running repairs could be completed, and refits of warships had to be undertaken in British or American ports. The committee also recommended that a new floating dock of at least 3000 tons, capable of handling the largest escort vessel, replace the recently acquired 1800-ton facility at St. John's as soon as possible. At the same time, planned improvements to the naval facilities needed to be "completed and manned as quickly as possible" and the labour force at the Newfoundland Dockyard augmented with skilled labour from Britain "without delay."[481]

Unfortunately, the committee's findings did nothing to dissipate the storm that was brewing in Ottawa between CNS Admiral Percy Nelles and Naval Minister, Angus Macdonald. The discontent both at sea and ashore concerning the equipment crisis on RCN ships had reached the minister in August. The month before, the Assistant Director of Naval Intelligence Captain W. Strange had sailed to Britain aboard HMS *Duncan* under the command of Commander Peter Gretton, RN, one of the Royal Navy's most successful escort commanders. During his conversations with Strange about the state of equipment on RCN ships, Gretton suggested that Strange talk to Commodore G.W.G. Simpson, Commodore (D) at Londonderry. Frustrated with the situation on Canadian ships, the irascible Simpson was frank in his criticisms of Naval Service Headquarters (NSHQ). Upon returning to Newfoundland, and possibly at the behest of the FONF Commodore Reid, Strange prepared a confidential report for Macdonald which the Minister received shortly after the Allied Repair Committee conference. Based on Strange's findings, Macdonald ordered Nelles to report on the state of equipment on RCN ships compared to the situation on RN warships. Nelles was not alarmed by the request because he felt many of the outstanding issues had been addressed, so he sent Macdonald a general overview of the state of affairs. But since this report did not answer many of the minister's specific queries, Macdonald immediately suspected a cover-up of some kind at NSHQ. The minister thus dispatched his executive assistant, J.J. Connolly, on a fact-finding mission to Britain, where Connolly interviewed several RCN and RN officers, including Simpson. Connolly returned in October with a somewhat lopsided, but still serious, critique of the state of RCN ships in particular and NSHQ in general. A series of increasingly acrimonious memoranda passed between the minister and the CNS over the next several months during which Macdonald downloaded all onus for the state of affairs onto Nelles and the staff at NSHQ.[482]

At the same time, Dönitz's U-boats returned to the fray in September with new weapons and tactics. While the basic goal was still to sink merchant ships, Dönitz's tactics now included eliminating rather

The "Newfyjohn" Solution

than avoiding the convoy's protection. Heavier anti-aircraft guns were mounted, and crews were admonished to stay on the surface and fight it out with attacking aircraft. To give warning of approaching planes, the radar warning device *Wanze* was installed on all boats; this sounded an alarm when ten-centimetre radar waves were detected. The *Zaunkonig* (Wren) homing torpedo, called GNAT (German Naval Acoustic Torpedo) by the Allies, was introduced as a defence against escort vessels. The torpedo was designed to follow the acoustic signature of an escort ship and to detonate against its stern. It was a GNAT that destroyed the Canadian EG.9 mentioned earlier.[483] Some successes were achieved, but because these torpedoes had to be launched while submerged, U-boat commanders could not confirm sinkings. Consequently, claims in no way reflected actual successes. Air defence tactics also proved ineffective, especially in the Bay of Biscay. After the first few confrontations with heavily armed U-boats in the bay, Coastal Command changed its tactics so that the spotting aircraft would call up reinforcements before going in for an attack. Even Dönitz's grouping of U-boats for mutual protection did not help, and eventually U-boat commanders were told to submerge at the first sign of aircraft. In January 1944, as monthly U-boat losses continued to soar, Dönitz abandoned pack tactics altogether, and the U-boats reverted to individual attacks. Whether he recognized it or not, this is when Dönitz changed the overall strategy of the Atlantic war. No longer was the priority to sever the lines of communication between the New World and the Old but rather to tie down naval forces until the new Type XXI "electro-boats" arrived from the builders.

Meanwhile, the Flag Officer Newfoundland Force (FONF) noted the September renewal in the Battle of the Atlantic and disbanded the ill-fated Escort Group 9 to reinforce the C Groups.[484] The floating dock also arrived during the month along with its commander, Engineering Lieutenant-Commander F. Burton, RCNR. Actually, a number of noteworthy people passed through the command during September. Capt. R.N. Wood, the Director of Naval Ordnance (DNO), arrived to discuss ordnance problems; Rear-Admiral Sir Francis Austin, RN, and Commander C.A. Moore, RN, held meetings in St. John's about the proposed Defensively Equipped Merchant Ships (DEMS) training facility; and the Director of Trade, Captain E.S. Brand, made a short visit towards the end of the month. At the same time, renovations began on the drill hall and the officers' wardroom at the naval barracks, which also accommodated 1170 men during this time. The daily average of warships alongside during the month decreased to thirty-two, with roughly fourteen merchant vessels in the harbour at the same time. Nineteen convoys were sailed, and 140 survivors were landed.[485] Despite the renewed U-boat offensive, on balance September turned out to be fairly uneventful for the Newfoundland Force.

This trend continued to the end of the year. After something of a lull in October, when the daily average of warships at St. John's was only twenty-nine, this figure rose in November and December to thirty-nine. As a result, more than 1200 men were accommodated monthly at the barracks during the fall, decreasing to a little over 1000 in December. Mines also became a problem during the fall, and U-boats were suspected off St. John's when a field of thirty-one German mines was discovered in the approaches to the port in October claiming two victims.[486] This concern persisted throughout the next two months, although no casualties were reported, and mine-clearing sweeps were eventually discontinued. Vice Chief of Naval Staff (VCNS) Rear Admiral C.G. Jones, and Murray's COS, Captain R.E.S. Bidwell, arrived in St. John's for separate meetings with base staff. Their appearance no doubt had something to do with the ongoing feud between Macdonald and Nelles, a dispute in which Jones was hardly an innocent bystander. Commodore Reid had been one of the many critics of the state of equipment of RCN forces in the spring and summer which may have precipitated a change in command in the Newfoundland Force, with Commodore C.R.H. Taylor replacing Reid, who departed for Ottawa in early November.[487]

The year ended as quietly as it had begun, although like the previous December, not without tragedy when on the night of 16 December a naval sentry on duty at the Naval Armament Depot on the Southside of the harbour mistakenly shot and killed an employee of E.G.M. Cape and Company.[488] Regardless, the transformation of the Battle of the Atlantic had been as swift as it was monumental. The transition from the disastrous mid-winter months when serious doubts arose about the effectiveness of the convoy system to the collapse of Dönitz's entire North Atlantic strategy had taken only three months. After May 1943, the Germans never regained the offensive in the Atlantic, and the initiative passed to the Allies. The U-boats became the hunted as escort groups were denuded of destroyers to form support and hunter/killer groups that exacted a terrible toll. Yet this change in fortune did not diminish St. John's' importance as a naval base. Indeed, plans were initiated to improve and expand HMCS *Avalon* as both a repair and maintenance facility and training centre. Although lingering suspicions among the various parties again caused some problems, the spirit of co-operation and compromise allayed the fears. The same could not be said, however, about relations in Ottawa, where a blame game and behind-the-

The "Newfyjohn" Solution

scenes power struggle was being played out between senior RCN officers and the naval minister.

Percy Nelles had been one of the country's first naval cadets and had spent much of his career in shore postings. Appointed CNS in 1934, he was a reasonably competent, if uninspired, officer and more a "senior public servant than [a] professional seadog."[489] Consequently, when Macdonald requested the equipment comparison between RCN and RN ships in the summer of 1943, Nelles seriously misjudged the situation. He thought that the majority of the complaints voiced about the RCN's equipment and training standards had been addressed. The paucity of RCN U-boat kills during the spring, a period when the RN and USN were racking up victory after victory, was an embarrassment to the Canadian government, and the minister was under tremendous pressure from his Cabinet colleagues to explain it. If Nelles was out of his depth, the same certainly applied to Angus Macdonald. The former premier of Nova Scotia had been happy enough to leave the running of the navy to NSHQ and took little interest in the RCN aside from routine administrative and intergovernmental matters. But as the year wore on, Macdonald's suspicions of incompetence at NSHQ were reinforced by Connolly's report on his mission to the UK and a whispering campaign by Nelles' VCNS, Vice-Admiral Jones.[490] Ultimately, Nelles was relieved of his duties in early 1944 and, after being replaced by Jones, was transferred to London as Senior Naval Officer, which really was a face-saving appointment. Disillusioned and justifiably bitter, Nelles retired from the RCN at the end of 1944. While deficient in planning and slow to react to the changing face of the Atlantic war, Nelles and the staff at NSHQ were unfairly blamed for a situation that was not their fault alone. Both the Canadian government and the British Admiralty contributed significantly to the crisis which eventually led to Nelles' removal.

The Liberal Government of Prime Minister Mackenzie King decided early in the conflict that if Canada was to participate, it was going to benefit the country's industrial base. Citing vulnerability and a scarcity of skilled labour in the Maritimes, the Minister of Munitions and Supply, C.D. Howe, concentrated the country's shipbuilding and repair facilities in Ontario and Quebec.[491] Unfortunately, putting all these eggs in one basket created a number of difficulties. The first was that most of these yards were inaccessible for months at a time due to winter ice in the St. Lawrence River, which often resulted in warships being released before the winter freeze up whether fully completed or not. These ships were often plagued by defects which had to be rectified in east coast shipyards, including the Newfoundland Dockyard. This situation was further exacerbated by the closures of the St. Lawrence in 1942 and 1944 due to enemy action. The other difficulty was that with all these yards occupied with new construction, there was little space available for repairs or upgrading. Not wanting to delay production, NSHQ decided to incorporate improvements in new construction rather than modernize current ships as circumstances warranted.[492] Unhappily, due to the aforementioned hazards in the St. Lawrence, as well as unforeseen difficulties at a number of yards, events at sea developed faster than these newer warships could be constructed. Had Ottawa developed shipbuilding and repair facilities on the east coast of the country as well as in central Canada, this may not have become the crisis that it did.[493] But with Ottawa's attention focussed on providing a spur to industrial development in central Canada, facilities in the Maritimes were neglected until it was too late. The result was that, when needed, repair facilities on the St. Lawrence were inaccessible or fully occupied with naval construction, and those on the east coast simply did not have the capacity or manpower to compensate. The only option available to the RCN was to send its ships to the UK or USA for upgrading, but these yards were also fully occupied. If the naval minister really wanted to get to the root of the equipment crisis, he should have started at his own government's door.

The British Admiralty, the RCN's most vociferous critic, also bore substantial responsibility for the shortcomings of the RCN. The protection of the trans-Atlantic lines of communication against U-boat attacks was the single most important responsibility in the Battle of the Atlantic. Before the war, confident that any submarine threat had been nullified by the development of ASDIC, the RN thought that the major threat would come from surface raiders. Yet within the first few months of the war it became evident that German U-boats were more than just a mere nuisance.[494] The RN was woefully short of escort craft, and Prime Minister Mackenzie King saw this as an area where Canada could make a major contribution to the war effort. To this end, NSHQ chose the corvette, which could be built to mercantile standards in Canadian shipyards. The first program, initiated in early 1940, called for twenty-eight corvettes by the end of the navigation season. This was soon followed by another order of thirty-six, bringing the total to sixty-four by the end of 1941.[495] With such a rapid production of vessels, manning became an issue.

When war was declared, the RCN consisted of 1719 officers and men, plus approximately 3700 retired officers and reserves. NSHQ quickly adopted a set of mobilization plans calling for 12,500 individuals of all ranks by the end of 1941.[496] NSHQ soon revised this estimate to a

The "Newfyjohn" Solution

compliment after three years of 1500 officers and 15,000 men. But when, by the end of 1940, the ships of the first building program were coming off the ways in rapid succession, the RCN was faced with the need to crew seventy-nine warships, including six vintage American destroyers, and an assortment of motor launches. As well, it was expected to find personnel to operate new shore establishments throughout eastern Canada and Newfoundland.[497] Although NSHQ thought that some relief would come when the Americans finally joined the hostilities, quite the opposite occurred.

When the RCN established the Newfoundland Escort Force (NEF) in May 1941, it was to be a temporary measure until the Americans entered the war and took over all convoy escort duties in the western Atlantic as specified in the ABC1 agreement. However, when it formally entered the European war in December the US withdrew all but two of its escorts from the Atlantic, and the RCN was forced to take up the slack. At the same time, with the U-boat onslaught along the eastern seaboard of the United States during the first six months of 1942, the RCN was obliged to initiate convoys to the Caribbean and between Halifax, Boston and the Western Ocean Meeting Point (WESTOMP) just east of the Newfoundland Grand Banks–the famous "Triangle Run." Suggestions as to what would have happened had the RCN not taken over these duties were not forthcoming, then or now. The RN did not have the resources to do it, and NSHQ rightly considered that any escorts were better than none. All the same, the result was that many Canadian ships and men went to war with minimal training and inadequate equipment. This was also partly the Admiralty's fault. In the case of radar, the RN initially agreed to send instructors to Canada to train personnel if the RCN seconded every qualified physics, mathematics, and engineering student it could enlist to train as radar officers. The RN, however, refused to return these men when requested, regardless of the severe shortage of such officers in Canadian ships and training facilities.[498]

In late 1942, NSHQ correctly argued that the lack of up-to-date equipment was the main culprit for the disproportionate losses in convoys escorted by the RCN. As with the training difficulties, the Admiralty was part of the problem, affording RCN ships a low priority in the allocation of equipment. Indeed, Nelles complained to Macdonald in 1943 that the RN had modernized its fleet "to the detriment of the RCN."[499] Macdonald may have boasted that he would have pulled the RCN out of the Atlantic if he had been informed of the equipment crisis, but this clearly would not have been an option in 1942.[500] Again using radar as an example, by December 1942, of the fifty-seven Allied warships in the North Atlantic that still required this essential equipment, forty-five (eighty percent) were Canadian.[501] This went further than just the supply of the various weapons and sensing systems to include the specifications for such systems as well.[502] Consequently, if the RCN wanted this vital equipment, the navy not only had to manufacture it but also design it.[503] Moreover, on the occasions that the Admiralty did supply specifications or prototypes to NSHQ, they were often a generation or two behind what was being used by RN vessels in the Battle of the Atlantic.[504] Exacerbating the situation, London's continued demands on the RCN for men and ships meant there was little opportunity for RCN ships to undergo refits to install the latest equipment even when it was available. Indeed, when the C Groups were pulled out of the Atlantic in early 1943 for training and upgrading, only twenty-three RCN corvettes were actually modernized.[505]

The Admiralty pointed to the heavy losses in RCN-escorted convoys in 1942 as justification for pulling the Canadians out of the North Atlantic in the winter of 1943. Yet it did not acknowledge that the St. John's-based Canadian forces escorted the slow SC convoys, which took longer to cross the Atlantic. Naturally, the enemy was able to find and remain in contact with these convoys much more easily than the faster convoys escorted by British and American escort groups. Indeed, C Groups were actually intercepted at twice the rate of the B Groups.[506] Furthermore, as has been previously mentioned, with the German's introduction of the "Triton" rotor to the *Kriegsmarine* Enigma machine in early 1942, there was a blackout in Ultra intelligence for most of the year which prevented RCN-escorted convoys from by-passing known U-boat concentrations. In January 1943, the Admiralty's *Monthly Anti-Submarine Report* pointed out that in the previous six months the RCN had borne the brunt of attacks in the Atlantic.[507] It is telling that after the RCN was pulled out of the North Atlantic, and British and American Groups took over the full burden, they fared no better than the Canadian Groups. As a matter of fact, the four hardest hit convoys during the "March Crisis"–when the Allies supposedly came closest to losing the Battle of the Atlantic–were all under British escort.[508]

While Nelles and the NSHQ deserve criticism for failing to provide proper training and equipment to the forces at sea, they should also be acknowledged for what they did accomplish. Canada was an insignificant naval power at the start of the war, but in the space of five years it built the third largest navy in the world. This unprecedented expansion could only be achieved by sacrificing quality for quantity since that was what was needed in the North Atlantic in 1941-1942. As

The "Newfyjohn" Solution

Marc Milner has noted, "[t]he significance of the RCN's contribution to the Battle of the Atlantic lay in its successful efforts to hold the line until the Allies could assume the offensive."[509] Unfortunately, the RCN could not do this and properly train and equip its ships, but Nelles and the staff at NSHQ did what they could with what they had. It is unfortunate that the British reaped the benefits of this effort without acknowledging from whence they came.

The Newfoundland Force continued to bear the brunt of the Atlantic war in early 1944 even though the enemy was an elusive foe. Throughout the winter months, the Force suffered through poor weather and short turnarounds, both of which took a toll on ships and men.[510] During the first five months of 1944, more than 300 naval vessels rotated through St. John's each month, and the naval barracks billeted a monthly average of approximately 1200 men daily. The FONF requested that layovers be increased, but this was not deemed possible by the ever-demanding Admiralty. When ice closed St. John's to traffic, escorts were diverted to Argentia.[511] Merchant vessels also suffered with the winter weather, especially the prefabricated Liberty ships, or "Kaiser's Coffins," as German propaganda labelled them.[512] Dr. Goebbels was probably not far off the mark in this characterization since these ships had a propensity to develop stress fractures in bad weather. In February, the Liberty ship SS *William Prescott* arrived in St. John's with a three-inch crack bisecting the ship behind the number two hold. Governor Walwyn was amazed that the ship had not simply broken in two. Nevertheless, the Newfoundland Dockyard welded the crack and then sent the ship on her way.[513] Regardless of such defects, approximately 400 of these "cookie-cutter" vessels were successfully escorted across the Atlantic in March.[514]

During the winter, the U-boats remained more a "fleet in being" than an actual threat. Dönitz felt that the Atlantic war had to continue despite the losses because "an extraordinarily large number of [enemy] forces [were] being tied up in this way"[515] To this end, several U-boats were posted in mid-Atlantic solely for the purpose of sending regular weather reports.[516] Their presence was revealed by sporadic wireless traffic, but their commanders demonstrated a marked reluctance to show their heads above water, so to speak, let alone to launch any attacks. Yet as Lt.-Commander A.G.S. Griffin, RCNVR, HMCS *Avalon*'s Staff Officer (Operations), noted in his monthly report, Dönitz still had "considerable sting in his U-boat arm."[517] This was amply shown when *U-538* sank the frigate HMS *Gould* of the British Support Group 1 with an acoustic torpedo during the month.[518] British and American forces continued to make kills in mid-ocean, but unsuccessful hunts off

Newfoundland and Halifax by the RCN in April for known contacts clearly showed that a "higher degree of skill than ever before" was needed for a successful conclusion.[519] Even when properly constituted and trained groups were involved, success still eluded the RCN. This was demonstrated in May with the torpedoing of HMCS *Valleyfield* and the failure to destroy the culprit off the south coast of Newfoundland.[520]

On 1 May 1944, a Liberator aircraft from No. 10 Squadron sighted *U-548* under *Kaptänleutnant* Heinrich Zimmermann east of Conception Bay. Zimmerman, thinking he had not been detected, dived and continued south. But a Salmon alert was broadcast,[521] and when *U-548* surfaced off Cape Broyle on the Southern Shore of the Avalon Peninsula late in the evening a couple of days later, the American-built destroyer/escort HMS *Hargood* was waiting. Zimmermann fired an acoustic torpedo at *Hargood* just as a Liberator aircraft from No. 10 Squadron arrived, and mistaking the aircraft's identification flare for an attack, Zimmermann fired at the plane. The Liberator thought that *Hargood* was attacking it and departed. Meanwhile, the U-boat took refuge close to the cliffs of Cape Broyle while the British warship tried to figure out who was friend or foe, staying bottomed until *Hargood* moved off about an hour later trailing her anti-torpedo, or CAT, gear.[522]

A couple of days later, Zimmermann encountered Escort Group C.1 with the Senior Officer Commander J. Byron RNR on board HMCS *Valleyfield* off the south coast on their way to Halifax after having escorted a convoy. Byron ordered the group to cease zigzagging shortly before midnight because ice condition presented a danger of collision if a ship had to zig to avoid a growler at the same time that a neighbour zagged in the ordered zigzag pattern. While understandable, this decision was unfortunate because shortly thereafter *U-548* hit *Valleyfield* with an acoustic torpedo, breaking her in two. Contrary to the Staff Officer (Operations)'s monthly report for May, C.1 did not institute the Salmon operation "immediately following the sinking of HMCS *Valleyfield*." Confusion reigned as the Officer of the Watch (OOW) of the next senior ship, HMCS *Edmundston*, tried to determine what had happened. As it was, HMCS *Giffard* was first on the scene and took over tactical command. The ships of C.1 streamed their CAT gear and started to conduct their search for *U-548*, often passing over the U-boat's position as it lay on the seafloor. Meanwhile, *Valleyfield*'s survivors were in the frigid water for almost an hour before *Giffard* broke off from the search to pick them up, and only thirty-eight of *Valleyfield*'s 165-man crew were still alive; most had died of exposure. After waiting three hours on the bottom, Zimmerman surfaced to find an empty ocean and moved off towards Halifax.[523] HMCS *Giffard* conveyed *Valleyfield*'s survivors and five bodies to St. John's, bringing the total number of distressed seamen landed at the port during the first five months of 1944 to 168, including fourteen German POWs. Funerals were held at the naval barracks for the five *Valleyfield* dead who were buried at the Joint Services Cemetery on Blackmarsh Road.[524]

With the upgrading of the Tactical Training Centre (TTC) under the 1943 expansion plan, training and advancement prospects improved at HMCS *Avalon*, and from February to the end of April twenty-two officers and more than 100 men of other ranks attended anti-submarine (A/S) training courses. In addition, a pair of two-week courses were run for petty officer and leading seamen candidates each month, resulting in eighty-three petty officer candidates and almost 250 leading seaman candidates being examined for advancement. Unfortunately, due to a shortage of staff, training for officers beyond the A/S courses was not possible.[525]

About this time, someone at NSHQ decided to ask that the British government pay Canada an agency fee for supervising the design and construction of the base at St. John's.[526] This was an odd request given that the British were already footing the bill for a facility that was exclusively Canadian. Furthermore, if the Canadians wanted to have any leverage for retaining the base after the war, such payments would in fact weaken their claim.[527] Considering NSHQ's initial offer to underwrite the base, and the Canadian government's fears of American entrenchment in Newfoundland, it is perplexing why the Canadians tried to download as much of the cost of the base as possible on the Admiralty, including furniture and household equipment.[528] Indeed, the Admiralty complained how difficult it was to get "a reasonable contribution from the Canadians."[529] The Admiralty ultimately told the Canadian government that, as far as it was concerned, Britain would be responsible for the major capital costs of the base, but the RCN would have to supply the normal "tenants' fittings which would presumably be standard items normally supplied for the Canadian Services." After all, the RCN was using the base rent-free for the duration.[530] The Admiralty used the same rationale when it came to refusing to pay an agency fee, noting that while Britain owned the St. John's base, it was always considered a Canadian base and Canada's contribution to the Battle of the Atlantic. Consequently, it felt that it was "inappropriate that [the Admiralty] should be charged an agency fee in respect to a base which is being operated entirely by the R.C.N., and without which the Canadian contribution could not have been made at all." Even more bluntly, if the Canadians wanted an agency fee, the Admiralty would start charging rent.[531] In the end, the matter was quietly dropped. After all, there were far more important events unfolding on the other side of the Atlantic.

When the Allies invaded Normandy in the early hours of 6 June 1944, Dönitz was on holiday at a hillside resort in the Black Forest. But the head of the U-Boat Arm was not caught unprepared. By the time he arrived at his headquarters just outside Berlin later that morning, his staff had already ordered the thirty-six U-boats at the Biscay bases (Brest, Lorient, St-Nazaire and La Pallice) and the twenty-two in Norway to prepare for immediate departure. A further seven stationed off Iceland were recalled, and those west of Norway were told to mark time until they received further orders. Only the eight schnorkel-equipped boats at Brest had any real prospect of getting to the invasion area, but Dönitz knew that their chances improved if they sortied with the other nine non-schnorkel boats.[532] In the meantime, the remaining Biscay boats formed a patrol line in the Bay to intercept any invasion fleet aimed at the French Atlantic coast.[533] Enigma decrypts kept the Admiralty's Operational Intelligence Centre (OIC) apprised of Dönitz's plans, and an almost unimaginable armada of naval and air forces were arrayed against the U-boats, including escort carriers, 286 destroyers, frigates and smaller A/S vessels, plus twenty-one squadrons of aircraft that flew continuous patrols over the Bay of Biscay.[534] Over the month, and despite several daring attempts, just one frigate, four freighters and a landing ship tank (LST) were sunk, and one frigate and one freighter damaged, at a cost of ten U-boats sunk, and damage to just about every other U-boat involved in the month-long operation.[535]

Some on Dönitz's staff wanted to send the surviving Biscay boats into the Atlantic even though their prospects of finding and attacking convoys were remote. They argued that the appearance of German submarines in those waters might induce the enemy to withdraw forces from the Channel to deal with them. Dönitz quite rightly disagreed, saying that such a move would only result in more losses without any results because he believed that the Allies had more than enough A/S forces available to deal with the additional threat without reducing their Channel assets. He also still feared a landing on the Biscay coast and preferred to keep the eighteen surviving boats in their pens while schnorkels were installed. Yet over the summer, as British, Canadian and American forces consolidated their gains and pushed the *Wehrmacht* out of Normandy, the Biscay bases were cut off, and the boats that survived the summer slaughter retreated to Norway with or without schnorkels.[536]

With all the activity on the other side of the Atlantic, the summer was quiet for the Newfoundland Command. The Staff Officer

The "Newfyjohn" Solution

(Operations) noted in his monthly report that the "outstanding feature of the month of June was its tranquillity." Scattered D/F readings indicated one or two U-boats were in the area, but these were "quite inoffensive and very prudent." Offensive operations against these submarines were limited to barrier patrols by aircraft, a strategy which unfortunately resulted in a few casualties among the pilots from three Merchant Aircraft Carriers (MAC) on the Grand Banks, demonstrating that the enemy was not the only danger in the North Atlantic. During the month, 267 warships passed through St. John's, and almost 1200 men were accommodated at the barracks. These figures remained fairly constant over the summer, with 248 warships and 1279 men in July and 276 ships and 1286 men in August.

In June the first large draft of Women's Royal Canadian Naval Service (WRCNS) personnel arrived in St. John's. The WRCNS, commonly referred to by their British moniker (WRENS), were formed in July 1942, and in many ways were the grease that kept Canadian naval operations moving. Modelled after their British counterparts, the Canadian Wrens took over many of the everyday duties that allowed HMCS *Avalon* to function smoothly under trying conditions: they drove staff cars and trucks through St. John's' narrow streets; coded, decoded and/or sent messages; maintained the plot in the Operations Room; handled the switchboards; made sure sailors were paid and even helped entertain them. By the end of the war, close to six hundred WRCNS served with HMCS *Avalon*, working in forty-eight trades, and the WRCNS establishment at. John's was second in size only to the one at HMCS *Stadacona*.[537]

Newfoundland was considered an "overseas posting" for these women and indeed, the hardships that many endured just getting here certainly brought this point home. However, it was the conditions they found when they arrived that really made them realize that they were on the front lines of the Battle of the Atlantic. They discovered that "being in Newfoundland was just like being in Britain. We felt under fire. We weren't really being shot at, but we could hear gunfire outside." German U-boats were an acknowledged menace, and one Wren remembers convoys being delayed in St. John's harbour for weeks because U-boats were reported just outside.[538]

In addition to rationing, blackouts, air raid drills and censorship, Wrens also had to endure the very tight security of a naval facility at war. Wrens reporting for their shifts at Fort William were met by "Navy guards carrying rifles, with fixed bayonets, [who] checked [their] passes and credentials several times" as they made their way to their work areas.[539] If any needed a further reminder that they were in a shooting war, the almost daily arrival of survivors, or worse–casualties - further exposed them to the stark realities of war. The loss of HMCS *Valleyfield*, previously mentioned, made a lasting impression on one Wren because she had attended high school with two of the "boys" on the ship.[540]

Despite the contributions, and sacrifices, these women and their counterparts in the army and air force made for the war effort, they were still subject to a malicious whispering campaign as the war dragged on. Supposedly, women in uniform were promiscuous and just interested in sex and snagging a man. The rumours had such a detrimental impact on morale and recruiting that the National Film Board (NFB) produced two shorts, *Proudly She Marches* and *Wings On Her Shoulders*. *These* films, along with a pay increase, helped restore morale and recruiting, and the various armed forces never lacked for female volunteers.[541]

One of the Wrens' most important duties at HMCS *Avalon* was to operate the training equipment at the Tactical Training Centre (TTC) and it was not long before they ran a petty officer and leading seaman course with fourteen ratings. As a result of their efforts, five Seamanship Boards promoted sixteen men to petty officer and forty-five to leading seamen. In addition, one officer attended a one-week course at the TTC. Training continued throughout the summer, with sixty-eight petty officers and leading seamen advancing in July. Unfortunately, a lack of available officers, both to teach and attend, curtailed officer training for the summer.

Meanwhile, work on the 1943 expansion plan was nearing completion by the end of September, with most delays being due to the non-arrival of essential equipment or materials. The Southside barracks and associated buildings were either complete or nearly so, awaiting the arrival of the aforementioned equipment and materials, and the improvements to the dockyard, including the various naval stores, were similarly almost complete, although again awaiting various items. The shore facilities for the floating dock were only half completed,[542] but the marine slipway at Bay Bulls had opened in April and had the advantage of being able to handle warships the size of a destroyer.[543] The Night Escort Teacher (NET) building was complete with the installation of the service equipment well in hand, and the new hospital on Topsail Road had been accepted from the contractors.[544]

By this time, the base compliment had grown to over 5000 officers and ratings including 596 Wrens.[545] By far, the largest commitment was at HMCS Dockyard which employed 1732 officers and men, followed by the Naval Barracks with 1345 including 234 Wrens,

The "Newfyjohn" Solution

the Naval Officer in Charge (NOIC) with 1194 including 328 Wrens, Captain (D) with 155 (5 Wrens) and FONF with 96 officers and ratings including 29 Wrens. The Manning Pool contained approximately 500 men, depending on demand.[546]

Despite the lull in action, the summer was not totally uneventful. A potentially serious fire started at the Imperial Oil facility on the Southside, which was contained fairly quickly using both naval personnel and vessels. This turned out to be a practice drill for an even more serious fire in Harbour Grace in August which was also quelled with the help of the navy.[547] Regardless, Enigma warnings, D/Fs, false sightings and contacts, and the apprehension that Dönitz's forces were rallying for another offensive kept Canadian forces tense.[548] No one thought that the Germans were avoiding battle because of cowardice, since they knew that "lack of courage [was] by no means an ingredient of the German character." Local commanders assumed that the Germans had accepted the power of Allied A/S measures and were simply biding their time before they once again engaged Allied forces with new weapons and tactics.[549] Intelligence showed that the *Kriegsmarine* had upgraded almost all its existing boats with schnorkels by the end of the summer; while slowing the rate of advance, this gave the U-boats back some of their invisibility. Furthermore, decrypts of both German and Japanese communications kept the OIC up to date on the fast electro-boats being built in German yards.[550] Local commanders also recognized an "awakening interest" in local waters by the enemy and anticipated some sort of offensive in the fall.[551] The tension, however, was taking its toll, and it was really not that surprising when aircraft from two MACs accompanying ONM-243 attacked the Free French submarine *La Perle* by mistake in July on her way from St. John's for refit in the United States.[552] SS *Empire MacColl* and SS *Empire MacCallum* were part of C.5 under the command of Commander George Stephen in HMCS *Dunver* as escort to ONM-243. Despite being in a safe lane and giving the correct recognition signals, the submarine was sunk with only one survivor.[553]

The expected return of U-boats to Canadian waters happened quietly in late August when *U-802* under *Kaptänleutnant* Helmut Schmoeckel surfaced 250 miles south of the Burin Peninsula, followed closely by *U-541* under *Kaptänleutnant* Kurt Petersen. In the new hostile environment of the North Atlantic, neither knew where the other was nor did they want to. Schmoeckel skirted St. Pierre and Miquelon and entered the Cabot Strait on the Newfoundland side. Despite finding patrols "extraordinarily light," the submarine was detected off Sable Island, and Canadian authorities suspected that this was not the only U-boat entering Canadian waters. This was confirmed when Petersen in *U-541* broke the St. John's-bound tanker SS *Livingston* in two with a GNAT 60 miles east of Scatarie Island Light in the first week of September. RCAF aircraft initiated a barrier patrol immediately, and Escort Group C.6 commenced a spiralling search outward from the flaming datum. By this time, however, Petersen was well inside the Gulf.[554]

Meanwhile, Schmoeckel penetrated the mouth of the St. Lawrence River by Bagot Bluff on Anticosti Island where, sitting on a thermal layer at periscope depth, he waited for prey. Unfortunately for Schmoeckel, the summer convoy cycle had ended, and coastal convoys sailed with full knowledge that U-boats were in the Gulf. To make matters worse, *U-802*'s hydrophones were inoperable, so all Schmoeckel could do was to sit in the hope that something passed by. Petersen, on the other hand, encountered a cacophony of alarms from his radar warning sets when he surfaced 28 miles south of South Point, Anticosti. Mistaking the shadow a few miles distant for an auxiliary aircraft carrier and the source of the alarms, Petersen headed for his target at full speed. Unbeknownst to the U-boat skipper, the aircraft carrier was actually the corvette HMCS *Nordsyd*, headed straight for the U-boat with a bone in her teeth and her 4-inch forward gun, 2-pound pompom, 2 20-mm oerlikons and depth charges and Hedgehogs all ready for action.[555] Alerted as to the true nature of her opponent by the flash of her 4-inch gun and the firing of star shells, Petersen dived while firing a GNAT. The GNAT's powerful end-of-run explosion misled Petersen into thinking he had sunk *Norsyd*, but this was not the case. An extensive search ensued, including EG.16, Group W-13, ships from the 71st and 79th M/L Flotillas as well as aircraft and HMCS *Magog* from Halifax. Petersen escaped undetected, passing through the middle of the Cabot Strait and after a few days patrolling south of Newfoundland, during which time he failed to intercept a large freighter, headed back to Norway.[556]

Meanwhile, in the course of a normal patrol, the frigates of Group W-13 stumbled across *U-802*'s hiding place. Thinking a convoy was coming up astern, Schmoeckel tried to slip through the screen only to be detected by HMCS *Stettler*. Schmoeckel fired a GNAT and upon hearing its detonation in *Stettin*'s wake, assumed he had made a kill. The U-boat safely avoided the expected counterattack by lying under a protective water layer at 170 metres and let the boat drift eastward with the Gaspé Current. Schmoeckel followed *U-541* through the Strait and into the deep Laurentian Channel, maintaining radio silence all the way, a tactic which caused U-Boat Headquarters to fear for its safety.[557]

The "Newfyjohn" Solution

The renewal of U-boat activity in the Canadian North West Atlantic Command (CNWAC) was actually more of an embarrassment than a threat to shipping. Contrary to the U-boat captains' claims, only one ship had actually been lost, and in the overall scheme, this was minor. What was more serious, however, was that even though the Canadian authorities knew there were at least two U-boats in the Gulf of St Lawrence and had deployed considerable resources against them, they were not able to find and sink them. This chagrin turned into more of a scandal as the fall wore on with the torpedoing of HMCS *Magog* in October and the grain carrier *Fort Thompson* in November, both victims of *U-1223*, and the sudden disappearance later in the month of HMCS *Shawinigan*, which was destroyed by a GNAT fired from *U-1228*. There were no survivors, and only six bodies were recovered.[558]

In the North Atlantic, winter weather appeared in October, scattering a number of convoys and forcing several vessels to seek the assistance of HMRT *Tenacity*. It soon became apparent that the five-ship, close-escort plan adopted for the summer months would not work during the winter because any casualties would leave the escort short-handed. As a result, Commodore Taylor, the FONF, and his staff decided to augment the C Groups with at least one frigate. This had the added advantage of giving each group an additional fast ship other than the Senior Officer, Escorts (SOE), for offensive action within the close escort. The local command also noticed that the enemy was experimenting not only with new weapons and equipment, particularly the GNAT and the schnorkel, but also with tactics. The U-boats had enjoyed tremendous success in UK waters by "bottoming," a tactic in which the submarine used wreckage and/or the contours of the seabed to disguise its presence from hunting warships and could simply lay in wait for its targets. Previous experience showed that Canadian inshore waters were particularly well suited for this tactic because thermal layers greatly inhibited ASDIC, and the various choke points were well known to the Germans. Consequently, the authorities had to consider this danger when routing convoys through shallow waters, particularly at the approaches to major ports. The authorities felt that the best defence was to conduct harassing patrols continually whether a target was confirmed or not. To this end, three frigate Escort Groups–EG.16, 25 and 27–carried out offensive operations with the co-operation of air patrols during October. With this close air/sea co-operation in mind, special classes were inaugurated in September for approximately 200 RCAF personnel in sailing and elementary seamanship in the event that they were forced down over open water. Regular seamanship and advancement courses were also scheduled at the TTC all through the fall.[559]

Poor weather continued to hamper operations in November with many convoys delayed or scattered, and coastal movements were continually restricted during the latter part of the month by strong winds. Shipping was generally not molested, but authorities were cognizant of the shallow water threat on both sides of the Atlantic. Local forces kept up offensive patrols, especially EG-16 and EG-27, and while no concrete results were forthcoming, the local command felt that the constant harassment had a detrimental effect on the crews of any U-boats in Canadian coastal waters. That a coastal offensive was imminent seemed obvious to senior officers, who felt that coastal or feeder convoys would bear the brunt. As a result, "a high degree of fluidity in the allocation of escorts" would be necessary to address it. To this end, NSHQ proposed to shift the emphasis on the allocation of resources from the Mid-Ocean Escort Force (MOEF) to the Western Ocean Escort Force (WOEF).[560]

Ashore, Commander H. Kingsley, RCN, arrived in St. John's to take up his appointment as Commander of the Port (COP) from Commander H.W. Balfour, who left for Halifax to assume his new position as Commanding Officer of HMCS *Stadacona*, something of a dubious appointment as future events would prove. In the meantime, 299 naval vessels rotated through St. John's during the month, and almost 1600 men were accommodated at the naval barracks. It was probably fortunate that the Southside Barracks were accepted from the contractors later in the month. Training continued apace, despite the bad weather. To acquaint RCAF aircrew undergoing RCN seamanship instruction with the conditions they would encounter if forced to ditch in the ocean, a dingy was put in place in Quidi Vidi Lake in front of the American Fort Pepperell. Sixteen candidates for leading seaman or petty officer attended a two-week advancement course, and two qualification boards were held which advanced seventeen to the rank of petty officer and twenty to leading seaman. Three ratings were drafted for radar courses and two for torpedo courses, while thirteen gunnery ratings were drafted for higher training. In addition, a three-week course commenced for harbour craft personnel who wanted to advance to the rating of harbour craft coxswain. Unfortunately, the course had a twenty-five percent failure rate. While off-duty, RCN personnel enjoyed a USO show at the barracks drill hall in early November, the locally produced "Up Spirits" variety show in mid-month which was attended by 12,000 people, and the Massey Harris "Combines" Musical Revue at month's end. The Thanksgiving Day parade to the Church of England Cathedral was cancelled due to inclement weather.[561]

The Submarine Tracking Room (STR) at NSHQ placed four U-Boats in Canadian waters by the first of December. Friedrich

The "Newfyjohn" Solution

Marienfeld's *U-1228* was patrolling the Cabot Strait after sinking *Shawinigan*; Hermann Lessing in *U-1231* was off Gaspé; *U-1230* under the command of *Kaptänleutnant* Hans Hilbig was southeast of Nova Scotia after having landed agents in Maine; and Klaus Hornbostel, conducting his first and only cruise in *U-806*, was headed towards Halifax. Hilbig scored the first kill of the month when he torpedoed the Canadian National Steamship's SS *Cornwallis* shortly after landing his passengers in the Gulf of Maine. But it was Hornbostel in *U-806* who enjoyed the most spectacular, and for Canadians the most frustrating, exploits. *U-806* arrived off Halifax at mid-month but did not strike until a week later when Hornbostel tracked the four-ship HHX-327 forming up for departure. His first shot missed its target, but the second hit SS *Samtuky*, which lost headway and started to settle by the stern. Hornbostel fired another torpedo which again hit its target but still did not sink it (indeed, it was eventually put back in service). Three days later, *U-806* was again off Halifax when the Halifax-to-Boston convoy XB-139 steamed out of port accompanied by the frigate HMCS *Kirkland Lake* and two Bangor minesweepers, *Clayoquot* and *Transcona*. Mistaking *Clayoquot*'s positioning manoeuvre as an attack run, Hornbostel fired a GNAT in the direction of the minesweeper and dove to fifty metres. Shortly thereafter, the minesweeper was hit astern and sank, taking eight men down with her. Following the attack, a massive hunt for the U-boat ensued; this ultimately consisted of a task force of twenty-one ships. Meanwhile, Hornbostel headed close to shore where he figured the Canadians would not expect him and bottomed his boat. After sitting quietly for ten hours, the U-boat lifted off and headed southward for deeper water. But instead of raising his schnorkel to replenish the air in the boat once the searching warships were far enough astern, Hornbostel waited another twenty-one hours before raising his schnorkel mast.[562]

Such U-boat activity off the mainland led the local command to fear that the same tactics would soon commence in Newfoundland coastal waters, particularly in the harbour approaches. Senior officers figured that after the "unpunished successes" off Halifax it was only be a matter of time before St. John's was targeted. As long as this threat remained, the authorities felt that serious thought should be given to shifting escorts from the MOEF to the Local Defence Force. They also noted that, as evidenced by the sinkings of HMCS *Clayoquot* and *Shawinigan*, the enemy no longer shied away from targeting escort vessels themselves in addition to the merchantmen they were protecting. Despite this, several offensive actions were taken during December, as C.5 hunted for a suspected U-boat around ONS-38, and HMCS *Swift*

Current investigated a periscope sighting by an American warship. Neither hunt was fruitful. Other than that, the Newfoundland Force remained on the defensive as EG.16 and EG.27 were employed as support for various convoys.[563]

Training continued to be a priority at HMCS *Avalon*. A further twenty-two ratings attended instructional classes, and three examination boards were held for fifty-four candidates (twenty-five petty officers and twenty-nine leading seamen) during December. Unfortunately, the failure rate for both ranks was fifty percent. Regardless, another twelve ratings were drafted for substantive and non-substantive training (radar, radio operators, leading torpedomen), and a second three-week Harbour Craft Coxswain's course was run with eight ratings. A daily average of thirteen merchant vessels shared the harbour with the more than 400 naval vessels that arrived or departed during the last month of 1944. The barracks accommodated a record 1616 men.[564]

By the end of 1944, the battle of the Atlantic was really all over but the shouting. Indeed, U-boat headquarters stopped making entries in its War Dairy after 15 January 1945.[565] Nevertheless, Dönitz steadfastly stuck to his strategy of sending boats into the Atlantic, particularly into coastal waters, to tie down Allied forces. One of the last major successes in the U-boat war occurred in Canadian coastal waters when *U-1232* under the command of *Kapitän sur See* Kurt Dobratz sank three ships out of the nineteen- vessel BX-14 as it entered Halifax. Despite the efforts of EG.27, Dobratz escaped and was awarded the Knight's Cross when he returned to Germany.[566] Still, this was essentially a pointless exercise since the Allies had overwhelming superiority on all fronts, and the forces the U-boats were tying down were essentially only employed in killing them. During the last four months of the war approximately 150 U-boats were lost to enemy action, a useless waste of life. Some of these were sent to Canadian waters. Actually, one of the last casualties of the war was *U-881*, which USS *Farquar* destroyed southeast of Cape Race on 6 May 1945.[567] On the Canadian side, the last RCN warship sunk by a U-boat during the war was HMCS *Esquimalt*, torpedoed by *U-190* off Halifax less than a month before the end of the war.[568] In the end, there were three U-Boats in Canadian waters when Germany finally surrendered on 8 May 1945–*U-190*, *U-889* and *U-805*. The first two surrendered to Canadian forces; U-190 was taken to Bay Bulls and *U-889* to Shelburne, NS. Even though *U-805* surrendered less than fifteen miles south of Cape Race, USN forces from Argentia took it to Casco Bay, Maine.[569]

By January, the Newfoundland Force also felt that the Atlantic

The "Newfyjohn" Solution

war was slowly dragging its way to conclusion. Senior officers acknowledged that if the U-boats continued to have success in Canadian inshore waters, it was only a matter of time before they tested the defences of St. John's. They also recognized, however, that with the relatively clear bottom along the approaches to St. John's and the minimal volume of merchant shipping moving in and out, it was unlikely that the port was subject to "as extensive a threat" as elsewhere. Consequently, aside from brief searches by TG 22.1 and W.4, no offensive operations were carried out in Newfoundland waters during the month. A false alarm in March did give the A/S organization a practice drill, though, when an RCAF aircraft reported sighting a U-boat in the vicinity of St. John's. Captain (D) despatched all available ships, and even though there were no results, the Newfoundland Command nevertheless felt that it was a beneficial exercise for both the ships involved and the operational and communications staffs ashore. This was especially so for the new communications organization which had been set up next to the Operations Room at headquarters. Deficiencies had come to light in Operation Shambles, a combined exercise involving both offensive forces and shore staffs, held in January. The false alarm in March indicated that these problems had been rectified. Actually, weather and pack ice seemed to be the main enemies during the winter months, and both caused delays which in turn shortened turnarounds for the escorts.[570] On average, 300 warships per month rotated through St. John's during the winter months, and over 1800 men were accommodated monthly at the naval barracks.[571] The short layovers also strained the base maintenance staff, which still managed to sail all mid-ocean groups on time to meet their charges during daylight hours. In an effort to prevent the complete sealing of St. John's harbour by ice, the icebreaker *Saurel* was kept on standby to sail for St. John's to open up the entrance if necessary.[572]

The Commander of US TG 22.1 and his staff and ships' commanding officers met with the FONF and his staff in April to see how RCN operations were conducted in St. John's and to exchange ideas on A/S warfare. The main topics of discussion were communications, air cover and the differing methods of operational control between RCN escort groups and US task forces. Commodore Taylor, who was surprised to learn from the TG commander that American forces had destroyed three U-boats during the month without his knowledge, complained that US operational authorities were not as forthcoming with reports of their sinkings as were Canadians.[573] Considering the RCN's lack of success in this area, however, this might have been just sour grapes.

With little more than false alarms and exercises to keep the Newfoundland Force occupied, training seemed to be a priority during the winter. Advancement courses for petty officers and leading seamen resumed, but the failure rate continued to be high at the seamanship boards. As only twenty-four of the forty-six men examined had attended the month's course, the base training officer felt that many candidates would benefit from the training, especially in the art of "taking charge of men," and that results would improve if they did so. Unfortunately, February's boards did not show any improvement. The three-week Harbour Craft Coxswain's course was more successful, and a large number of ratings were drafted for more advanced training in various technologies. At the same time, a large number of sub-lieutenants had been appointed to HMCS *Avalon* (over 2000 men were accommodated in the naval barracks in April 1945)[574], and arrangements were made to offer instruction in Extended Defence (XD), Commercial Vessel Defence (CVD) and Naval Stores in addition to the regular classes at the TTC.[575]

The end of the war was almost anti-climactic for the base at St. John's. There were the usual parties and ceremonies marking the defeat of Germany, but unlike in Halifax, VE Day passed fairly quietly. Whereas all the tensions and resentments between city residents and naval personnel exploded in an orgy of rioting and looting in that Nova Scotia port, both naval personnel and the people in St. John's merely breathed a sigh of relief that it was finally over and things could get back to normal.

The last twenty-four months of the war had been a period of growth at HMCS *Avalon*. After the climatic defeat of Dönitz's U-boats in May 1943, things were quiet as the mid-ocean groups were raided for ships to form support and hunter/killer groups in the eastern Atlantic, and the convoy cycle was opened up. By this time, the RCN was almost exclusively responsible for their safety; on average, some 300 naval vessels rotated through St. John's monthly. Fortunately, the expansion plans from the year before were progressing well, particularly at Bay Bulls which could now handle larger warships than the floating dock at St. John's. However, the U-boats were still a threat as was amply demonstrated in the spring of 1944 with the sinking of HMCS *Valleyfield* by *U-548* off the south coast of Newfoundland.

D-Day brought another lull as Dönitz once again recalled his forces to the eastern Atlantic, but this gave naval authorities time to complete the additional facilities at *Avalon* in time for the next onslaught. Recognizing that the Gulf of St. Lawrence was a hub of shipping and that its difficult ASDIC conditions gave U-boats some immunity from attack,

The "Newfyjohn" Solution

Dönitz sent some of his best young commanders to the east coast of Canada where they were particularly successful against escort vessels, sinking four by the end of hostilities. The U-boats also developed new tactics and chose to lay in wait for vessels going in or out of port, sinking a number off Halifax. Local naval authorities feared that the waters off St. John's were next and fine-tuned the combined operations apparatus. Yet aside from a few false alarms, the Newfoundland zone was quiet and remained so until the U-boats hoisted their black flags and radioed their positions in May 1945. It was somewhat appropriate that *U-190*, which sank the last RCN casualty of the war, was brought to St. John's after its surrender.

---

[468] Library and Archives Canada (LAC), Record Group (RG) 24, Flag Officer Newfoundland Force (FONF), Vol. 11,505, FONF, monthly reports, June and July 1943.

[469] V.E. Tarrant, *The U-Boat Offensive, 1914-1945* (Annapolis: Naval Institute Press, 1989), 123-124.

[470] LAC, RG 24, FONF, Vol. 11,505, FONF, monthly reports, August 1943.

[471] Marc Milner, *North Atlantic Run: The Royal Canadian Navy and the Battle for the Convoys* (Toronto: University of Toronto Press, 1985), 272-274. See also Fraser McKee and Robert Darlington, *The Canadian Naval Chronicle, 1939-1945* (St. Catharines: Vanwell Publishing, 1996), 102-105.

[472] Great Britain, National Archives (TNA/PRO), Dominions Office (DO) 35/1369, DO memorandum, August 1943. Indeed, Admiral Murray felt that the British would "sell [the Canadians] down the river" to the Americans if it would keep the latter in the Western Atlantic. Canada, FONF, RG 24, Vol. 11,979/51-15, Murray to Reid, 5 October 941.

[473] *Ibid.*, Admiralty (ADM) 6/494, British Admiralty Delegation, Washington (BAD) to Admiralty, 2 April 1943.

[474] *Ibid.*, DO 35/1369, Treasury to Clutterbuck, Dominions Office, 7 August 943.

[475] *Ibid.*, DO 35/1369, Woods to Clutterbuck, 7 August 943.

[476] *Ibid.*, ADM116/4941, Comments on extract from letter from Sir Wilfred Woods to Clutterbuck, August 1943.

[477] LAC, RG 25, Series 62, Vol. 3198, file 5206-40, Malcolm MacDonald, High Commissioner for the United Kingdom to A. Robertson, Under-Secretary for External Affairs, Ottawa, 12 April 1943. See also TNA/PRO, ADM 6/494, MacDonald to Robertson, 12 April 1942.

[478] LAC, RG 24, FONF, Vol. 11,505, War Diary of NOIC, Administrative War Diaries, 1445-102-3, sub. 1, vol. 1, May 1943.

[479] Milner, *North Atlantic Run*, 250-251.

[480] LAC, RG 24, FONF, Vol. 11,505, War Diary of NOIC, Administrative War Diaries, 1445-102-3, sub. 1, vol. 1, June, July and August 1943.

[481] *Ibid.*, RG 28, Vol. 129, File C-3-2,1 Minutes of Combined Canadian, United Kingdom and United States Committee to Examine Repair Problem for Warships and Merchant Vessels on the East Coast of Canada and Newfoundland, 12 August 1943. See also TNA/PRO, ADM 116/4941, Minutes of Combined Canadian, United Kingdom and United States Committee to Examine Repair Problem for Warships and Merchant Vessels on the East Coast of Canada and Newfoundland, 12 August 1943.

[482] Milner, *North Atlantic Run*, 252-258; and Marc Milner, *The U-Boat Hunters: The Royal Canadian Navy and the Offensive against Germany's Submarines* (Annapolis: Naval Institute Press, 1994), 49-52. For an extensive account of the equipment crisis and the back channels used to bring the issue to a head in the fall of 1943, see Richard O. Mayne, *Betrayed: Scandal, Politics and Canadian Naval Leadership* (Vancouver: UBC Press, 2006); and David Zimmerman, *The Great Naval Battle of Ottawa: How Admirals, Scientists, and Politicians Impeded the Development of High Technology in Canada's Wartime Navy* (Toronto: University of Toronto Press, 1989).

[483] HMCS *St. Croix* was first hit by a GNAT, and her survivors were rescued by her group mate, HMS *Itchen*. Unfortunately, *Itchen* was hit two days later and only one man from each crew survived.

[484] The Town-class destroyer HMCS *St. Francis* and the corvettes HMCS *Chambly, Morden* and *Sackville*. Milner, *North Atlantic Run*, 272-273.

[485] LAC, RG 24, FONF, Vol.11 ,505, Naval Control Staff Officer, report, October, November and December 1943; and War Diary of NOIC, Administrative War Diaries, 1445-102-3, sub. 1, vol. 1, October, November and December 1943.

[486] These were laid by U-220 (Barber) and claimed two ships, but U-220 was sunk two weeks later off the Azores with the loss of all hands. Modern sources claim that the U-boat laid 66 mines rather than just the 31 noted in the Administrative War Diary.Roger Sarty, *War in the St. Lawrence: The Forgotten Battles on Canada's Shores* (Toronto: Allen Lane, 2012), 256; John F. White, *U-boat Tankers, 1941-45: Submarine Suppliers to Atlantic Wolf Packs* (Shrewsbury: Airlife Publishing, 1998), 184-5; Kenneth Wynn, *U-Boat Operations of the Second World War, Vol. 1: Career Histories U1-U510* (London: Chatham Publishing, 1997), 170. Jürgen Rohwer, *Axis Submarine Successes, 1939-1945*. Cambridge: Patrick Stephens, 1983, 173. LAC, RG 24, FONF, Vol. 11,505, Naval Control Staff Officer, report, October, November and December 1943; and War Diary of NOIC, Administrative War Diaries, 1445-102-3, sub. 1, vol. 1, October, November and December 1943

[487] Mayne, *Betrayed*, 204-205.

[488] *Ibid.*, War Diary of NOIC, Administrative War Diaries, 1445-102-3, sub. 1, vol. 1, December 1943.

[489] Tony German, *The Sea is at Our Gates: The History of the Canadian Navy* (Toronto: McClelland and Stewart, 990), 6. See also Roger Sarty, "Admiral Percy W. Nelles: Diligent Guardian of the Vision," in Michael Whitby, Richard H. Gimblett and Peter Haydon (eds.), *The Admirals: Canada's*

Senior Naval Leadership in the Twentieth Century (Toronto: Dundurn Press, 2006); Mac Johnston, *Corvettes Canada: Convoy Veterans of WWII Tell Their True Stories* (Toronto: McGraw-Hill Pyerson, 1994; reprint, Toronto: John Wiley and Sons, 2008), 231-233; and Joseph Schull, *Far Distant Ships: An Official Account of Canadian Naval Operations in World War II* (Ottawa: Edmond Cloutier, 1950; 2nd ed., Toronto: Stoddart Publishing, 1987), 2-3.

[490] Milner, *U-Boat Hunters*, 51-52.

[491] Ernest R. Forbes, "Consolidating Disparity: The Maritimes and the Industrialization of Canada during the Second World War," *Acadiensis*, XV, No. 2 (Spring 1986), 3-27, argues that this was a purely partisan decision based more on politics and close personal friendships with leading central Canadian industrialists than on practical or military considerations.

[492] W.A.B. Douglas, et al., *A Blue Water Navy: The Official Operational History of the Royal Canadian Navy in the Second World War, 1943-1945, Volume II, Part 2* (St. Catharines: Vanwell Publishing., 2007), 4. Indeed, it was that the smaller section of the Vickers floating dock in Montreal was needed for new construction that NSHQ denied the BAD's request that it be sent to St. John's to help relieve repair problems there.

[493] Forbes, "Consolidating Disparity," 3-27.

[494] During the first four months of the war (September-December 1939), U-boats sank over a half million tons of British shipping, including the aircraft carrier HMS *Courageous* and the battleship *Royal Oak*, the latter at anchor at Scapa Flow. See Tarrant, *U-Boat Offensive*, 84.

[495] Johnston, Corvettes Canada, 3.

[496] Milner, North Atlantic Run, 14.

[497] *Ibid.*, 27.

[498] Zimmerman, *Great Naval Battle*, 34 and 42.

[499] Marc Milner, "Squaring Some of the Corners," in Timothy J. Runyan and Jan M. Copes (eds.), *To Die Gallantly: The Battle of the Atlantic* (Boulder, CO: Westview Press, 1994), 35.

[500] Milner, *U-Boat Hunters*, 80-82. See also Marc Milner, *Canada's Navy: The First Century* (Toronto: University of Toronto Press, 1999), 136.

[501] Zimmerman, Great Naval Battle, 84.

[502] It took the personal intervention of C.D. Howe, Canada's Minister of Munitions and Supply, with Lord Beaverbrook to obtain prototypes of the air-to-surface vessel radar being developed by the British Ministry of Aircraft Production. *Ibid.*, 66.

[503] Thanks to the lack of co-operation from the British, Canadian scientists had to practically "reinvent radar, using civilian tubes and circuitry." *Ibid.*, 33.

[504] *Ibid.*, 4, 69 and 73.

[505] Milner, U-Boat Hunters, 43.

[506] Milner, *North Atlantic Run*, 190. One other problem was that the German Intelligence service B-Dienst had broken the Admiralty's Naval Cipher 3, used by all Canadian, British and American convoy escort forces. Some have

suggested that this lapse "very nearly cost [the Allies] the war." Andrew Williams, *The Battle of the Atlantic: The Allies' Submarine Fight against Hitler's Gray Wolves of the Sea* (London: BBC Worldwide, 2002), 186.

[507] Milner, "Squaring Some of the Corners," 132.

[508] Douglas, et al., Blue Water Navy, 30.

[509] Milner, North Atlantic Run, 277.

[510] LAC, RG 24, FONF, Vol. 11,505, file 1445-102-3, vol. 1, Staff Officer (Operations), monthly reports, January, February and March 1944.

[511] *Ibid.*, monthly reports, Administrative War Diaries, January-May 1944.

[512] *Ibid.*, monthly reports, Operational War Diaries, March 1944.

[513] TNA/PRO, DO 35/357, Governor's Quarterly Report, April 1944.

[514] LAC, RG 24, FONF, Vol. 11,505, File 1445-102-3, Sub. I, Vol. 1, monthly reports, Operational War Diaries, March 1944.

[515] Minutes of the Conference of the C-in-C, Navy and the Fuehrer at Headquarters, Berghof, on April 2 and 3, 1944, in *Fuehrer Conferences on Naval Affairs, 1939-1945* (Annapolis: Naval Institute Press, 1990), 390.

[516] F.H. Hinsley, *et al.*, *British Intelligence in the Second World War* (3 vols., London: HMSO, 1970-1990), III, part 2, 238.

[517] LAC, RG 24, FONF, Vol. 11,505, file 1445-102/3, vol. 1, Staff Officer (Operations), monthly reports, January-April 1944.

[518] *Ibid.*, Staff Officer (Operations), monthly reports, March 1944. See also Clay Blair, *Hitler's U-Boat War: The Hunted, 1942-1945* (New York: Random House, 1998), 502.

[519] LAC, RG 24, FONF, Vol. 11,505, file 1445-102/3, vol. 1, Staff Officer (Operations), monthly reports, February-April 1944.

[520] *Ibid.*, May 1944. See also Marc Milner, "Inshore ASW: The Canadian Experience in Home Waters," in W.A.B. Douglas (ed.), *The RCN in Transition 1910-1985* (Vancouver: University of British Columbia Press, 1988), 143-158; and Michael L. Hadley, "Inshore ASW in the Second World War: The U-boat Experience," in Douglas (ed.), *RCN in Transition* , 127-142.

[521] During the war, the RN developed a number of search strategies for finding and destroying U-boats after they had been initially detected either through sightings, intelligence or a "flaming datum" (a torpedoed ship). The patterns varied depending upon factors such as bottom conditions but were predicated on the fact that a submerged U-boat could only travel so far for so long. Consequently, the search pattern would expand outward from the starting point and continue until the U-boat was destroyed or reached "the point of exhaustion" when it would have to surface and fight or make a run for it.

[522] CAT stood for Canadian Anti-Torpedo gear which basically consisted of three pipes on an A-shaped frame. When towed behind a ship, its loud rattle attracted German acoustic torpedoes rather than the ship's propellers. Douglas, *et al.*, *Blue Water Navy*, 421 See also W.A.B. Douglas, *The Creation of a National Air Force: The Official History of the Royal Canadian Air Force, Volume II* (Toronto: University of Toronto Press, 1986.), 579; and Michael L.

Hadley, *U-Boats against Canada: German Submarines in Canadian Waters* (Kingston: McGill-Queen's University Press, 1985), 209.

[523] McKee and Darlington, *Canadian Naval Chronicle*, 147-158. See also Douglas, *et al.*, *Blue Water Navy*, 421-425; and Douglas, *Creation of a National Air Force*, 579-580.

[524] Hadley, *U-Boats against Canada*, 217-218; and LAC, RG 24, FONF, Vol. 11,505, Commanding Officer HMCS *Avalon*, monthly report, May 1944.

[525] LAC, RG 24, FONF, Vol. 11,505, file 1445-102/3, vol. 1, Training Officer, HMCS *Avalon*, monthly reports, February-April 1944.

[526] TNA/PRO, ADM 116/4941, Admiralty to BAD, 24 July 1944.

[527] *Ibid.*

[528] *Ibid.*, ADM 116/4540, memorandum, financial responsibility, division between Admiralty and Canada, 8 December 1941.

[529] *Ibid.*, Morrison to Seal, 17 December, 1941.

[530] *Ibid.*, memorandum, financial responsibility, division between Admiralty and Canada, 8 December 1941.

[531] *Ibid.*, ADM 116/4941, Admiralty to BAD, 26 September 1944.

[532] A schnorkel was a valved tube which could be raised while a U-boat was submerged at periscope depth enabling the diesel engines to be run for propulsion rather than the batteries which had a limited life before requiring recharging. While running this way greatly reduced the boats radius of action, it provided some safety against Allied detection.

[533] V.E. Tarrant, *The Last Year of the Kriegsmarine, May 1944-May 1945* (Annapolis: Naval Institute Press, 1994), 71-80. See also Tarrant, *U-Boat Offensive*, 131-132.

[534] Tarrant, *Last Year of the Kriegsmarine*, 53.

[535] *Ibid.*, 80.

[536] *Ibid.*, 81-82. From D-Day to the end of the summer, the Admiralty estimated that forty-four U-boats took part in operations in the Channel. Of that number, twenty-five were sunk and three probably sunk, for a return of ten merchant ships, four escorts and three other commissioned ships sunk, and seven merchant ships and six naval vessels damaged. See Hinsley, *et al.*, *British Intelligence*, III, part 2, 463-466.

[537] Lisa Banister (ed.), *Equal to the Challenge: An Anthology of Women's Experiences during WW II* (Ottawa: Department of National Defence, 200), xvi.; Barbara Winters, "The Wrens of the Second World War: Their Place in the History of Canadian Service Women," in Michael L. Hadley, Rob Huebert and Fred W. Crickard (eds.), *A Nation's Navy: In Quest of Canadian Naval Identity* (Montreal: McGill-Queen's University Press, 996), 280-296; "Wren Establishment Here Second Largest in the R.C.N.," *Evening Telegram* (St. John's), 8 August 944; and Gilbert Tucker, *The Naval Service of Canada* (2 vols., Ottawa: King's Printer, 1952), II, 322. See also Verity Sweeny Purdy, *As Luck Would Have It: Adventures with the Canadian Army Show 1943-1946* (St. Catharine's, ON: Vanwell Publishing Ltd., 2003).

[538] *Equal to the Challenge*, 177.
[539] *Equal to the Challenge*, 454.
[540] *Equal to the Challenge*, 458.
[541] *Equal to the Challenge*, xvii.
[542] TNA/PRO, ADM 116/4941, HMC Naval Base, St, John's, Newfoundland, progress report for the period 1 September to 3 September 1944.
[543] *Ibid.*, DO 35/1357, Governor's quarterly report ending 30 June 1944. See also Governor's quarterly report ending 30 September 1944.
[544] *Ibid.*, ADM 116/4941, HMC Naval Base, St, John's, Newfoundland, progress report for the period 1 September to 30 September 1944.
[545] This total includes personnel posted at Botwood (109) and Bay Bulls (172), as well as a Manning Pool of approximately 500 men.
[546] LAC, RG 24, Vol. 11,949, 30-1-1-Vol. 3, Base Compliment, September 9-11, 1943, and *Ibid.*, Vol. 2, FONF to Capt. (D), NOIC, CO HMCS *Avalon*, CENC, 26 May 1943
[547] LAC, RG 24, FONF, Vol. 11,505, file 1445-102-3, sub. 1, vol. 1, monthly reports, Administrative War Diary, August 1944.
[548] Hadley, *U-Boats against Canada*, 225.
[549] LAC, RG 24, FONF, Vol. 11,505, monthly reports, Operational War Diary, July 1944.
[550] Hinsley, *et al., British Intelligence*, III, part 2, 473-487. See also Douglas, *et al., Blue Water Navy*, 446-447.
[551] LAC, RG 24, FONF, Vol. ,11505, monthly reports, Operational War Diary, August 1944.
[552] *Ibid.*, monthly Reports, Operational War Diary, July 1944.
[553] Paul Kemp, *Submarine Action* (Stroud: Sutton Publishing, 1999; reprint, London: Chancellor Press, 2000) 41-43. See also Douglas, *et al., Blue Water Navy*, 426-428.
[554] Hadley, *U-boats against Canada*, 226-234.
[555] Pompoms and oerlikons were rapid-firing weapons that could be used for anti-aircraft defence or in surface-to-surface confrontations, such as against a surfaced submarine. Hedgehog fired a cluster of mortars ahead of an attacking warship which only detonated when they struck the submerged U-boat's hull.
[556] Douglas, et al., Blue Water Navy, 429-431.
[557] Hadley, U-boats against Canada, 232-234.
[558] Nathan M. Greenfield, *The Battle of the St. Lawrence: The Second World War in Canada* (Toronto: Harper Collins, 2005), 229-234, see also McKee and Darlington, *Canadian Naval Chronicles* 93-95; Hadley, "Inshore ASW in the Second World War," 27-42; and Milner, "Inshore ASW, 43-58.
[559] LAC, RG 24, FONF, Vol. 11,505, monthly reports, Operational War Diary, September-October 1944. For a discussion of RAF/RCAF survival training and equipment, see Graham Pitchfork, *Shot Down and In the Drink: RAF and Commonwealth Aircrews Saved from the Sea, 1939-1945* (Kew:

National Archives, 2005).

[560] *Ibid.*, monthly reports, Operational War Diary, November 1944.

[561] *Ibid.*, Vol. 11,505, monthly reports, Administrative War Diary, Commanding Officer and Training Officer, HMCS *Avalon*, monthly reports, November 1944.

[562] McKee and Darlington, *Canadian Naval Chronicles*, 96-99. See also Doug M. McLean, "Muddling Through: Canadian Anti-Submarine Doctrine and Practice, 1942-1945," in Hadley, Huebert and Crickard (eds.), A Nation's Navy, 173-189; and Hadley, *U-boats against Canada*, 232-234 and 249-271.

[563] LAC, RG 24, FONF, Vol. 11,505, monthly reports, Administrative War Diary, December 1944.

[564] *Ibid.*, monthly reports, Administrative War Diary, Commanding Officer and Training Officer, HMCS *Avalon*, monthly reports, December 1944.

[565] Hadley, *U-boats against Canada*, 271.

[566] German, *Sea is at Our Gates*, 179, See also Marc Milner, *The Battle of the Atlantic* (St. Catharines: Vanwell Publishing, 2003), 220-221, and McLean, "Muddling Through," 173-189.

[567] Tarrant, *U-Boat Offensive*, 137-142.

[568] Greenfield, *Battle of the St. Lawrence*, 238-240, See also McKee and Darlington, Canadian Naval Chronicle, 220-223.

[569] Hadley, *U-boats against Canada*, 289-296.

[570] LAC, RG 24, FONF, Vol. 11,505, file 1445-102-3, sub. 2, vol. 2, monthly reports, Operational War Diary, January-March 1945.

[571] *Ibid.*, sub. 1, vol. 1, monthly reports, Administrative War Diary, January-March 1945.

[572] *Ibid.*, sub 2, vol. 2, monthly reports, Operational War Diary, January-March 1945.

[573] *Ibid.*, monthly reports, Operational War Diary, April 1945.

[574] *Ibid.* file 1445-102/3, sub 1, vol.1, Administrative War Diary, April 1945.

[575] *Ibid.*, sub. 2, vol.1, HMCS *Avalon* Training Officer, monthly reports, January-February 1945.

Conclusion

As can be seen, HMCS *Avalon* faced and overcame a number of enormous challenges. Most of them were due to one important factor. Considering that it became the RCN's most important overseas commitment, and ultimately one of the most important escort bases in the North Atlantic, there was a complete lack of initial planning. Indeed, from the Admiralty's first queries to the arrival of the first ships of the NEF and the start of operation took less than two weeks. This is really not surprising for a number of reasons. First, the base was borne out of crisis. It was the westerly advance of Donitz's U-boats, necessitating continuous convoy protection, that prompted the Admiralty's establishment of the base at St. John's. Even then, it was to be only a temporary measure until the Americans entered the war and took over all escort responsibilities in the western Atlantic. In addition, the Admiralty was considering just a small force which would have found only a dozen ships alongside at any one time. The Admiralty originally had proposed to run a sort of shuttle service between Newfoundland and Iceland. The Newfoundland Escort Force (NEF) would escort a convoy to a meeting point west of Iceland (WESTOMP); from there an Iceland-based force would escort it to the Eastern Ocean Meeting Point (EASTOMP) where it would be passed to the Royal Navy (RN).

This plan was shelved when the Admiralty decided that it was a more effective use of scarce resources to extend both the WESTOMP and EASTOMP into a Mid-Ocean Meeting Point (MOMP) and to use Iceland only for refuelling. To facilitate this, the strength of the NEF was increased to thirty destroyers, twenty-four corvettes and nine sloops; of this number, it was estimated that only sixteen would be in St. John's at any one time, but as events unfolded, it was not unusual to find more than thirty escorts alongside daily.

As has been pointed out elsewhere, St. John's had the leanest of facilities to offer the Newfoundland Escort Force in May 1941. Initially, both administrative and personnel accommodation were afloat or in rental space, and repair facilities were supplied by a depot ship and the Newfoundland Dockyard. Thus, the base was actually designed and built while operations were carried out. This was a tall order. Unlike the Americans and the Canadian Army and Air Force, who built their facilities on the sparsely populated outskirts of St. John's, the RCN had to develop its facilities in the centre of Newfoundland's capital city and major seaport. The harbour was already heavily congested with mercantile shipping and there were no vacant harbour front properties readily at hand. The RCN had to acquire land from property owners, most of whom just wanted to be left alone. In addition, negotiations were carried out through the auspices of the Newfoundland Government. Considering the state of Canada/Newfoundland relations, this was not easy. There were tensions between Canadian authorities and Newfoundland Government and city of St. John's officials, and regularly the Canadians bypassed the Newfoundland Government representatives altogether and dealt directly with the British. Nevertheless, deals were made and land purchased or leased. Often, the RCN upgraded and shared a waterfront property with its mercantile owner. Even after the land was acquired, the facilities themselves had to be built from scratch, and most of the materials and skilled labour to build them had to be imported from Canada, and this led to further problems.

Throughout its construction, and the expansion program in 1943, the base suffered from the non-arrival of necessary equipment. The naval hospital had to operate for several months during the winter of 1942 without a proper heating system which did not arrive until June. The problem had a number of causes. Of course, the most obvious is that mostly all materials and equipment had to come from Canada or the United States through waters that, from the latter's entry into the war in December 1941, became the prime hunting ground for Hitler's U-boats. Starting in January 1942, U-boats ranged from the Gulf of St. Lawrence to the Gulf of Mexico. During the first six months, hundreds of ships were sunk, all carrying valuable war supplies. In reaction to this onslaught, coastal shipping was formed into convoys which slowed shipments, and the Canadian Government was forced to close the St. Lawrence River. This in turn, meant that vital building materials and equipment earmarked for HMCS *Avalon* had to travel overland from Quebec or Ontario to the already overworked ports of St. John, New Brunswick, or Sydney and Halifax for shipment to St. John's. Even when they arrived at St. John's, the cargoes could languish in the harbour awaiting warehouse space ashore; that is if the local longshoremen were not causing problems.

As has been noted, events at sea had a drastic impact on the development of HMCS *Avalon*. With the arrival of the U-boats in Newfoundland waters, Admiral Murray had to institute local convoys even though he was already short on escorts due to their diversion to the Mediterranean for the Torch Invasion of North Africa and to escort tanker convoys to the Caribbean. Murray had to make due with what he had available: minesweepers, motor launches, rescue tugs and even Royal Navy anti-submarine trawlers in transit to the United States. This put tremendous strain on these ships and their crews which in turn overburdened the repair and replenishment facilities at St. John's.

One of the other complicating factors affecting HMCS *Avalon* was the convoluted command structure. Thanks the Anglo-American ABC 1 Agreement, the western Atlantic was under the jurisdiction of the United States. Consequently, the NEF was under the overall command of the American admiral in Argentia, Admiral Bristol. What is really confounding about this is that the United States really had few assets in the North Atlantic. Thus, you had a Canadian naval force of some 70 warships, under a Canadian Admiral, operating in traditionally Canadian waters taking direction from an American admiral who had very few of his own forces. The difficulty of this situation was more than demonstrated when, after the Japanese attack on Pearl Harbor, Bristol ordered the RCN to commence hostilities against Japan even before the Canadian Government had declared war on that country. It is indeed fortunate that Admiral Bristol was a consummate diplomat and relations between his command and the Newfoundland Command were always cordial.

However, this situation demonstrates that many of the factors affecting the development and operation of HMCS *Avalon* were really out of FONF's control. Often, FONF had to implement decisions that were made in Argentia, Ottawa, London, or Washington, sometimes without any consultation. The effects of the closure of the St. Lawrence River on base construction has already been mentioned, but there were many others. For instance, despite Murray's complaints as to the short turnaround times in harbour being experience by the WEF, in March 1942, NSHQ still decided to push WOMP further east, thus extending the WEF's time at sea and further reducing its turnaround in port. Similarly, in May 1942, Murray was forced to reduce the MOEF Groups from 14 to 12 Groups to release seven corvettes for duty escorting the newly formed tanker convoys to the Caribbean. At the same time, the Admiralty decided to reduce the number of Groups even further to eleven so as to release one of the British B Groups for the same purpose. Unfortunately, this shortened the layover time for the remaining Groups which led to crew fatigue, and congestion and repair problems at St. John's. To help relieve the pressure, Murray was forced to stagger the A, B and C Groups. This effort proved unsuccessful as there were still times that St. John's Harbour was overcrowded and others when it was empty. Of course, the most significant decision which impacted on HMCS

The "Newfyjohn" Solution

Avalon was the Admiralty's move to recall all of FONF Canadian escorts to the eastern Atlantic for training in early 1943. Supposedly, the better equipped and trained RN and USN ships would take up the strain, but unfortunately, these forces experienced the same problems of short turnaround times, damaged equipment, crew fatigue, and last minute group substitution as the RCN Groups with similar results.

As has been shown, a multitude of factors determined how HMCS *Avalon* was developed and operated. Right from the beginning, its evolution was determined by events at sea and decisions ashore, many out of the control of the FONF. Yet, despite these challenges, the base managed to keep the forces afloat in a reasonable state of readiness. Contrary to the derision and condescension of the British, the RCN accomplished exactly what it was supposed to. It held the line against the U-boats under difficult conditions when to do otherwise would have dramatically altered the course of the war. The fact that the better trained and equipped RN suffered a similar loss rate when it took over the duty in the winter of 1943 illustrates the challenges the RCN had faced. Nobody disputed that Canadian training and equipment lagged behind the RN, but the RCN persevered and deserves an important place in the history of the Battle of the Atlantic.

If the RCN "solved the problem of the Atlantic convoys," then HMCS *Avalon* solved the problem of the RCN's trans-Atlantic escorts. The transformation from a poorly defended harbour in 1939 to one of the most important escort bases in the North Atlantic at war's end was quite an accomplishment for both Canada and its Newfoundland hosts. Over the course of the war, over 500 warships, not to mention the ubiquitous motor launches, tugs and harbour craft, were posted at St. John's. The number of personnel rose from less than 1000 in 1941 to over 5000 four years later, not including the thousands of men who crewed the ships of the Newfoundland Force and were accommodated at the naval barracks of HMCS *Avalon*.

This was not accomplished in isolation from the residents of St. John's, who also had to contend with other Canadian and American armed forces. Despite suspicions and tensions between the various government and military authorities, concessions were offered and accommodations made for the sake of the war effort. The general public opened their homes, arranged activities, and volunteered at the various hostels that appeared in St. John's to take care of the visiting forces, many away from home for the first time. Overall, HMCS *Avalon* offers a unique case study in Allied "hostilities-only" naval base development during the Second World War. Hundreds of such bases ringed the North

Atlantic during the war, and some survived to the end of the Cold War. No doubt all required the co-operation of local governments and civilian populations. But in the case of HMCS *Avalon*, the base was developed in a small, fully utilized harbour, surrounded by a city already occupied by two armed forces, where most of the materials and skilled labour had to be imported through the co-operation of the British, Canadian, American and Newfoundland governments, all of whom had their own agendas. That the base was developed at all, to say nothing of reaching the operational level it did, is a truly remarkable story.

This study provides the foundation narrative for understanding the development of St. John's as a major naval facility during the Second World War. It sought to answer two important questions: How did St. John's develop from a poorly defended harbour in September 1939 to a major Allied naval base a mere two years later? Secondly, if the RCN "solved the problem of the Atlantic convoys" as suggested by Commander-in-Chief, Admiral Sir Percy Noble, then how did HMCS *Avalon* contribute to this accomplishment? This narrative has attempted to answer these questions thusly. It chronicles the evolution of the port from a mere defended harbour in 1939 through the arrival of the NEF and the creation of HMCS *Avalon* as a forward operating base in 1941 and ultimately the centre of the RCN's campaign in the Atlantic with the MOEF a year later. It was further enlarged and upgraded in 1943 as the Allies planned the invasion of Hitler's Fortress Europe and the RCN assumed sole responsibility for trans-Atlantic escort. Further, this study examines how external and internal factors determined the development and operation of HMCS *Avalon*.

Overall, several conclusions can be made. Canada developed HMCS *Avalon* as much to enhance its international stature and stake out its special interest in Newfoundland as to aid in the Allied war effort; intergovernmental suspicions and tensions, labour difficulties, events at sea, decisions ashore, and even the weather all conspired to hamper the development and/or operation of the base; and finally, despite its many difficulties, HMCS *Avalon* contributed significantly towards the RCN's success in ensuring the "safe and timely" arrival of the all-important North Atlantic convoys by providing the logistical and administrative support necessary to allow a naval force of the size and composition of the NEF/MOEF to operate on a continual basis. This was *The Newfyjohn Solution*.

About the Author

Paul W. Collins is a native Newfoundlander, with a doctoral degree in History from Memorial University of Newfoundland (MUN). He is a recognized author, speaker and consultant on Newfoundland during the Second World War and an expert on Newfoundland's role in the Battle of the Atlantic.

Dr. Collins has contributed to such respected academic journals as *The Northern Mariner, Newfoundland and Labrador Studies* and *The Newfoundland Quarterly,* as well as, the *Newfoundland and Labrador Heritage Website*. In 2010, his essay "From Defended Harbour to Trans-Atlantic Base" on St. John's' development as a Second World War naval base appeared in the award-winning *Occupied St. John's: A Social History of a City at War 1939-1945* published by McGill-Queen's University Press. *The "Newfyjohn" Solution: St. John's, Newfoundland as a Case Study of Second World War Allied Naval Base Development During the Battle of the Atlantic* is the result of extensive research at The National Archives (TNA/PRO), Kew, London, UK; Libraries and Archives Canada (LARC); the Provincial Archives of Newfoundland and Labrador (PANL); and The City of St. John's Archives.

Acknowledgements

First and foremost I thank my parents, Eileen M. and the late James J. Collins, for their tremendous support throughout my university career, and also my two children, Caitlin and Ryan, for their love and support. I would like to acknowledge the friendship, guidance, and support of my graduate supervisor, Dr. Lewis "Skip" Fischer, over the past ten years as well as that of Drs. Kurt Korneski, Mike O'Brien and Jeff Webb, who were always available to answer any of my many questions and to offer sound advice. I would like to thank the Department of History and the School of Graduate Studies at Memorial University for financial support during my graduate program.

I also owe a debt of gratitude to Dr. Marc Milner of the University of New Brunswick and Dr. Roger Sarty of Wilfrid Laurier University, both of whom have been very free with their advice and guidance over the years. I would also like to acknowledge the financial support of the Johnson Family Foundation and the Michael Harrington Foundation.

Abbreviations

A/	Acting
AA	Anti–Aircraft
A/Capt	Acting Captain
ACNS	Assistant Chief of the Naval Staff
ADM	Admiralty Document
AMC	Armed Merchant Cruiser
A/NCSO	Acting Naval Control Service Officer
AND	Admiralty Net Defence
AOC	Air Officer Commanding
ARO	Admiralty Record Office
A/S	Anti–Submarine
A/SO (CO)	Acting Staff Officer (Combined Operations)
A/T	Anti–Torpedo
BAD	British Admiralty Delegation
BATM	British Admiralty Technical Mission
BDO	Boom Defence Officer
BPC	Base Planning Committee
CAMS	Catapult Aircraft Merchant Ships
Capt. (D)	Captain (Destroyers)
CAS	Chief of the Air Staff
CCCS	Captain (later Commodore) Commanding Canadian Ships and Establishments in the United Kingdom
CCNF	Commodore Commanding Newfoundland Force
CCO	Communications, Coding and Ciphering Arrangements
Cdr	Commander
Cdr. (D)	Commander (Destroyers)
Cdre.	Commodore
CGS	Canadian Government Ship
CHOP Line	Change of Operational Control Line near 47th Meridian divided the British and Canadian areas of responsibility

C–in–C	Commander in Chief
C–in–C, A and WI	Commander in Chief, Atlantic and West Indies Station
C–in–C, CNA	Commander in Chief, Canadian Northwest Atlantic
CINCLANT	Commander in Chief, US Atlantic Fleet
CNEC	Chief of Naval Engineering and Construction
CNES	Chief of Naval Equipment and Supply
CNMO	Canadian Naval Mission Overseas
CNO	Canadian Naval Order
CNP	Chief of Naval Personnel
CNS	Chief of the Naval Staff
CNW	Canadian Naval War Plan
CO	Commanding Officer
COAC	Commanding Officer Atlantic Coast
COMINCH	Commander in Chief, US Fleet
Commander (D)	Commander (Destroyers)
Comm. of Customs	Commissioner of Customs
COP	Commander of Port; Captain of Port
CPO	Chief Petty Officer
CSC	Chiefs of Staff Committee
CTF	Commander Task Force
CWSF	Commander Western Sea Frontier
D.A/S	Director of Anti–submarine
D/C	Depth Charge
D/C D	Depth Charge Driller
DCNP	Deputy Chief of Naval Personnel
DCNS	Deputy Chief of the Naval Staff
D/DEMS	Director of Defensively Equipped Merchant Ships
DEMS	Defensively Equipped Merchant Ships
DG	Degaussing Gear
D/G	Degaussing
DHD	Director of Harbour Defence
DNI	Director of Naval Intelligence

DNI and P	Director of Naval Intelligence and Plans
DNI and T	Director of Naval Intelligence and Trade
DNO	Director of Naval Ordnance
DNOT	Director of Naval Operations and Training
DNP	Director of Naval Personnel
DNS	Director of Naval Stores
DNT	Director of Naval Training
DOD	Director of Operations Division
D of P	Director of Plans
D of T	Director of Trade
DO	Dominions Office
DPD	Director of Plans Division
DSD	Desirable Sailing Date
DSR	Director of Ship Repairs
DTD	Director of Trade Division
D WRCNS	Director of Women's Royal Canadian Naval Service
DWS	Director of Women's Service
DWT	Director of Warfare and Training; Director of Weapons and Tactics
EA	Electrical Artificer
EAM/BMO	Electrical Anti–mining Base Maintenance Officer
EASTOMP	Eastern Ocean Meeting Point
EG	Escort Group
E–in–C	Engineer in Chief
ERA	Engine Room Artificer
ER Ratings	Engine Room Ratings
FEO	Fleet Engineer Officer
FONF	Flag Officer, Newfoundland Force
FR	Fishermen's Reserve
(G)	Gunnery
GN	Government of Newfoundland Document
Gunner (T)	Torpedo Gunner
HF/DF	High Frequency Direction Finding

HMCS	His Majesty's Canadian Ship
HMS	His Majesty's Ship
HMT	His Majesty's Transport
HMRT	His Majesty's Rescue Tug
HQ	Headquarters
IE	Increased Endurance
LARC	Library and Archives Canada
LCT	Landing Craft Tank
Lieut.	Lieutenant
LN	Quebec–Labrador convoy
LST	Landing Ship Tank
LTO	Leading Torpedoman
MAC	Merchant Ship Aircraft Carrier
M and S	Munitions and Supply
M A/S TU	Mobile ASDIC Training Unit
MCI	Mercantile Convoy Instructions
MGB	Motor Gun Boat
M/L	Motor Launch
MO	Medical Officer
MOEF	Mid–Ocean Escort Force
MOIC	Maintenance Officer in Charge
MOMP	Mid–Ocean Meeting Point
M/T	Motor Transport
MTB	Motor Torpedo Boat
MWT	(British) Ministry of War Transport
NCSO	Naval Control Service Officer
NEF	Newfoundland Escort Force
NET	Night Escort Trainer
NL	Labrador–Quebec convoy
NOB	Naval Operating Base
NOIC	Naval Officer in Charge
NRC	National Research Council
NSHQ	Naval Service Headquarters
NSO	Naval Stores Officer

The "Newfyjohn" Solution

OIC	Operational Intelligence Centre
ON	United Kingdom–North America convoy
ONS	United Kingdom–North America slow convoy
OOD	Officer of the Deck
PANL	Public Archives of Newfoundland and Labrador
PDO	Port Defence Officer
PJBD	Permanent Joint Board on Defence
PMO	Principal Medical Officer
PO	Petty Officer
PRO	Public Records Office
QS	Quebec–Sydney convoy
RA 3rd BS	Rear Admiral Third Battle Squadron
RCA	Royal Canadian Artillery
RCAF	Royal Canadian Air Force
RCMP	Royal Canadian Mounted Police
RCN	Royal Canadian Navy
RCNB	Royal Canadian Naval Barracks
RCNR	Royal Canadian Naval Reserve
RCNVR	Royal Canadian Naval Volunteer Reserve
RDF	Radio Direction Finding (later Radar)
RDFO	Radio Direction Finding Officer
RG	Record Group
RN	Royal Navy
RNR	Royal Naval Reserve
RNVR	Royal Naval Volunteer Reserve
R/T	Radio Telephony
SBD	Superintendent of Boom Defence
SBT	Submarine Bubble Target
SC	New York (Halifax, Sydney)–U.K. convoy
SCFO (O)	Senior Canadian Flag Officer (Overseas)
SCNO	Senior Canadian Naval Officer
S/D	Submarine Detector
SDI	Submarine Detector Instructor
SNO	Senior Naval Officer

SO	Senior Officer; Signal Officer
SOE	Senior Officer Escorts
SO (CO)	Staff Officer (Combined Operations)
SO (I)	Staff Officer (Intelligence)
SO (O)	Staff Officer (Operations)
SO (P)	Staff Officer (Plans)
SQ	Sydney–Quebec convoy
SSB	Superintendent of Shipbuilding
ST	Seaman Torpedoman
STO	Squadron Torpedo Officer
TF	Task Force
TGM	Torpedo Gunner's Mate
TNA	The National Archives (UK)
TTC	Tactical Training Centre
UG	United States–Gibraltar convoy
UK	United Kingdom
USCG	United States Coast Guard
USN	United States Navy
USNR	United States Naval Reserve
USO	United Service Organization
VCNS	Vice Chief of the Naval Staff
VLR	Very Long Range
V/S	Visual Signalling
WACI	Western Approaches Convoy Instructions
WESTOMP	Western Ocean Meeting Point
WEF	Western Escort Force
WO	Watch Officer
WRCNS	Women's Royal Canadian Naval Service
WRNS	Women's Royal Naval Service (Wrens)
WSF	Western Support Force
W/T	Wireless Telegraphy
XB	Halifax–Boston Convoy
XDO	Extended Defence Officer
XO	Executive Officer

Maps and Photographs

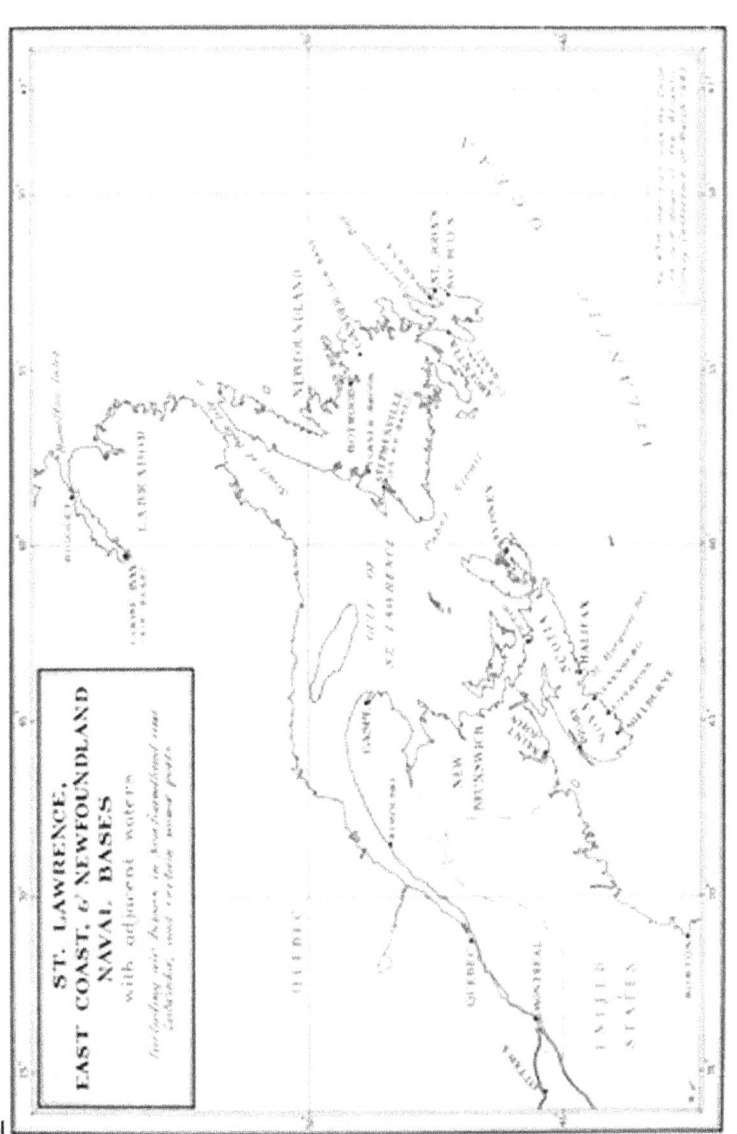

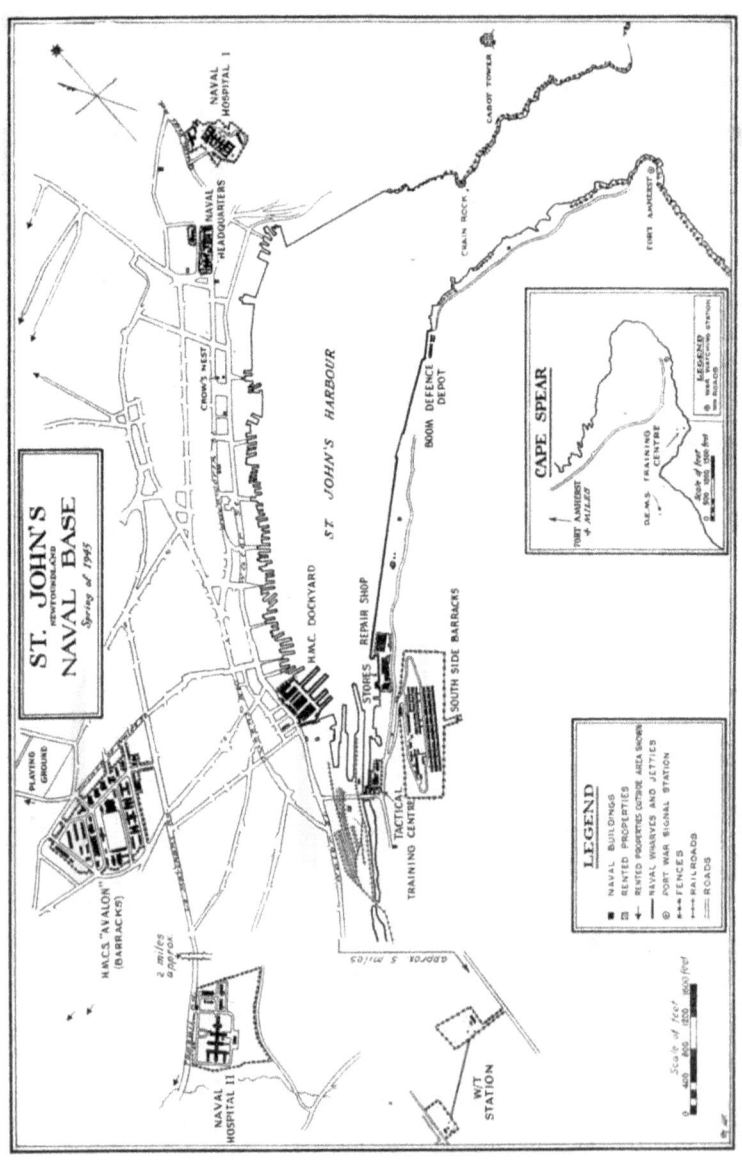

St. John's, Newfoundland, Naval Base, Spring of 1945 (Naval Service of Canada, Volume 2; Tucker, G.N., Ottawa, 1952)

The "Newfyjohn" Solution

Chief of Naval Staff (CNS)
Admiral Percy Nelles RCN

FONF Admiral Leonard Murray RCN

Newfoundland Commissioner of Justice & Defence L. Edward Emerson

Newfoundland Governor
Admiral Sir Humphrey Walwyn RN

Admiral Murray, Governor Walwyn, Comdr. James D. Prentice, Mrs. Prentice

Comdr. James D. "Chummy" Prentice

Captain "D" E. R. Mainguy, RCN

The "Newfyjohn" Solution

Founder of the 'Crow's Nest'
Vice-Admiral E.R. Mainguy,
R.C.N
(July 1951)

St. John's Harbour, Newfoundland during the Second World War. Painting by Thomas Beamont [Beaverbrook Collection of War Art, Canadian War Museum, artifact # 19710261 - 1048] Reproduced with permission.

Bibliography

Adams, Thomas A. "The Control of British Merchant Shipping." In Howarth, Stephen and Law, Derek (eds.). *The Battle of the Atlantic, 1939–1945: The 50th Anniversary International Naval Conference.* Annapolis: Naval Institute Press, 1994, pp. 158–178.

Armstrong, John Griffith. *The Halifax Explosion and the Royal Canadian Navy: Inquiry and Intrigue.* Vancouver: UBC Press, 2002.

Badgley, Kerry. "'Rigorously Applied in Practice:' A Scorched Earth Policy for Canada and Newfoundland during the Second World War." *The Archivist*, No. 446 (1998), pp. 38–43.

Bannister, Jerry. *The Rule of the Admirals: Law, Custom and Naval Government in Newfoundland, 1699–1832.* Toronto: University of Toronto Press, 2003.

Bannister, Lisa (ed.). *Equal to the Challenge: An Anthology of Women's Experiences during World War II.* Ottawa: Department of National Defence, 2001.

Barton, Jonathan. *A History of Ulster.* Belfast: Blackstaff Press, 1992; rev. ed., Belfast: Blackstaff Press, 2005.

Bassler, Gerhard P. *Vikings to U–Boats: The German Experience in Newfoundland and Labrador.* Montreal: McGill–Queen's University Press, 2006.

Beatty, David. "'The Canadian Corollary' to the Monroe Doctrine and the Ogdensburg Agreement of 1940." *The Northern Mariner/Le Marin du nord*, I, No. 1 (1991), pp. 3–22.

Beeby, Dean. *Cargo of Lies: The True Story of a Nazi Double Agent in Canada.* Toronto: University of Toronto Press, 1996.

Bergsma, Daniel. "Sex in Newfoundland: A US Army View." In Granatstein, J.L. and Hillmer, Norman (eds.). *First Drafts: Eyewitness Accounts from Canada's Past.* Toronto: Thomas Allen Publishers, 2002.

Bishop, Chris. *Kriegsmarine U–Boats 1939–45: The Essential Submarine Identification Guide.* London: Amber Books, 2006.

Blair, Clay. *Hitler's U–Boat War: The Hunted, 1942–1945.* New York: Random House, 1998.

_____. *Hitler's U–Boat War: The Hunters, 1939–1942.* New York: Random House, 1996.

Blake, John W. *Northern Ireland in the Second World War.*

Belfast: HMSO, 1956; reprint, Belfast: Blackstaff Press, 2000.

Borden, Robert Laird. *Letters to Limbo*. Henry Borden (ed.). Toronto: University of Toronto Press, 1971.

Boutilier, James A. (ed.). *The RCN in Retrospect, 1910–1968*. Vancouver: University of British Columbia Press, 1982.

Bradham, Randolph. *Hitler's U–Boat Fortresses*. Westport, CT: Praeger Press, 2003.

Brebner, John Bartlett. *North Atlantic Triangle: The Interplay of Canada, the United States, and Great Britain*. New Haven: Yale University Press, 1945.

Bridle, Paul (ed.). *Documents on Relations between Canada and Newfoundland*. 2 vols. Ottawa: Department of External Affairs, 1974–1984.

Brown, Robert Craig. *Robert Laird Borden: A Biography*. 2 vols. Toronto: Macmillan of Canada, 1975.

Brock, P. Willet. "Commander E.A.E. Nixon and the Royal College of Canada." In Boutilier, James A. (ed.). *The RCN in Retrospect, 1910–1968*. Vancouver: University of British Columbia Press, 1982, pp. 33–43.

Brodeur, Nigel. "L.P. Brodeur and the Origins of the Royal Canadian Navy." In Boutilier, James A. (ed.). *The RCN in Retrospect, 1910–1968*. Vancouver: University of British Columbia Press, 1982, pp. 13–32.

Byers, Daniel. "Canada's 'Zombies:' A Portrait of Canadian Conscripts and Their Experiences during the Second World War." In Horn, Bernd (ed.). *Forging a Nation: Perspectives on the Canadian Military Experience*. St. Catharines: Vanwell Publishing, 2002, pp. 155–176.

Cadigan, Sean T. *Newfoundland and Labrador: A History*. Toronto: University of Toronto Press, 2009.

Caldwell, R.H. "The VE Day Riots in Halifax, 7–8 May 1945." *The Northern Mariner/Le Marin du nord*, X, No. 1 (January 2000), pp. 3–20.

Cameron, James M. *Murray: The Martyred Admiral*. Hantsport, NS: Lancelot Press, 1980.

Canada. Department of National Defence. Directorate of History and Heritage. Flag Officer Monthly Reports, NSS–1000–5–20, Vol. I.

_____."Harbour Training in St. John's - Summary of General Development." 28 June 1945. NHS 8000.

_____. Lt. Stuart Keats, "The Royal Canadian Navy in Newfoundland, 1940–1944." October 1944, NHS 8000.

_____. Flag Officer Monthly Report on Proceedings, NSS–1000–5–13.5, various years.

_____. Flag Officer Monthly Report on Proceedings, NSS–1000–5–20, various years.

_____. Directorate of History and Heritage. DHH81/520/1440–166/25 II (1).

Canada. Library and Archives Canada. Record Group 28, Vol. 129, File C–3–21, Minutes of Combined Canadian, United Kingdom, and United States Committee to Examine Repair Problem for Warship and Merchant Vessels on the East Coast of Canada and Newfoundland, 12 August 1943.

_____. RG 25, Series 62, Vol. 3198, File 5206–40.

_____. Flag Officer Newfoundland Force (FONF) RG 24, Vol. 3892, NSS1033–6–1, Pt. 1.'Nfld. Convoy Escort Forces. Gen. Data and Correspondence.'

_____. FONF, RG 24, Vol. 5256, File HQS–22–1–13.

_____. FONF, RG 24, Vol. 11,505, File MS1550–14631–1.

_____. FONF, RG24, Vol. 11, 505, Monthly Reports, 1445–100–3, Vol. 1.

_____. FONF, RG24, Vol. 11, 505, Monthly Reports, 1445–102–3, Sub1, Vol.1.

_____. FONF, RG24, Vol. 11, 505, Monthly Reports, 1445–102–3, Sub 2, Vol.2.

_____. FONF, RG24, Vol. 11,505; 335.4.1, Vol. 1.

_____. FONF, RG 24, Vol. 11,927, MS1400–4, Vol. 1.

_____. FONF, RG 24, Vol. 11,949.

_____. FONF, RG 24, Vol. 11,951.

_____. FONF, RG 24, Vol. 11,953, File 1–1–1, Vol. I.

_____. FONF, RG 24, Vol. 11,956.

_____. FONF, RG 24, Vol. 11,956, NFM 2–8.

Cardolis, John N. *A Friendly Invasion: The American Military in Newfoundland, 1940 to 1990*. St. John's: Breakwater Books, 1990.

_____. *A Friendly Invasion II: A Personal Touch*. St. John's: Creative Publishers, 1993.

Carroll, Joseph T. *Ireland in the War Years 1939–1945*. Newton

Abbot: David and Charles, 1975.

Churchill, Winston S. *The Second World War: The Hinge of Fate*, 11th ed. New York: Bantam Books, 1962.

_____. *The Gathering Storm*. 18th ed. New York: Bantam Books, 1961.

Christie, Carl A. *Ocean Bridge: The History of RAF Ferry Command*. Toronto: University of Toronto Press, 1997.

City of St. John's Archives. Jackman Collection, MG40, 2–2–2, File 38.

Collins, Paul. "Fortress Newfoundland: How the Fear of Nazi Attack Turned Newfoundland into an Armed Camp During the Second World War," *Newfoundland and Labrador Studies*, XXVI, No. 2, (Fall 2011), pp. 197–213.

_____."The Battle for Bell Island: The U–boat Attacks at Wabana, Bell Island in the Fall of

1942 and Their Impact on the People of Newfoundland," *The Newfoundland Quarterly*, Vol. 104, No. 3, (Fall 2011), pp. 48–53.

_____. "From Defended Harbour to Transatlantic Base." In High, Steven (ed.). *Occupied St. John's: A Social History of a City at War, 1939–1945*. Montreal: McGill–Queen's University Press, 2010, pp. 81–109.

_____. "'Canada's Plan to Torch St. John's during the Second World War: Upper Canadian Arrogance or Tabloid Journalism?" *Newfoundland and Labrador Studies*, XXIV, No. 2 (Fall 2009), pp. 261–270.

_____. "'First Line of Defence:' The Establishment and Development of St. John's, Newfoundland, as the Royal Canadian Navy's Premier Naval Base in the Second World War." *The Northern Mariner/Le Marin du nord*, XVI, No. 3 (July 2006), pp. 15–32.

Conn, Stetson; Engelman, Rose C.; and Fairchild, Byron. *Guarding The United States and Its Outposts*. Washington, DC: Office of the Chief of Military History, 1964; reprint, Washington, DC: US Government Printing Office, 2000.

Dönitz, Karl. *Memoirs: Ten Years and Twenty Days*. Annapolis: Naval Institute Press, 1990.

Douglas, W.A.B. *The Creation of a National Air Force: The Official History of the Royal Canadian Air Force*. Volume II. Toronto: University of Toronto Press, 1986.

_, et al. *No Higher Purpose*: *The Official Operational History of*

the Royal Canadian Navy in the Second World War, 1939–1945, Volume II, Part 1. St. Catharines: Vanwell Publishing, 2002.

_____, et al. *A Blue Water Navy: The Official Operational History of the Royal Canadian Navy in the Second World War, 1939–1945.* Volume II, Part 2. St. Catharines: Vanwell Publishing, 2007.

_____ (ed.) *The RCN in Transition, 1910–1985.* Vancouver: University of British Columbia Press, 1988.

Duley, Margaret. *The Caribou Hut.* Toronto: Ryerson Press, 1949.

Dunmore, Spencer. *In Great Waters: The Epic Story of the Battle of the Atlantic, 1939–45.* Toronto: McClelland and Stewart, 1999.

Dyer, Gwynne. "The Strategic Importance of Newfoundland and Labrador to Canada." In Newfoundland. *Royal Commission on Renewing and Strengthening Our Place in Canada.* St. John's: Government of Newfoundland and Labrador, 2003.

Easton, Alan. *50 North: An Atlantic Battleground.* London: Eyre and Spottiswoode, 1963; 2nd ed. Markham, ON: Paperjacks, 1980.

Eayrs, James (ed.) *In Defence of Canada.* 3 vols. Toronto: University of Toronto Press, 1965.

Edwards, Bernard. *Dönitz and the Wolfpacks.* London: Arms and Armour Press, 1996; reprint, London: Brockhampton Press, 1999.

Erskine, Ralph, "Breaking German Naval Enigma on Both Sides of the Atlantic." In Smith, Michael and Erskine, Ralph (eds.). *Action This Day: Bletchley Park from the Breaking of the Enigma Code to the Birth of the Modern Computer.* London: Bantam Press, 2001, pp. 174–196.

Evening Telegram (St. John's). 1939–1945.

Facey–Crowther, David. "Newfiejohn: Garrison Town." Unpublished paper presented at the Newfoundland Museum Lecture Series, St. John's, June 1995.

Farago, Ladislas. *The Tenth Fleet: The True Story of the US Navy's "Phantom" Fleet Battling U–Boats during World War II.* New York: Drum Books, 1986.

Fingard, Judith. *Jack in Port: Sailortowns of Eastern Canada.* Toronto: University of Toronto Press, 1982.

Fisher, Robert C. "'We'll Get Our Own:' Canada and the Oil Shipping Crisis of 1942." *The Northern Mariner/Le Marin du nord,* III, No. 2 (April 1993), pp. 33–39.

FitzGerald, John Edward. "'The Difficult Little Island' that 'Must Be Taken In:' Canadian Interest in Newfoundland During World

War Two." *Newfoundland Quarterly*, XCIV, No. 2 (Spring 2001), 21–28.

Forbes, Ernest R. "Cutting the Pie into Smaller Pieces: Matching Grants and Relief in the Maritime Provinces during the 1930s." *Acadiensis*, XVII, No. 1 (Autumn 1987), pp. 34–55.

____. "Consolidating Disparity: The Maritimes and the Industrialization of Canada during the Second World War." *Acadiensis*, XV, No. 2 (Spring 1986), pp. 3–27.

Forward, E.G. "Leadmark to Confederation: The Second World War Militarization of Newfoundland." Unpublished MA Thesis, Canadian Forces College, 2009.

Fraser, A. *History of the Participation of Newfoundland in World War II*. Peter Neary and

Melvin Baker (eds). St John's: Centre for Newfoundland Studies, 2010.

Fuehrer Conferences on Naval Affairs 1939–1945. Annapolis: Naval Institute Press, 1990.

Gannon, Michael. *Black May: The Epic Story of the Allies' Defeat of the German U–Boats in May 1943*. New York: Harper Collins, 1998.

____. *Operation Drumbeat: The Dramatic True Story of Germany's First U–boat Attacks along the American Coast in World War II*. New York: Harper and Row, 1990.

German, Tony. *The Sea is at Our Gates: The History of the Canadian Navy*. Toronto: McClelland and Stewart, 1990.

Gibson–Harris, Derrick. *Life–Line to Freedom: Ulster in the Second World War*. Lurgan: Ulster Society, 1990.

Gilmore, William C. "Law, Constitutional Convention, and the Union of Newfoundland with Canada," *Acadiensis*, XVIII, No. 2 (Spring 1989), pp. 111–126.

Glover, William. "The RCN: Royal Colonial or Royal Canadian Navy?" In Hadley, Michael L.; Huebert, Rob; and Crickard, Fred W. (eds.). *A Nation's Navy: In Quest of a Canadian Naval Identity*. Montreal: McGill–Queen's University Press, 1996, pp. 71–90.

Goodhart, Philip. *Fifty Ships that Saved the World: The Foundation of the Anglo–American Alliance*. New York: Doubleday and Co., 1965.

Goodspeed, Donald (ed.). *The Armed Forces of Canada, 1867–1967: A Century of Achievement*. Ottawa: Queen's Printer, 1967.

Gough, Barry M. "The End of *Pax Britannica* and the Origins of the Royal Canadian Navy: Shifting Strategic Demands of an Empire at Sea." In Douglas, W.A.B. (ed.). *The RCN in Transition, 1910–1985*. Vancouver: University of British Columbia Press, 1988, pp. 90–102.

_and Sarty, Roger. "Sailors and Soldiers: The Royal Navy, the Canadian Forces, and the Defence of Atlantic Canada, 1890–1918." In Hadley, Michael L.; Huebert, Rob; and Crickard, Fred W. (eds.). *A Nation's Navy: In Quest of a Canadian Naval Identity*. Montreal: McGill–Queen's University Press, 1996, 112–130.

Granatstein, J.L. *Canada's War: The Politics of the Mackenzie King Government, 1939–1945*. Toronto: Oxford University Press, 1975.

_____. and Neary, Peter (eds.). *The Good Fight: Canadians and World War II*. Toronto: Copp Clark, 1995.

Great Britain. Ministry of Information. *What Britain Has Done 1939–1945*. London: HMSO, 1945; reprint, London: Atlantic Books, 2007.

_. National Archives. Admiralty 116/4387. Copies at National Defence Headquarters, Ottawa, Directorate of History and Heritage.

_____. . Admiralty File ADM 1/4387.

_____. . Admiralty File ADM 1/4388.

_. . Admiralty File ADM 1/10608.

_____. . Admiralty File ADM 116/4409.

_____. . Admiralty File ADM 116/4526.

_____. . Admiralty File ADM 116/4540.

_____. . Admiralty File ADM 116/4540, Minute Series M 1272/42.

_____. . Admiralty File ADM 116/4701.

_____. . Admiralty File ADM 116/4941

_____. . Admiralty File ADM 116/4941, British Merchant Shipping Mission.

_____. . Admiralty File ADM 199/2096, Review of the U–Boat War For The Year 1943.

_____. . Cabinet File CAB 122/85.

_____. . Dominions Office File DO 35/1354, Governor's Quarterly Report, Jan. 1943.

_____. . Dominions Office File DO 35/1355, Governor's Quarterly Report June 1943.

_____. . Dominions Office File DO 35/1357, Governor's Quarterly Report April 1944.

_____. . Dominions Office File DO 35/1357, Governor's Quarterly Report June 1944.

_____. . Dominions Office File DO 35/1358, Governor's Quarterly Report Oct.1944.

_____. . Dominions Office File DO 35/1358, Governor's Quarterly Report Dec. 1944.

_____. . Dominions Office File DO 35/1359, Governor's Quarterly Report April 1945.

_____. . Dominions Office File DO 35/1359, Governor's Quarterly Report June 1945.

_____. . Dominions Office File DO 35/1368.

_____. . Dominions Office File DO 35/1369.

_____. . Prime Minister's Office. Premier 4/44/3, Parliamentary Mission to St. John's.

_____. . War Office. WO 106/4874, Memorandum on "The Defence of Canada."

Greenfield, Nathan M. *The Battle of the St. Lawrence: The Second World War in Canada*. Toronto: Harper Collins, 2005.

Grove, Eric J. (ed.). *The Defeat of the Enemy Attack on Shipping, 1939–1945*. Naval Records Society Vol. 137. Aldershot: Ashgate Publishing, 1997.

Hadley, Michael L. "The Popular Image of the Canadian Navy." In Hadley, Michael L.; Huebert, Rob; and Crickard, Fred W. (eds.). *A Nation's Navy: In Quest of Canadian Naval Identity*. Montreal: McGill–Queen's University Press, 1996, pp. 35–56.

_____. *U–Boats against Canada: German Submarines in Canadian Waters*. Montreal/Kingston: McGill–Queen's University Press, 1985.

_____. "Inshore ASW in the Second World War: The U–boat Experience." In Douglas, W.A.B. (ed.). *The RCN in Transition, 1910–1985*. Vancouver: University of British Columbia Press, 1988, pp. 127–142.

_____; Huebert, Rob; and Crickard, Fred W. *A Nation's Navy: In Quest of Canadian Naval Identity*. Montreal: McGill–Queen's University Press, 1996.

_____ and Sarty, Roger. *Tin Pots and Pirate Ships: Canadian*

Naval Forces and German Sea Raiders, 1880–1918. Montreal: McGill–Queen's University Press, 1991.

Hague, Arnold. *The Allied Convoy System, 1939–1945: Its Organization, Defence and Operation*. St. Catharines: Vanwell Publishing, 2000.

Halford, Robert G. *The Unknown Navy: Canada's World War II Merchant Navy*. St. Catharines: Vanwell Publishing, 1995.

Hall, H. Duncan. *Commonwealth: A History of the British Commonwealth of Nations*. London: Van Nostrand Reinhold, 1971.

_____. *North American Supply*. London: HMSO, 1955.

Hansen, Kenneth P. "Kingsmill's Cruisers: The Cruiser Tradition in the Early Royal Canadian Navy." *The Northern Mariner/Le Marin du nord*, XIII, No. 1 (January 2003), pp. 37–52.

_____. "The Superior–Simple Ship Fleet Construct," *Canadian Naval Review*, III, No. 2 (Summer 2007), pp. 4–7.

Hennessy, Michael. "The Industrial Front: The Scale and Scope of Canadian Industrial Mobilization during the Second World War." In Horn, Bernd (ed.). *Forging a Nation: Perspectives on the Canadian Military Experience*. St. Catharines: Vanwell Publishing 2002, pp. 135–154.

Hessler, Günther. *The U–Boat War in the Atlantic, 1939–1945*. 3 vols. London: HMSO, 1989.

Hickam, Homer H., Jr. *Torpedo Junction: U–Boat War off America's East Coast, 1942*. Annapolis: Naval Institute Press, 1989.

High, Steven. *Base Colonies in the Western Hemisphere, 1940–1967*. New York: Palgrave Macmillan, 2009.

_. "Rethinking the Friendly Invasion." In High, Steven (ed.). *Occupied St. John's: A Social History of a City at War, 1939–1945* Montreal: McGill–Queen's University Press, 2010, pp. 151–190.

_(ed.). *Occupied St. John's: A Social History of a City at War, 1939–1945*. Montreal: McGill–Queen's University Press, 2010.

Hinsley, F.H., et al. *British Intelligence in the Second World War: Its Influence on Strategy and Operations*. 4 vols. London: HMSO, 1979–1990.

Hirschmann, Werner with Graves, Donald E. *Another Place, Another Time: A U–Boat Officer's Wartime Album*. Annapolis: Naval Institute Press, 2004.

Horn, Bernd (ed.). *Forging a Nation: Perspectives on the Canadian Military Experience*. St. Catharines: Vanwell Publishing,

2002.

_____ and Harris, Stephen (eds.). *Warrior Chiefs: Perspectives on Senior Canadian Military Leaders*. Toronto: Dundurn Press, 2001.

Horth, Lillie B. and Horth, Arthur C. *101 Things to Do In War Time 1940*. London: B.T. Batsford, 1940; reprint, London: B.T. Batsford, 2007.

How, Douglas. *Night of the Caribou*. Hantsport, NS: Lancelot Press, 1988.

Howarth, Stephen and Law, Derek (eds.). *The Battle of the Atlantic, 1939–1945: The 50th Anniversary International Naval Conference*. Annapolis: Naval Institute Press, 1994.

Hunt, Barry D. "The Road to Washington: Canada and Empire Naval Defence, 1918–1921." In Boutilier, James A. (ed.). *The RCN in Retrospect, 1910–1968*. Vancouver: University of British Columbia Press, 1982, pp. 49–57.

Hunter, Mark C. *To Employ and Uplift Them: The Newfoundland Naval Reserve, 1899–1926*. St. John's: Institute of Social and Economic Research, 2009.

Jackson, Robert. *The German Navy in World War II*. London: Brown Books, 1999.

Johnman, Lewis and Murphy, Hugh. "The British Merchant Shipping Mission in the United States and British Merchant Shipping in the Second World War." *The Northern Mariner/Le Marin du nord*, XII, No. 3 (July 2002), pp. 1–16.

Johnston, Mac. *Corvettes Canada: Convoy Veterans of World War II Tell Their True Stories*. Toronto: McGraw–Hill Ryerson, 1994; reprint, Toronto: John Wiley and Sons, 2008.

Jones, Geoffrey P. *Defeat of the Wolfpacks*. London: Kimber, 1986; reprint, Bristol: Cerberus Publishing, 2004.

_____. *Autumn of the U–Boats*. London: Kimber, 1984.

Jordan, David. *Wolfpack: The U–Boat War and the Allied Counter–Attack, 1939–1945*. Staplehurst: Spellmount, 2002.

Kaplan, Philip and Currie, Jack. *Wolfpack: U–Boats at War, 1939–1945*. London: Aurum Press, 1997; reprint, London: Aurum Press, 1999.

Kavanagh, Robert. "W Force: The Canadian Army and the Defence of Newfoundland in the Second World War." Unpublished MA Thesis, Memorial University of Newfoundland, 1995.

Kealey, Gregory S. and Whitaker, Reg (eds.). *R.C.M.P. Security*

Bulletins: The War Series, 1939–1941. St. John's: Canadian Committee on Labour History, 1989.

_____ and _(eds.). *R.C.M.P. Security Bulletins: The War Series, Part II, 1942–45.* St. John's: Canadian Committee on Labour History, 1993.

Kelshall, Gaylord T.M. *The U–Boat War in the Caribbean.* Port-of-Spain: Paria Publishing, 1988; reprint, Annapolis: Naval Institute Press, 1994.

Kemp, Paul. *Submarine Action.* Stroud: Sutton Publishing, 1999; reprint, London: Chancellor Press, 2000.

Kennedy, Paul. "Naval Mastery: The Canadian Context." In Douglas, W.A.B. (ed.). *The RCN in Transition, 1910–1985.* Vancouver: University of British Columbia Press, 1988, pp. 15–33.

Klein, Sandor S. "Roosevelt, Churchill Map War Aims at Sea." *New York World–Telegram,* 14 August 1941.

Knox, John H.W. "An Engineer's Outline of RCN History: Part I." In Boutilier, James A. (ed.). *The RCN in Retrospect, 1910–1968.* Vancouver: University of British Columbia Press, 1982, pp. 96–116.

Koechl, Marc. "'Sailors Ashore:' A Comparative Analysis of Wartime Recreation and Leisure in Halifax and St. John's." Unpublished MA Thesis, St. Mary's University, 2003.

Konstam, Angus and Malmann Showell, Jak P. *7th U–Boat Flotilla: Dönitz's Atlantic Wolves.* London: Ian Allan, 2003.

Lacy, Brian. *Seige City: The Story of Derry and Londonderry.* Belfast: Blackstaff Press, 1990.

Lamb, James B. *On the Triangle Run.* Toronto: Macmillan of Canada, 1986.

_____. *The Corvette Navy: True Stories from Canada's Atlantic War.* Toronto: Macmillan of Canada, 1977; 2nd ed., Toronto: Fitzhenry and Whiteside, 2000.

Lane, Tony. "The Human Economy of the British Merchant Navy." In Howarth, Stephen and Law, Derek (eds.). *The Battle of the Atlantic, 1939–1945: The 50th Anniversary International Naval Conference.* Annapolis: Naval Institute Press, 1994, pp. 45–59.

Lapierre, Laurier L. *Sir Wilfred Laurier and the Romance of Canada.* Toronto: Stoddart Publishing, 1996.

Lavery, Brian (comp. and intro.). *The Royal Navy Officer's Pocket–Book 1944.* London: Conway Maritime Books, 2007.

Lawrence, Hal. *A Bloody War: One Man's Memories of the*

Canadian Navy, 1939-45. Toronto: Macmillan of Canada, 1979.

_____. *Tales of the North Atlantic*. Toronto: McClelland and Stewart, 1985.

Lay, H. Nelson. *Memoirs of a Mariner*. Stittsville, ON: Canada's Wings, 1982.

Loewenheim, Francis L.; Langley, Harold D.; and Jonas, Manfred (eds.). *Roosevelt and Churchill: Their Secret Wartime Correspondence*. London: Barrie and Jenkins, 1975.

Lower, A.R.M. "Transition to Atlantic Bastion." in MacKay, R.A. (ed.). *Newfoundland: Economic, Diplomatic and Strategic Studies*. Toronto: Oxford University Press, 1946, pp. 484–508.

Lund, Wilfred G.D. "Vice–Admiral Howard Emmerson Reid and Vice–Admiral Harold Taylor Wood Grant: Forging the New 'Canadian' Navy." In Whitby, Michael; Gimblett, Richard H.; and Haydon, Peter (eds.). *The Admirals: Canada's Senior Naval Leadership in the Twentieth Century*. Toronto: Dundurn Press, 2006, pp. 157–186.

_____. "Vice–Admiral E. Rollo Mainguy: Sailor's Admiral." In Whitby, Michael; Gimblett, Richard H.; and Haydon, Peter (eds.). *The Admirals: Canada's Senior Naval Leadership in the Twentieth Century*. Toronto: Dundurn Press, 2006, pp. 187–212.

_____. "The Royal Canadian Navy's Quest for Autonomy in the North West Atlantic: 1941–43." In Boutilier, James A. (ed.). *The RCN in Retrospect, 1910–1968*. Vancouver: University of British Columbia Press, 1982, pp. 138–157.

Lynch, Mack (ed.). *Salty Dips*. Ottawa: Naval Officers' Association of Canada, 1983.

Lyon, David J. "The British Order of Battle." In Howarth, Stephen and Law, Derek (eds.). *The Battle of the Atlantic, 1939–1945: The 50th Anniversary International Naval Conference*. Annapolis: Naval Institute Press, 1994, pp. 266–275.

Macbeth, Jack. *Ready, Aye, Ready: An Illustrated History of the Royal Canadian Navy*. Toronto: Key Porter Books, 1989.

Macintyre, Donald. *U–Boat Killer: Fighting the U–boats in the Battle of the Atlantic*. London: Weidenfeld and Nicolson, 1956.

MacKay, RA. *Newfoundland in North Atlantic Strategy in the Second World War*. Ottawa: Information Canada, 1974.

_____. "The Problem of Newfoundland." In MacKay, R.A. (ed.). *Newfoundland: Economic, Diplomatic and Strategic Studies*. Toronto: Oxford University Press, 1946, pp. 3–38.

_____. (ed.). *Newfoundland: Economic, Diplomatic and Strategic Studies*. Toronto: Oxford University Press, 1946.

MacKenzie, David. "A North Atlantic Outpost: The American Military in Newfoundland, 1941–1945." *War & Society*, XXII, No. 2 (October 2004), pp. 51–74.

_____. *Inside the Atlantic Triangle: Canada and the Entrance of Newfoundland into Confederation, 1939–1949*. Toronto: University of Toronto Press, 1986.

MacLeod, Malcolm. *Peace of the Continent: The Impact of the Second World War Canadian and American Bases in Newfoundland*. St. John's: Harry Cuff Publishing, 1986.

_____ and Penny, Brad. "Sailors Ashore: RCN Interaction with the Civilian Society of St. John's, 1941–45." Unpublished paper presented to the Newfoundland Historical Society Symposium on Newfoundland in World War Two, St. John's, 2002.

Macpherson, Ken and Milner, Marc. *Corvettes of the Royal Canadian Navy, 1939–1945*. St. Catharines: Vanwell Publishing, 1993.

Major, Kevin. *As Near to Heaven by Sea: A History of Newfoundland and Labrador*. Toronto: Penguin Books, 2001.

Mallmann Showell, Jak P. *Hitler's U–Boat Bases*. Stroud: Sutton Press, 2007.

_____. *U–Boats under the Swastika: A Guide to German Submarines, 1935–1945*. London: Ian Allan, 1973; 2nd ed., Annapolis, Naval Institute Press, 2000.

_____. *U–Boats at War: Landings on Hostile* Shores. London: Ian Allan Publishing, 2000.

_____. *U–Boat Command and the Battle of the Atlantic*. St. Catharines: Vanwell Publishing, 1989.

Mayne, Richard O. *Betrayed: Scandal, Politics, and Canadian Naval Leadership*. Vancouver: UBC Press, 2006.

_____. "Vice–Admiral George C Jones: The Political Career of a Naval Officer." In Whitby, Michael; Gimblett, Richard H.; and Haydon, Peter (eds.). *The Admirals: Canada's Senior Naval Leadership in the Twentieth Century*. Toronto: Dundurn Press, 2006, pp. 125–155.

_____. "Keeping Up With The Joneses: Admiralship, Culture and Careerism in the Royal Canadian Navy, 1911–1946." Unpublished paper, Canadian Forces Leadership Institute, 2002.

McCrostie, James. "'Women and Seamen Don't Mix:' VD in Canada's Merchant Navy, 1942– 1945." *The Northern Mariner/Le Marin du Nord*, IX, No. 4 (October 1999), pp. 1–12.

McGrath, Darrin. *Last Dance: The Knights of Columbus Fire*. St. John's: Flanker Press, 2002.

McKay John and Harland John. *Anatomy of the Ship: The Flower Class Corvette AGASSIZ*. London: Conway Maritime Press, 1993; rev. ed., London: Conway Maritime Press, 2004.

McKee, Fraser. *'Sink all the Shipping There': The Wartime Loss of Canada's Merchant Ships and Fishing Schooners*. St. Catharines, ON: Vanwell Publishing Ltd., 2004.

_____. and Darlington, Robert. *The Canadian Naval Chronicle, 1939–1945*. St. Catharines: Vanwell Publishing, 1996.

_____. "Some Revisionist History in the Battle of the Atlantic." *The Northern Mariner/Le Marin du nord*, I, No. 4 (October 1991), pp. 27–32.

McKercher, B.J.C. "The Canadian Way of War 1939–1945." In Horn, Bernd (ed.). *Forging a Nation: Perspectives on the Canadian Military Experience*. St. Catharines: Vanwell Publishing, 2002, pp. 123–134.

McLean, Doug M. "Muddling Through: Canadian Anti–Submarine Doctrine and Practice, 1942–1945." In Hadley, Michael L.; Huebert, Rob; and Crickard, Fred W. (eds.). *A Nation's Navy: In Quest of a Canadian Naval Identity*. Montreal: McGill–Queen's University Press, 1996, pp. 173–189.

McNaught, Siobhan J. "The Rise of Proto–Nationalism: Sir Wilfred Laurier and the Founding of the Naval Service of Canada, 1902–1910." In Hadley, Michael L.; Huebert, Rob; and Crickard, Fred W. (eds.). *A Nation's Navy: In Quest of a Canadian Naval Identity*. Montreal: McGill–Queen's University Press, 1996, pp. 102–111.

Miller, D.C. (ed.). *St. John's Naval Guide Book*. St. John's: Robinson Blackmore, 1942.

Miller, David. *U–Boats: The Illustrated History of the Raiders of the Deep*. Washington, DC: Brassey's, 2000.

Miller, Nathan. *War at Sea: A Naval History of World War II*. New York: Scribner, 1995; reprint, New York: Oxford University Press, 1997.

Milner, Marc. "The Newfoundland Escort Force: Navy, Part 29." *Legion Magazine*. 3 October 2008. http://www.legionmagazine.com/en/index.php/author/marc_milner.

_____. "The Rise of Leonard Murray: Navy, Part 30."*Legion*

Magazine. 12 December 2008. http://www.legionmagazine.com/en/index.php/author/marc_milner.

_____."The Training Gap: Navy, Part 31." *Legion Magazine*. February 20, 2009.http://www.legionmagazine.com/ http://www.legionmagazine.com/en/index.php/author/marc_milner.

_____." Caught Between Powers: Navy, Part 32." *Legion Magazine*. 18 April 2009.http://www.legionmagazine.com/ http://www.legionmagazine.com/en/index.php/author/marc_milner.

_____. "A Sad State of Affairs: Navy, Part 34. *Legion Magazine*. 20 August 2009.http://www.legionmagazine.com/ http://www.legionmagazine.com/en/index.php/author/marc_milner.

_____. "The Cruelest Months: Navy, Part 35. *Legion Magazine*. 15 October 2009.http://www.legionmagazine.com/ http://www.legionmagazine.com/en/index.php/author/marc_milner.

_____. "Rear–Admiral Leonard Warren Murray: Canada's Most Important Operational Commander." In Whitby, Michael; Gimblett, Richard H.; and Haydon, Peter (eds.). *The Admirals: Canada's Senior Naval Leadership in the Twentieth Century*. Toronto: Dundurn Press, 2006, pp. 97–124.

_____. "The Historiography of the Canadian Navy." In Hadley, Michael L.; Huebert, Rob; and Crickard, Fred W. (eds.). *A Nation's Navy: In Quest of a Canadian Naval Identity*. Montreal: McGill–Queen's University Press, 1996, pp. 23–34.

_____. "Royal Canadian Navy in the Battle of the Atlantic Crisis of 1943." In Granatstein, J.L. and Neary, Peter (eds.). *The Good Fight: Canadians and World War II*. Toronto: Copp Clark, 1995, pp. 65–81.

_____. "Squaring Some of the Corners." In Runyan, Timothy J. and Copes, Jan M. (eds.). *To Die Gallantly: The Battle of the Atlantic*. Boulder, CO: Westview Press, 1994, pp. 121–136.

_____. *The Battle of the Atlantic*. St. Catharines: Vanwell Publishing, 2003.

_____. *Canada's Navy: The First Century*. Toronto: University of Toronto Press, 1999.

_____. *HMCS Sackville 1941–1945*. Halifax: Canadian Naval Memorial Trust, 1998.

_____. *The U–Boat Hunters: The Royal Canadian Navy and the Offensive against Germany's Submarines*. Annapolis: Naval Institute Press, 1994.

_____. "The Battle of the Atlantic." *Journal of Strategic Studies*,

XIII, No. 4 (March 1990), pp. 44–66.

_____. "Reflections on the State of Canadian Army History in the Two World Wars." *Acadiensis*, XVIII, No. 2 (Spring 1989), pp. 135–150.

_____. "Inshore ASW: The Canadian Experience in Home Waters." In Douglas, W.A.B. (ed.). *The RCN in Transition, 1910–1985*. Vancouver: University of British Columbia Press, 1988, pp. 143–158.

_____. *North Atlantic Run: The Royal Canadian Navy and the Battle for the Convoys*. Toronto: University of Toronto Press, 1985.

Morison, Samuel Eliot. *History of United States Naval Operations in World War II. Vol. I: The Battle of the Atlantic, September 1939–May 1943*. Boston: Little, Brown, and Co. 1947; reprint, Urbana: University of Illinois Press, 2002.

_____. *History of United States Naval Operations in World War II, Vol. 3: The Rising Sun in the Pacific, 1931–April 1942*. Boston: Little, Brown and Co., 1948; reprint: Urbana: University of Illinois Press, 2002.

_____. *History of United States Naval Operations in World War II. Vol. 10: The Atlantic Battle Won, May 1944–May 1945*. Boston: Little, Brown and Co., 1956; reprint, Urbana: University of Illinois Press, 2002.

_____. *The Two–Ocean War: A Short History of the United States Navy in the Second World War*. Boston: Little, Brown, 1963; reprint, Annapolis: Naval Institute Press, 2007.

Murphy, Heather. "The Relationship between Canadian Military Personnel Stationed in St. John's and the Civilian Population between October 1940 and December 1942." Unpublished Honours Thesis, Memorial University of Newfoundland, 1981.

Naftel, William D. *Halifax at War: Searchlights, Squadrons and Submarines, 1939–1945*. Halifax: Formac Publishing, 2008.

Neary, Peter. *Newfoundland in the North Atlantic World, 1929–1949*. Montreal: McGill–Queen's University Press, 1988; 2nd ed., Montreal: McGill–Queen's University Press, 1996.

_____. "Newfoundland and the Anglo–American Leased Bases Agreement of 27 March 1941." *Canadian Historical Review*, LXVII, No. 4 (December 1986), pp. 491–519.

_____. "Clement Attlee's Visit to Newfoundland, September 1942." *Acadiensis*, XIII, No. 2 (Spring 1984), pp. 101–109.

Neary, Steve. *The Enemy on Our Doorstep: The German Attacks at Bell Island, Newfoundland, 1942*. St. John's: Jespersen Press, 1994.

"New AEF Lands In N. Ireland - Thousands Cheered: Band Played." *New York Post*, 26 January 1942.

Newfoundland. Provincial Archives of Newfoundland and Labrador. Government of Newfoundland. Department of Justice and Defence. GN 38:S4–1–2.

    _____. . . . GN 38: S4–1–4.

    _____. . . . GN 38: S4–1–6.

    _____. . . . GN 38: S4–1–7.

    _____. . . . GN 38: S4–2–1.1, File 9, 578–42.

    _____. . . . GN 38: S4–2–1.2.

    _____. . . . GN 38: S4–2–2.

    _____. . . . GN 38: S4–2–3.1.

    _____. . . . GN 38: S4–2–3.2.

    _____. . . . GN 38: S4–2 –3.3, File 4.

    _____. . . . GN 38: S4–2–4, Files 2–3 and 5.

    _____. . . . GN 38: S4–2–5.

    _____. . . . GN 38: S4–2–6, File 8.

    _____. . . . GN 38: S4–2–7, File 16.

    _____. . . . Department of Public Utilities. GN 38: S5–1–2, File 9, P.U. 38(a)–41, "Regulations for the Control of Small Boats Plying for Hire or Reward in the Harbour of St. John's," 17 June 1942.

O'Brien, Mike. "Out of a Clear Sky: The Mobilization of the Newfoundland Regiment, 1914–1915." *Newfoundland and Labrador Studies*, XXII, No. 2 (Fall 2007), pp. 401–427.

O'Connor, Edward. *The Corvette Years: The Lower Deck Story*. Vancouver: Cordillera Publishing, 1995.

O'Neill, Paul. *The Oldest City: The Story of St. John's, Newfoundland*. Erin, ON: Press Porcepic, 1975.

Padfield, Peter. *Dönitz: The Last Fuhrer*. London: Victor Gollancz, 1984.

Parker, Mike. *Running the Gauntlet: An Oral History of Canadian Merchant Seamen in World War II*. Halifax: Nimbus Publishing, 1994.

Parrish, Thomas. *The Submarine: A History*. New York: Viking Penguin, 2004.

Pickersgill, J.W. *The Mackenzie King Record*. 4 vols. Toronto: University of Toronto Press, 1960.

Pierson, Ruth Roach. *They're Still Women After All: The Second World War and Canadian Womanhood*. Toronto: McClelland and Stewart, 1986.

Pitchfork, Graham. *Shot Down and In the Drink: RAF and Commonwealth Aircrews Saved from the Sea, 1939–1945*. Kew: National Archives, 2005.

Pope, Peter E. *Fish into Wine: The Newfoundland Plantation in the Seventeenth Century*. Chapel Hill: University of North Carolina Press, 2004.

Porter, Helen, "An Excerpt from *Below the Bridge: Memories of the South Side of St. John's*." In Rompkey, Bill (ed.). *St. John's and the Battle of the Atlantic*. St. John's: Flanker Press, 2009, pp. 199–214.

Poulter, Gillian, and Baldwin, Douglas O. "'Never a Dull Moment in this Port:' Mona Wilson and the Canadian Red Cross in Wartime St. John's." In High, Steven (ed.). *Occupied St. John's: A Social History of a City at War, 1939–1945* Montreal: McGill–Queen's University Press, 2010, pp. 220–250.

Preston, Antony (ed.). *History of the Royal Navy in the 20th Century*. London: Hamlyn, 1987.

Preston, Richard A. *Canada and "Imperial Defence:" A Study of the Origins of the British Commonwealth's Defence Organization, 1867–1919*. Durham, NC: Duke University Press, 1967.

Pritchard, James. *Anatomy of a Naval Disaster: The 1746 French Expedition to North America*. Montreal and Kingston: McGill–Queen's University Press, 1995.

Prim, Joseph and McCarthy, John. *Those in Peril: The U–Boat Menace to Allied Shipping in Newfoundland and Labrador Waters, World War I and World War II*. St. John's: Jespersen Press, 1995.

Prowse, D.W. *A History of Newfoundland*. London: Macmillan, 1895; reprint, Portugal Cove/St. Philips: Boulder Publications, 2002.

Pugh, Philip, "Military Needs and Civil Necessity." In Howarth, Stephen and Law Derek (eds.). *The Battle of the Atlantic, 1939–1945: The 50th Anniversary International Naval Conference*. Annapolis: Naval Institute Press, 1994, pp. 30–44.

Pullen, Hugh Francis. "The Royal Canadian Navy between the Wars, 1922–39." In Boutilier, James A. (ed.). *The RCN in Retrospect, 1910–1968*. Vancouver: University of British Columbia Press, 1982, pp. 62–73.

Purdy, Verity Sweeny. *As Luck Would Have It: Adventures With the Canadian Army Show 1943-1946.* St. Catharine's ON: Vanwell Publishing Limited, 2003.

Ransom, Bernard. "Canada's 'Newfyjohn' Tenancy: The Royal Canadian Navy in St. John's 1941-1945." *Acadiensis,* XXIII, No. 2 (Spring 1994), pp. 58-81.

___. "A Nursery of Fighting Seamen? The Newfoundland Royal Naval Reserve, 1901-1920." In Hadley, Michael L.; Huebert, Rob; and Crickard, Fred W. (eds.). *A Nation's Navy: In Quest of Canadian Naval Identity.* Montreal: McGill-Queen's University Press, 1996, pp. 239-255.

Robertson, Barbara. *Sir Wilfred Laurier: The Great Conciliator.* Toronto: Oxford University Press, 1971; reprint, Kingston: Quarry Press, 1991.

Rohwer, Jürgen. "The Wireless War." In Howarth, Stephen and Law, Derek (eds.). *The Battle of the Atlantic, 1939-1945: The 50th Anniversary International Naval Conference.* Annapolis: Naval Institute Press, 1994, pp. 408-417.

___. *Axis Submarine Successes, 1939-1945.* Cambridge: Patrick Stephens, 1983.

___. *The Critical Convoy Battles of March 1943: The Battle for HX. 229/SC122*: London: Ian Allan, 1977.

___. and Gümmelchen, Gerhard. *Chronology of the War at Sea, 1939-1945: The Naval History of World War Two.* London: Ian Allan, 1972; 3rd rev. ed., London: Chatham Publishing, 1992.

Rompkey, Bill (ed.). *St. John's and the Battle of the Atlantic.* St. John's: Flanker Press, 2009.

Roskill, Stephen W. *Naval Policy between the Wars. Vol. 1: The Period of Anglo-American Antagonism, 1919-1929.* London: Collins, 1968.

___. *Naval Policy between the Wars. Vol. 2: The Period of Reluctant Rearmament, 1930-1939.* Annapolis: Naval Institute Press, 1976.

___. *The War at Sea, 1939-1945.* 3 vols. London: HMSO, 1954-1961; reprint, Uckfield, Naval and Military Press, 2004.

Rössler, Eberhard. *The U-Boat: The Evolution and Technical History of German Submarines.* London: Arms and Armour Press, 1981.

Runyan, Timothy J. and Copes, Jan M. (eds.) *To Die Gallantly: The Battle of the Atlantic.* Boulder, CO: Westview Press, 1994.

Salisbury, Harrison. "U-Boats' Defeat Total This Month -

Churchill: 'We'll Fight until Japan Bites Dust.'" *New York World–Telegram*, 30 June 1943.

Sarty, Roger. *War in the St. Lawrence: The Forgotten Battles on Canada's Shores.* Toronto: Allen Lane, 2012.

_____. "Admiral Percy W. Nelles: Diligent Guardian of the Vision." In Whitby, Michael; Gimblett, Richard H.; and Haydon, Peter (eds.). *The Admirals: Canada's Senior Naval Leadership in the Twentieth Century.* Toronto: Dundurn Press, 2006, pp. 69–95.

_____. "The Halifax Military Lands Board: Civil–Military Relations and the Development of Halifax as a Strategic Port, 1905–1928." *The Northern Mariner/Le Marin du nord*, XII, No. 2 (April 2002), pp. 45–68.

_____. "Rear–Admiral L.W. Murray and the Battle of the Atlantic: The Professional Who Led Canada's Citizen Sailors." In Horn, Bernd and Harris, Stephen (eds.). *Warrior Chiefs: Perspectives on Senior Canadian Military Leaders.* Toronto: Dundurn Press, 2001, pp. 165–192.

_____. "The Incident on Lucknow Street: Defenders and the Defended in Halifax, 1915." *Canadian Military History*, X, No. 2 (Spring 2001), pp. 58–67.

_____. "Canada's Coastal Fortifications of the Second World War and Their Origins." In Sarty, Roger (ed.). *The Maritime Defence of Canada.* Toronto: Canadian Institute of Strategic Studies, 1996.

_____. "Ultra, Air Power, and the Second Battle of the St. Lawrence, 1944." In Runyan, Timothy J. and Copes, Jan M. (eds.). *To Die Gallantly: The Battle of the Atlantic.* Boulder, CO: Westview Press, 1994, pp. 186–209.

_____. "Hard Luck Flotilla: The RCN's Atlantic Coast Patrol, 1914–18." In Douglas, W.A.B. (ed.). *The RCN in Transition, 1910–1985.* Vancouver: University of British Columbia Press, 1988, pp. 103–125.

_____ (ed.). *The Maritime Defence of Canada.* Toronto: Canadian Institute of Strategic Studies, 1996.

_____ and Knight, Doug. *Saint John Fortifications, 1630–1956.* Fredericton, NB: Goose Lane Books, 2003.

Schull, Joseph. *Far Distant Ships: An Official Account of Canadian Naval Operations in World War II.* Ottawa: Edmond Cloutier, 1950; 2nd ed., Toronto: Stoddart Publishing, 1987.

Sharpe, Christopher A. and Shawyer, A.J. "Building a Wartime Landscape." In High, Steven (ed.). *Occupied St. John's: A Social History of a City at War, 1939–1945.* Montreal: McGill–Queen's University

Press, 2010, pp. 21–80.

Smith, Michael and Erskine, Ralph (eds.). *Action This Day: Bletchley Park from the Breaking of the Enigma Code to the Birth of the Modern Computer.* London: Bantam Press, 2001.

Stacey, C.P. *Six Years of War: The Army in Canada, Britain and the Pacific.* Ottawa: Queen's Printer, 1956.

_____. *Arms, Men and Governments: The War Policies of Canada, 1939–1945.* Ottawa: Queen's Printer, 1970.

Stalin's Correspondence with Churchill, Atlee, Roosevelt and Truman 1941–45. New York: E.P. Dutton, 1958.

Stern, Robert C. *Type VII U–Boats.* Annapolis: Naval Institute Press, 1991.

Syrett, David. "The Battle for Convoy HX 133, 23–29 June 1941." *The Northern Mariner/Le Marin du nord*, XII, No. 3 (July 2002), pp. 43–50.

_____. *The Defeat of the German U–Boats: The Battle of the Atlantic.* Columbia: University of South Carolina Press, 1994.

Tarrant, V.E. *The Last Year of the Kriegsmarine, May 1944–May 1945.* Annapolis: Naval Institute Press, 1994.

_____. *The U–Boat Offensive, 1914–1945.* Annapolis: Naval Institute Press, 1989.

Tennyson, Brian and Sarty, Roger. *Guardian of the Gulf: Sydney, Cape Breton, and the Atlantic Wars.* Toronto: University of Toronto Press, 2000.

Till, Geoffrey. "The Battle of the Atlantic as History." In Howarth, Stephen and Law, Derek (eds.). *The Battle of the Atlantic, 1939–1945: The 50th Anniversary International Naval Conference.* Annapolis: Naval Institute Press, 1994, pp. 584–595.

Tracy, Nicholas. *Attack on Maritime Trade.* Toronto: University of Toronto Press, 1991.

Tucker, Gilbert. *The Naval Service of Canada.* 2 vols. Ottawa: King's Printer, 1952.

Tweedie, Graeme R. "The Roots of the Royal Canadian Navy: Sovereignty versus Nationalism, 1812–1910." In Hadley, Michael L.; Huebert, Rob; and Crickard, Fred W. (eds.). *A Nation's Navy: In Quest of a Canadian Naval Identity.* Montreal: McGill–Queen's University Press, 1996, pp. 91–101.

Type IX U–Boats: German Type IX Submarine, German Submarine U–110, German Submarine U–155, German Submarine U–

505, German Submarine U–862. Memphis, TN: Books LLC, 2010.

US Naval Intelligence. *German Naval Vessels of World War Two*. Annapolis: Naval Institute Press, 1991.

Van der Vat, Dan. *The Atlantic Campaign: The Great Struggle at Sea, 1939–1945*. New York: Harper and Row, 1988.

Vause, Jordan. *Wolf: U–Boat Commanders in World War II*. Annapolis: Naval Institute Press, 1997.

Waters, John M., Jr. *Bloody Winter*. Princeton: Van Nostrand, 1967; reprint, Annapolis: Naval Institute Press, 1994.

Watson, Mark B. *Sea Logistics: Keeping the Navy Ready Aye Ready*. St. Catharines, ON: Vanwell Publishing Ltd., 2004.

Webb, Jeff A. *The Voice of Newfoundland: A Social History of the Broadcasting Corporation of Newfoundland, 1939–1949*. Toronto: University of Toronto Press, 2008.

_____. "Gate Keeping and Newfoundland Popular Culture." In High, Steven (ed.). *Occupied St. John's: A Social History of a City at War, 1939–1945* Montreal: McGill–Queen's University Press, 2010, pp. 191–219.

Wemyss, D.E.G. *Relentless Pursuit: The Story of Capt. F.J. Walker, CB, DSO, RN, U–Boat Hunter and Destroyer*. London: Wren's Park Publishing, 1955; reprint, Bristol: Cerberus Publishing, 2003.

Westwood, David. *Anatomy of the Ship: The Type VII U–Boat*. London: Conway Maritime Press, 1984; rev. ed., London: Conway Maritime Press, 2003.

Whitby, Michael. "Instruments of Security: The Royal Canadian Navy's Procurement of the Tribal–Class Destroyers, 1938–1943." *The Northern Mariner/Le Marin du nord*, II, No. 3 (July 1992), pp. 1–15.

_____. "In Defence of Home Waters: Doctrine and Training in the Canadian Navy during the 1930s." *Mariner's Mirror*, LXXV, No. 2 (May 1991), pp.167–177.

_____. Gimblett, Richard H.; and Haydon, Peter (eds.) *The Admirals: Canada's Senior Naval Leadership in the Twentieth Century*. Toronto: Dundurn Press, 2006.

White, John F. *U–boat Tankers, 1941–45: Submarine Suppliers to Atlantic Wolf Packs*. Shrewsbury: Airlife Publishing, 1998.

Williams, Andrew. *The Battle of the Atlantic: The Allies' Submarine Fight against Hitler's Gray Wolves of the Sea*. London: BBC Worldwide, 2002.

Williamson, Gordon. *Wolf Pack: The Story of the U–Boat in*

World War II. Oxford: Osprey Publishing, 2005.

_____. *U–Boat Bases and Bunkers, 1941–45.* Oxford: Osprey Publishing, 2003.

Wilson, Harold A. *The Imperial Policy of Sir Robert Borden.* Gainesville: University of Florida Press, 1966.

Winters, Barbara. "The Wrens of the Second World War: Their Place in the History of Canadian Service Women." In Hadley, Michael L.; Huebert, Rob; and Crickard, Fred W. (eds.). *A Nation's Navy: In Quest of Canadian Naval Identity.* Montreal: McGill–Queen's University Press, 1996, pp. 280–296.

Wynn, Kenneth. *U–Boat Operations of the Second World War, Vol. 2: Career Histories U511–UIT25.* London: Chatham Publishing, 1998.

_____. *U–Boat Operations of the Second World War, Vol. 1: Career Histories U1–U510.* London: Chatham Publishing, 1997.

Zimmerman, David. "The Social Background of the Wartime Navy: Some Statistical Data." In Hadley, Michael L.; Huebert, Rob; and Crickard, Fred W. (eds.). *A Nation's Navy: In Quest of a Canadian Naval Identity.* Montreal: McGill–Queen's University Press, 1996, pp. 256–279.

_____. "Technology and Tactics." In Howarth, Stephen and Law, Derek (eds.). *The Battle of the Atlantic, 1939–1945: The 50th Anniversary International Naval Conference.* Annapolis: Naval Institute Press, 1994, pp. 476–489.

_____. *The Great Naval Battle of Ottawa: How Admirals, Scientists, and Politicians Impeded the Development of High Technology in Canada's Wartime Navy.* Toronto: University of Toronto Press, 1989.

_____. "The Royal Canadian Navy and the National Research Council, 1939–1945." *Canadian Historical Review*, LXIX, No. 2 (June 1988), pp. 203–221.

Index

71st Motor Launch Flotilla, 103, 156
73rd Motor Launch Flotilla, 103
79th Motor Launch Flotilla, 156
Admiral Hipper, 31
Agassiz HMCS, 201
Alberni HMCS, 30
Allied Anti-Submarine Survey Board, 141
Amber HMCS, 29
Anderson, Major-General T.V., Chief of the General Staff, 28, 29
Andrews, Officer in Charge of Works in Bermuda, 50, 64
Anglo-American Leased Bases Agreement ("destroyers for bases" deal), 17, 25, 33, 39, 40, 56, 57, 84, 85
Anglo-American Staff Agreement (ABC1), 36
anti-torpedo baffle, 30, 49, 76
Arakaka SS, 37
Argentia, 12, 15, 33, 53, 60, 61, 66, 72, 75, 79, 93, 100, 109, 111, 117, 149, 160, 172
ASDIC, 21, 36, 107, 117, 146, 157, 162, 180
Assiniboine HMCS, 100, 101, 102, 117
Austin, Rear-Admiral Sir Francis, 143
Avalon, 8
Avalon HMCS, 7, 9, 10, 11, 12, 13, 14, 15, 16, 24, 37, 42, 56, 58, 62, 63, 67, 69, 72, 81, 84, 96, 98, 99, 100, 102, 104, 108, 110, 112, 115, 124, 125, 128, 129, 132, 133, 140, 144, 149, 151, 153, 154, 160, 162, 167, 168, 169, 170, 171, 172, 173, 174
Avalon Peninsula, 28, 65, 96, 109, 150
Battle of the Atlantic, i, 7, 8, 10, 11, 12, 13, 14, 15, 18, 19, 25, 30, 31, 33, 36, 55, 63, 69, 70, 71, 77, 85, 86, 90, 116, 118, 120, 121, 125, 126, 127, 128, 135, 136, 137, 138, 139, 143, 144, 146, 148, 149, 151, 153, 165, 166, 169, 173, 175, 188, 192, 197, 198, 199, 200, 201, 202, 203, 205, 206, 207, 208, 210
Bay Bulls, 15, 28, 67, 70, 76, 103, 125, 154, 160, 162, 168
Bay of Biscay, 140, 143, 152

Beaverbrook, Lord (Maxwell "Max" Aitken), British Minister of Supply, 32, 57, 165
Bell Island (Wabana), 26, 28, 109, 110, 115, 191
Bermuda, 32, 33, 50, 64
Bidwell, Captain R.E.S, 96, 100, 101, 144
Bismarck, 34
Black Watch of Canada, 28
Bletchley Park. *see Government Code and Cipher School*
Blitzkrieg, 28, 39
Botwood, 26, 27, 28, 35, 101, 105, 108, 168
Bowring Brothers Ltd, 50
Brand, Captain E., Director of Trade, 38, 143
Bristol, Admiral A.L.,, 33, 53, 60, 71, 100, 111, 172
British Admiralty, 10, 35, 145, 146
British Admiralty Delegation, 50, 85, 123, 141
British Home Fleet, 34
Buchans, 26
Bulldog, 33
Byron, Commander J.,, 17, 84, 150, 191
Cabot Tower (Port War Signal Station, 29, 30
Camp Lester, 29
Canada, 7, 9, 10, 11, 13, 15, 16, 17, 18, 19, 22, 24, 27, 28, 35, 36, 37, 38, 39, 40, 41, 42, 43, 44, 45, 46, 47, 48, 60, 66, 69, 77, 82, 84, 85, 89, 90, 91, 92, 93, 95, 100, 101, 105, 106, 114, 124, 130, 131, 132, 133, 134, 136, 137, 138, 140, 141, 145, 146, 147, 148, 151, 163, 164, 165, 167, 168, 169, 171, 173, 174, 175, 180, 188, 189, 190, 191, 192, 193, 194, 195, 196, 197, 198, 199, 200, 201, 202, 205, 206, 207, 208, 209, 210
Canadian Mutual Aid Fund, 140
Cape Breton, 17, 28, 99, 208
Cape Race, 28, 40, 57, 65, 66, 109, 160
Cape Spear, 29, 30, 58, 63, 72, 99, 104, 124, 126
Capt. R.N. Wood, the Director of Naval Ordnance (DNO), 143
Caribou SS, 95, 105, 107, 109, 114, 115, 133, 192, 197
CAT gear, 150
Central Atlantic Neutrality Patrol., 33

Chambly HMCS, 30, 48, 54, 79, 164
Chesterfield HMS, 49
Chief of the Naval Staff (CNS), 100, 141
Christoph von Doornum, 27
Churchill, Prime Minister Winston S, 21, 23, 32, 36, 46, 52, 68, 73, 86, 90, 115, 118, 136, 139, 191, 198, 199, 207, 208
City of Toronto SS, 37
Clayoquot HMCS, 159
Coastal Command, 31, 68, 143
Cobalt HMCS, 30
Collingwood HMCS, 30, 48
Combined Canadian, British and American committee "to examine repair problems for warships and merchant ships" in the northwest Atlantic, 141
Commission of Government, 8, 17, 19, 20, 24, 26, 27, 37, 38, 44, 45, 46, 52, 56, 83, 86, 87, 125, 140
Commodore Commanding Canadian Ships (CCCS), 35, 49
Commodore Commanding, Newfoundland Force (CCNF), 49, 85
Connolly, J. J., 142, 145
Convoys
  BX-14, 160
  HHX-327, 159
  HX-129, 48
  HX-217, 111
  HX-222, 116
  HX-228, 120
  HX-229, 122
  HX-233, 123
  HX-72, 23
  HX-79, 23
  JH-HJ, 116, 118
  OB-126, 34
  OB-318, 34
  ON-100, 96
  ON-102, 96

ON-113, 98
ON-115, 98, 99, 101
ON-122, 102
ON-127, 102
ON-139, 105
ON-144, 108, 109
ON-145, 108
ON-152, 111
ON-153, 111
ON-154, 111
ON-163, 117
ON-166, 117
ON-169, 122
ON-175, 123
ON-5, 128
ON-60, 71
ONM-243, 155
ONS-38, 159
SC 7, 23
SC-107, 108
SC-121, 120
SC-122, 122
SC-130, 128
SC-42, 54
SC-44, 54
SC-45, 54
SC-52, 57
SC-61, 60
SC-67, 71
SC-94, 100, 101
TC-14, 53
XB-139, 159
Cook, Rear-Admiral, 33
Corner Brook, 26, 28

Courageous HMS, 21, 42, 165
Croil, Chief Air Vice Marshal G.M, 28
Defensively Equipped Merchant Ship (DEMS),, 22, 124
Defensively Equipped Merchant Ships (DEMS), 102, 143
Department of Posts and Telegraphs, 52
Devers, General Jacob L, 33
Dobratz, Klt. Kurt, 160
Dominions Office, 27, 46, 84, 85, 91, 110, 132, 133, 138, 163, 179, 194, 195
Dönitz, Admiral Karl, 14, 30, 63, 65, 66, 68, 69, 89, 95, 96, 98, 101, 102, 115, 117, 119, 121, 122, 126, 128, 140, 142, 143, 144, 149, 152, 155, 160, 162, 163, 191, 192, 198, 204
Duncan HMS, 142
Dunver HMCS, 155
Earnshaw, Brigadier P., Commander, Combined Newfoundland and Canadian Military Forces, 29, 60
Eastern Ocean Meeting Point (EASTOMP), 11, 44, 170
Edmund B Alexander USAT, 29
Edmundston HMCS, 150
Emergency Powers Defense Order, 51
Emerson, Leonard E., Commissioner of Finance and Defense, 28, 46, 60, 61, 73, 84, 92, 97, 131, 185
Enigma, 33, 127, 128, 148, 152, 155, 192, 208
Escort Group
  TG 22.1, 161
  W.4, 161
Escort Groups
  A Group, 129
  A.3, 117, 123
  B.1, 102
  B.4, 122, 123
  BGroups, 79, 100, 129, 148, 172
  C Group, 78, 116, 117, 120, 129, 130, 136, 143, 148, 157, 172
  C.1, 101, 150
  C.2, 129

C.3, 117, 123
C.5, 155, 159
C.6, 156
E.25, 157
E.27, 157
EG.16, 156, 157, 160
EG.27, 160
EG.3, 123
EG.9, 143
EG-27, 158
W.13, 156

Esquimalt HMCS, 160
Examination Battery, 30
Examination Service, 29, 30
Farquar USS, 160
First World War, 22, 36, 40
Flower-class corvettes, 23
Fort Amherst, 29, 30, 72, 91, 104
Forth HMS, 49, 55
German Naval Acoustic Torpedo (GNAT), 143, 156, 157, 159, 164
Germany, 15, 21, 26, 27, 31, 89, 160, 162, 164, 193, 202
Giffard HMCS, 150
Gneisenua, 31
Government Code and Cipher School (Bletchley Park), 33, 128, 138
Grand Banks, 11, 19, 20, 34, 65, 147, 153
Grand Falls, 28
Greenslade (Greenslade Board), Admiral John W, 33
Gretton, Commander Peter, 142
Griffin, Lt.-Commander A.G.S, 149
Griffiss, Lt. Colonel Townsend E., 33
Halifax, Nova Scotia, 10, 34
Harbour Grace, 29, 47, 55, 76, 79, 103, 111, 125, 155
Hargood HMS, 150
High Frequency Direction Finding (Huff Duff, H/F D/F), 101, 126

Hilbig, Klt. Hans, 159
Hornbostel, Klt. Klaus, 159
Iceland, 11, 24, 33, 34, 44, 55, 67, 68, 82, 83, 129, 152, 170
Imperial Oil, 50, 74, 76, 117, 155
Jeckell, Lt A. W., 50
Job Brothers, 50, 58, 98
Jones, Rear Admiral C.G, 144, 145, 197, 200
Kaufman, Admiral J. L, 141
King George V, 34
Kingsley, Commander H., 158
Kirkland Lake HMCS, 159
Knights of Columbus, 47, 58, 62, 112, 114, 115, 135, 201
La Perle, Free French Submarine, 155
Lemcke, Kptlt. Rudolf, 102
Lessing, KzS Hermann, 159
Lewisporte, 26, 29, 105
Liberty ships, 120, 149
Liverpool, 11, 25, 33, 69
London, 12, 15, 18, 19, 20, 24, 27, 33, 35, 38, 41, 45, 46, 47, 51, 53, 72, 85, 86, 89, 91, 92, 115, 128, 130, 132, 135, 136, 138, 145, 148, 164, 166, 168, 172, 175, 188, 192, 194, 196, 197, 198, 199, 200, 201, 204, 205, 206, 208, 209, 210
Macdonald, Hon. Angus L., Canadian Naval Minister, 117, 142, 144, 145, 147
MacDonald, Malcolm, British High Commissioner to Ottawa, 141
Mackenzie King, Prime Minister William Lyon, 22, 23, 27, 36, 39, 45, 82, 145, 146, 194, 205
Magog HMCS, 156, 157
Mainguy, Captain Edmund Rollo, 35, 42, 49, 74, 91, 102, 103, 105, 106, 136, 186, 187, 199
Malony, Harry J, 33
Mansfield, Rear Admiral J.M., 141
Marvita HMCS/CNAV, 30
Merchant Aircraft Carriers (MAC), 153
Mid-Ocean Meeting Point (MOMP), 11, 44, 170

Ministry of War Transport (MWT), 44, 49, 99, 106
Monthly Anti-Submarine Report, 148
Moore, Commander C.A.,, 143
Murray, Rear Admiral L.W, 14, 35, 48, 49, 52, 53, 54, 55, 56, 57, 59, 60, 61, 62, 67, 71, 73, 74, 75, 77, 78, 79, 80, 81, 82, 83, 85, 87, 88, 96, 97, 98, 99, 100, 101, 102, 125, 131, 138, 144, 163, 171, 172, 185, 186, 189, 202, 207
Naval Armament Depot, 81, 144
Naval Control Service (NCS), 26, 99, 129, 177, 180
Naval Examination Service (NES), 29
Naval Officer in Charge (NOIC), 26, 29, 40, 49, 99, 134, 155
Naval Officer In Charge (NOIC), 81
Naval Service Headquarters (NSHQ), 8, 10, 13, 29, 35, 57, 85, 138, 142, 180
Nazis, 27, 118
Nelles, Vice-Admiral Percy, 28, 35, 42, 100, 130, 142, 144, 145, 147, 148, 149, 164, 185, 207
Newfoundland Airport (Gander), 27, 29
Newfoundland Defence Force (NDF), 30
Newfoundland Defence Scheme, 26, 38
Newfoundland Defense Force, 75
Newfoundland Dockyard, 26, 50, 53, 124, 141, 145, 149, 170
Newfoundland Escort Force (NEF), 11, 30, 44, 147, 170, 180, 201
Newfoundland Hotel, 12, 49, 53, 58, 80, 99
Newfoundland Railway, 20, 29, 59, 71, 76
Newfyjohn, 7, 9, 10, 16, 18, 19, 174, 175, 206
Niblack USS, 33
Night Escort Teacher (NET), 124, 154
Noble, Admiral Sir Percy, C-in-C, Northwest Approaches, 10, 49, 174
North Atlantic, 7, 9, 11, 12, 14, 16, 17, 18, 24, 25, 31, 34, 37, 38, 39, 41, 42, 43, 47, 55, 63, 64, 67, 76, 83, 85, 86, 88, 90, 91, 98, 105, 115, 116, 117, 119, 120, 121, 126, 129, 133, 135, 139, 140, 144, 148, 153, 155, 157, 163, 164, 165, 166, 170, 172, 173, 174, 189, 199, 200, 203
Oberkommando der Wehrmacht (OKW), Supreme High Command of the German Armed Forces, 30
Ogdensburg, New York, 23, 45

The "Newfyjohn" Solution

Operation *Rheinubung*, 34
Operation Shambles, 161
Operation Torch, 92, 171, 191
Orillia HMCS, 30, 48
Ottawa, 8, 9, 10, 12, 13, 15, 16, 27, 28, 30, 35, 38, 39, 40, 41, 42, 43, 48, 57, 75, 84, 85, 90, 95, 99, 101, 106, 109, 116, 123, 128, 131, 134, 136, 138, 141, 142, 144, 146, 163, 164, 165, 167, 172, 188, 189, 194, 199, 207, 208, 210
Ottawa HMCS, 102, 104
P-514 HMS/m, 79, 96, 97
Permanent Joint Board on Defense (PJBD), 23, 40, 41, 45
Petersen, Klt. Kurt, 155, 156
Phony War, 14, 28
Port War Signal station, 58
Port War Signal Station, 29, 30, 55, 62, 63, 72, 104
Prentice, Commander James "Chummy,", 30, 54, 79, 186
Prinz Eugen, 34
Proudly She Marches, 154
Radar (RDF), 55, 81
Ralston, Hon. J.L., Canadian Minister of Defense, 36
repair facilities, 15, 45, 68, 69, 124, 141, 145, 170
Rodney HMS, 34
Roosevelt, US President Franklin D., 23, 32, 39, 45, 52, 73, 84, 86, 198, 199, 208
Royal Canadian Air Force (RCAF), 28, 47, 84, 99, 166, 181, 191
Royal Canadian Navy (RCN), 7, 9, 10, 11, 17, 18, 28, 42, 47, 85, 93, 95, 113, 131, 133, 163, 164, 165, 181, 188, 189, 190, 191, 192, 193, 194, 196, 199, 200, 202, 203, 205, 206, 208, 209, 210
Royal Navy (RN), 11, 21, 26, 32, 44, 109, 135, 142, 170, 172, 181, 194, 198, 205
Rudeltaktik, 23, 69
Saurel CCGS, 161
Scharnhorst, 31
Schmoeckel, Klt. Helmut, 155, 156
schnorkel, 152, 157, 159, 167

Schwerdt, Captain C.M.R, 26, 29, 30, 35, 37, 38, 40, 42, 46, 49, 55, 57, 58, 59, 70, 71, 75, 76, 77, 78, 79, 80, 81, 82, 86, 87, 88, 92, 98, 99, 110

Scorched Earth Policy, 73, 75, 92, 188

Seal, E A.(codename Britman), 50, 56, 123, 137, 167

Second World War, 7, 9, 10, 14, 16, 17, 18, 19, 20, 21, 24, 26, 40, 41, 42, 43, 58, 80, 90, 91, 92, 93, 112, 114, 121, 131, 136, 138, 164, 165, 166, 167, 168, 173, 174, 175, 187, 188, 189, 191, 192, 193, 195, 196, 197, 199, 200, 203, 205, 207, 210

Senior Officer Escort (SOE), 32

Shawinigan HMCS, 157, 159

Sheridan, Rear Admiral, 46, 49

Shulamite HMCS/CNAV, 30

Signal Hill, 29, 99

Simpson, Commodore G.W.G, 142

Somalia HMS, 33

Sonar. *See ASDIC*

Southern Shore, 28, 76, 109, 150

St. John's, 7, 9, 10, 11, 12, 13, 14, 15, 19, 20, 26, 28, 29, 30, 32, 34, 35, 36, 37, 44, 45, 47, 48, 49, 50, 51, 52, 54, 55, 58, 60, 61, 62, 66, 68, 70, 71, 72, 73, 74, 75, 76, 77, 78, 79, 82, 97, 99, 100, 101, 102, 103, 105, 108, 109, 110, 111, 112, 113, 115, 116,☐117, 118, 122, 123, 124, 125, 128, 129, 130, 131, 140, 141, 142, 143, 144, 148, 149, 151, 153, 155, 158, 159, 161, 162, 170, 171, 172, 173, 175, 189, 190, 192, 196, 198, 200, 201, 203, 204, 205, 206, 208, 209

St. Lawrence, 67, 72, 95, 96, 106, 110, 115, 145, 146, 156, 162, 171, 172

St. Lawrence (Gulf of, River), 28

Stephen, Commander George H, 46, 118, 155

Stephens, Rear-Admiral G.L., 125, 141

Stettler HMCS, 156

Support Force, Atlantic Fleet, 33

Swift Current HMCS, 160

Taylor, Commodore C.R.H.,, 87, 144, 157, 161

Tenacity HMRT, 76, 112, 157

Thompson, R. C.,, 49, 50, 51

Trade Division, 22

training facilities, 15, 69, 116, 124, 130, 147
Trepassey, 28, 72
Triangle Run, 18, 147, 198
U-110, 33, 127, 139
U-1223, 157
U-1228, 157, 159
U-1230, 159
U-1231, 159
U-1232, 160
U-190, 160, 163
U-538, 149
U-541, 155, 156
U-548, 150, 162
U-802, 155, 156
U-805, 160
U-806, 159
U-881, 160
U-889, 160
U-boat, 13, 14, 21, 22, 30, 31, 33, 34, 40, 42, 54, 63, 64, 66, 67, 70, 72, 78, 79, 89, 91, 95, 96, 98, 102, 105, 107, 108, 109, 111, 116, 117, 118, 119, 120, 121, 122, 126, 128, 130, 136, 138, 140, 143, 144, 145, 146, 147, 148, 149, 150, 152, 156, 157, 159, 160, 161, 164, 166, 167, 168
United States, 11, 13, 14, 17, 23, 27, 32, 36, 37, 39, 41, 45, 46, 63, 67, 68, 69, 73, 75, 77, 83, 84, 86, 91, 99, 115, 119, 120, 121, 141, 147, 155, 164, 171, 172, 182, 189, 190, 191, 197, 203
US TF 24, 91, 109
US TF 4, 53, 60
US TG 22.1, 161
US *TG 7.3*, 33
Valleyfield HMCS, 150, 151, 154, 162
Vice Chief of Naval Staff (VCNS, 144
Walwyn, Vice-Admiral Sir Humphrey, Governor of Newfoundland, 26, 27, 28, 46, 60, 88, 98, 99, 108, 110, 118, 125, 149, 185, 186
War Cabinet, 36, 39, 74, 125, 132
Washington, 12, 15, 17, 41, 50, 53, 64, 67, 84, 85, 88, 96, 123, 128, 138,

163, 172, 191, 197, 201
Western Approaches Command (WAC), 11, 33, 49, 116
Western Atlantic, 19, 36, 52, 53, 54, 63, 67, 83, 163
Western Ocean Meeting Point (WESTOMP), 11, 44, 147
Wetaskiwin HMCS, 30, 99, 101
Wings On Her Shoulders, 154
Women's Royal Canadian Naval Service (WRCNS), 153
Woods, Sir Wilfrid, Commissioner of Public Utilities, 8, 29, 50, 51, 56, 59, 72, 100
Zimmermann, Klt. Heinrich, 150

The "Newfyjohn" Solution

www.ingramcontent.com/pod-product-compliance
Lightning Source LLC
Chambersburg PA
CBHW060514100426
42743CB00009B/1314